Miners, Unions and Politics, 1910-47

MINERS, UNIONS AND

POLITICS, 1910-47

Edited by

ALAN CAMPBELL
NINA FISHMAN
DAVID HOWELL

Published by
SCOLAR PRESS
Gower House
Croft Road
Aldershot
Hants GU11 3HR
England

Ashgate Publishing Company
Old Post Road
Brookfield
Vermont 05036
USA

British Library Cataloguing in Publication Data

Miners, Unions and Politics, 1910-47
  I. Campbell, Alan
331.881223340941

ISBN 1-85928-269-5

Library of Congress Cataloging-in-Publication Data

Miners, unions, and politics, 1910-47/edited by Alan Campbell, Nina Fishman, David Howell.
    p.   cm.
  Includes index.
  ISBN 1-85928-269-5 (hc)
    1. Trade-unions--Coal miners--Great Britain--Political activity--History--20th century. 2. Coal miners--Great Britain--History--20th century. 3. Labor movement--Great Britain--History--20th century. 4. Miners' Federation of Great Britain--History. 5. National Union of Mineworkers--History. I. Campbell, Alan, 1949- . II. Fishman, Nina. III. Howell, David, 1945- .
HD6668.M615M58   1996
331.88'122334'0941-dc20   95-38640
                                                                          CIP

ISBN 1 85928 269 5
Printed and Bound in Great Britain by
Hartnolls Limited, Bodmin, Cornwall.

Contents

Contributors

Alan Campbell lectures in the Department of Economic and Social History, University of Liverpool. He is the author of *The Lanarkshire Miners: a social history of their trade unions, 1775-1874* and is currently writing a book on politics and trade unionism in the Scots coalfields during the period 1874-1939.

David Egan teaches at the Cardiff Institute of Higher Education. As well as a number of articles on syndicalism, his writing on South Wales includes *Coal Society: a history of the South Wales mining valleys, 1840-1980*.

Nina Fishman teaches history, politics and industrial relations at the University of Westminster. Her recent publications include *The British Communist Party and the Trade Unions, 1933-45*. Together with Hywel Francis, she is currently researching a biography of Arthur Horner.

Hywel Francis is Professor in the Department of Adult Continuing Education, University of Wales, Swansea. His previous publications include *The Fed: a history of the South Wales miners in the twentieth century* (with David Smith) and *Miners Against Fascism: Wales and the Spanish Civil War*.

David Gilbert lectures in the Department of Geography, Royal Holloway and Bedford New College, University of London. He is the author of *Class, Community and Collective Action: social change in two British coalfields, 1850-1926*.

Trevor Griffiths has recently completed his doctorate on the coalmining and cotton industries in Lancashire. He is currently a lecturer in the Department of Economic and Social History, University of Edinburgh.

David Howell is Professor in the Department of Politics, University of York.   His publications include *British Workers and the Independent Labour Party, 1888-1906*, *A Lost Left*, and *The Politics of the NUM: a Lancashire view*.

Duncan Tanner is Professor of Modern History at the University College of North Wales, Bangor.   He is the author of *Political Change and the Labour Party, 1900-1918* as well as a number of articles on electoral politics.

Andrew Taylor teaches politics at the University of Huddersfield. His publications include *The Politics of the Yorkshire Miners* and *The Trade Unions and the Labour Party*.

Chris Williams lectures in the School of History and Archaeology, University of Wales, Cardiff.   His doctoral thesis was on the political and social history of the Rhondda and his publications include articles on this topic.

List of Tables

List of Maps

The editors gratefully acknowledge the work of Justin Jacyno in preparing the maps.

List of Abbreviations

AEU	Amalgamated Engineering Union
BLA	Bolton Library Archives
BLPES	British Library of Economic and Political Science
BMPL	Buckhaven and Methil Public Library
BSP	British Socialist Party
BWL	British Workers' League
CP	Communist Party
CPGB	Communist Party of Great Britain
CRO	County Record Office
DLP	Divisional Labour Party
DMA	Durham Miners' Association
EWO	Essential Works Order
HCDeb	House of Commons Debates
HRF	Hulton Colliery Disaster Relief Fund
ILP	Independent Labour Party
IRA	Irish Republican Army
LCMF	Lancashire and Cheshire Miners' Federation
LMWU	Lanarkshire Mine Workers' Union
LP	Labour Party
LRO	Lancashire Record Office
MFGB	Miners' Federation of Great Britain
MIU	Miners' Industrial Union
MMM	Miners' Minority Movement
MRU	Mineworkers' Reform Union
NCB	National Coal Board
NCOA	Nottinghamshire Coal Owners' Association
NLS	National Library of Scotland
NMA	Nottinghamshire Mineworkers' Association
NMFU	Nottinghamshire and District Miners' Federated Union
NMIU	Nottinghamshire Miners' Industrial Union
NMLH	National Museum of Labour History, Manchester

NSSWCM	National Shop Stewards and Workers' Committee Movement
NUM	National Union of Mineworkers
NUSMW	National Union of Scottish Mine Workers
PLP	Parliamentary Labour Party
PPC	Pit Production Committee
PRO	Public Record Office
PRS	Lancashire and Cheshire Miners' Permanent Relief Society
RDC	Rural District Council
RILU	Red International of Labour Unions
SLP	Socialist Labour Party
SMF	Scottish Miners' Federation
SRO	Scottish Record Office
SWMF	South Wales Miners' Federation
SWMIU	South Wales Miners' Industrial Union
SYCTA	South Yorkshire Coal Trades Association
TGWU	Transport and General Workers Union
TUC	Trades Union Congress
UDM	Union of Democratic Mineworkers
UDC	Urban District Council
UMS	United Mineworkers of Scotland
URC	Unofficial Reform Committee
WA	Wigan Archives
WRCC	West Riding County Council
WYCOA	West Yorkshire Coal Owners' Association
YMITU	Yorkshire Miners' Industrial Trade Union
YMWA	Yorkshire Mine Workers' Association

'The tradition of all the dead generations ...'

Mining trade unions offer powerful examples of the invention of tradition, the construction of what might be characterised as usable pasts. These can be found in the iconography of banners and in the architecture of union offices; they form the content of influential union histories. But as with any invented tradition, there are selective myths, significant absences and limiting closures. These not only restrict understanding of the past; they might propose misleading models for contemporary practice.

Early in 1987 a Lancashire NUM (National Union of Mineworkers) activist reflecting on the history of the national union commended Robin Page Arnot's work as vital.[1] He had in mind its treatment of 1926, and of its divisive aftermath as offering insights into the plight of the NUM in the late 1980s. He had been a striker in 1984 at a colliery where most miners had worked through the dispute. A committed Scargillite, the assumptions and style of Page Arnot were clearly congenial. Yet a ready endorsement of Page Arnot's version of mining history would be mistaken.

The style is epic, the vision is heroic: the creation and consolidation of an effective national union, and the end of private ownership in the coal industry. Page Arnot seriously began his work during the Second World War. Quickly, the Miners' Federation of Great Britain (MFGB) was succeeded by the National Union of Mineworkers, and with the election of the postwar Labour government, public ownership was guaranteed. The texts were written and were read with an awareness of what seemed to be the decisive outcomes. The miners might have had their 'years of struggle', but these had ended successfully.

From the vantage point of 1995, the construction of such a history seems naive. The industry is tiny, employing no more than two per cent of the number employed in 1947, and the coalowners have

returned in the shape of Richard Budge.   Any notion that the
foundation of the NUM marked a significant shift from federation to
national union has had to be revised in the light of the disunity of
1984-5 and the subsequent secession of a minority into the Union of
Democratic Mineworkers (UDM).   Ironically the NUM could operate
as a national union only if local priorities were acknowledged and
typically respected; any conception of a naturally cohesive national
union was misleading.   Recent episodes suggest that perhaps the past
should be viewed differently.   Given the formation of the UDM, the
Spencer breakaway of 1926 could be reassessed.   Debate about
whether the NUM would have been wiser to endorse some kind of
settlement in the summer or autumn of 1984 raises similar questions
about the heroic moment of 1926.   The near disappearance of the
industry and of the NUM necessitates that the history of the mining
unions must be reconstructed.

Writing as official historian and as a member of the Communist
Party, Page Arnot tended to blur divisions within the MFGB.   The
only obvious villains are the 'renegades' such as George Spencer,
and, perhaps, Frank Hodges.   Otherwise, controversial moments
within the MFGB are not investigated seriously.   For example, with
the exception of a section in his book on the Scottish miners, there
is little on the left-right controversies that marked the MFGB in the
aftermath of 1926.   Potential solidarity is seen as more significant
than actual controversy.   Similarly miners' views are often understood in formal institutional terms.   Page Arnot tends to equate rank
and file opinion with union policy.   There is little suggestion that
outcomes were the result of factional competition, of bargaining, of
manipulation by officials, of accommodations around ambiguous
formulae.   The internal politics of the MFGB and of its constituent
bodies remain largely unexplored.   Equally there is no discussion of
how far the institutions and procedural rules might misrepresent the
sentiments of members.   A classic case is the defeat of the 'Bishops
Proposals' in the summer of 1926 against the MFGB executive
recommendation and effectively through the bloc votes of Lancashire,
South Wales and Yorkshire.

The limitations of Page Arnot's vision reflect not just his political
vantage point and assumptions, but also the contemporary state of
trade union historiography.   Over the last two decades, there have
been significant developments in methodology, not least in attempts

to connect the collective organisation of miners to their local societies. The pioneering collection of essays edited by Royden Harrison in 1978, *Independent Collier*, initiated this challenge to simplistic notions of the miner as 'archetypal proletarian'.[2] Other studies have focussed on examples which appear as exceptional within the broad framework of trade union solidarity and a strengthening Labour politics. Robert Moore's study of the Durham miners of the Deerness Valley showed how in villages notable for their strong Methodism, political Liberalism and the pursuit of consensual industrial relations survived into the 1920s.[3] Robert Waller's analysis of the Dukeries coalfield demonstrated how pervasive paternalism helped to ensure only a limited trade union presence when this district developed between the wars.[4] In contrast Stuart Macintyre's *Little Moscows* included two mining communities, one in Rhondda and one in Fife, where the Communist Party secured relatively significant influence.[5] Such studies seek to locate Lib-Labism, Spencerism, non-unionism and communist sympathies within specific patterns of employer strategy within both workplace and community, coupled with an awareness of the resources available or not available to trade unionists, and located within specific chronologies. The value of such studies is strengthened by a comparative dimension both within and between coalfields; hence the value of Alan Campbell's study of the influences on variations in trade union strength in Lanarkshire communities in the nineteenth century, and more recently David Gilbert's comparison of Ynysybwl and Hucknall where analysis of local class relations and resources are employed to explain the contrasting politics of the South Wales Miners' Federation and of the Nottinghamshire Miners' Association.[6]

Methodological innovations have also influenced the historiography of district unions. Hywel Francis and Dai Smith's presentation of the 'Fed' in South Wales retains something of the epic quality of Page Arnot, but there are two distinctive and significant elements.[7] The 'Fed' is presented as a lens through which to understand the development of South Wales society from the 1920s to the 1970s. The characterisation obviously marginalises other sections of the population, but it locates the union firmly within a wider context. Secondly, the book is informed by a strong sense of strategic options and choices made as activists attempted to revive the union after the disaster of 1926. Similarly, Huw Beynon and Terry Austrin's recent study of the Durham Miners' Association links the association's politics to the distinctive social and economic patterns of the coalfield.[8] This perspective is then used to explain the DMA's separatism under the Lib-Labs, and subsequently the emergence of a particular style of loyalist Labourism.

Overall, these developments have located mining unionism more sensitively within the distinctiveness of individual coalfields and local communities. The dominant sense is of diversity - of experience, and of response - and also of the contingent. Old certainties are eroded as choices appear more complex; there is no privileged progress to the national union and a publicly owned industry. One more specific consequence has been to produce more rounded understandings of key figures. They cease to be patriarchal paragons of virtue, or bearers of political positions. Instead they appear as political agents, often articulating local interests and culture. George Spencer, instead of simply a renegade, becomes a moderate, vain trade union official and Labour MP whose critical choice in 1926 could capitalise on a significant vein of support in Nottinghamshire. Peter Lee was not simply a venerable icon but an autocratic and wily administrator in the tradition of the Durham Miners' Association (DMA). MFGB general secretary A.J. Cook was not simply reducible to Beatrice Webb's portrait of 'an inspired idiot'; rather he was a pragmatic bargainer whose flexibility was perhaps a legacy of his syndicalism.[9]

The changing fortunes of industry and union, and historiographical developments in terms of both methodological awareness and empirical understanding combine to justify a new look at miners, their unions and politics. For if there is a gap in the historiography, it lies in the treatment of politics within the context of regional diversity. Roy Gregory's still valuable, but long out of print, comparative study was confined to the years 1906-14.[10] Our period is longer - from Tonypandy to nationalisation, and our definition of politics is broader and multi-dimensional.

The party political context is from the formal affiliation of the MFGB to the Labour Party to the election of the first majority Labour government. In terms of the state's involvement, one starting point is the minimum wage legislation of 1912, our conclusion is the advent of nationalisation. From the vantage point of the left outside the Labour Party, one theme concerns the complex continuities and ruptures between early syndicalist and 'direct action' mobilisations, and later commitment - often by the same people - to the Communist Party.

One emphasis within the treatment of 'party politics' is the complexity of political developments. As a result, old stereotypes are eroded, whether these be the increasingly straightforward commitment of mining communities to Labour, the relationship between the MFGB and the interwar Labour governments, the role of the Communist Party in mining unionism and the character and legacy of syndicalism. These portraits are revisionist in the sense that they contrast old images with new materials and interpretations. The outcome can be read not simply as new insights into mining unionism but as a significant contribution to broader debates. The imagery of 'the Forward March of Labour' is another example of a now discredited and invented tradition. In this teleology the miners from 1910 to 1947 played a pivotal role. The studies below help to replace the old certainties with a more nuanced understanding in which Labour strength in the coalfields grows at variable rates, and MFGB relationships with Labour governments do not fit easily into the language of either union dominance or incorporation. Similarly international events and archival liberalisation have massively increased the scope for serious study of the Communist Party and its trade union influence, whilst one of the Communist Party's predecessors, the syndicalist movement can be viewed now in its own right rather than as the primitive prelude to a more scientific politics.

A second dimension of miners' politics concerns competing factions, whether or not rallied under party banners, within district unions and the MFGB. 'Union politics' cannot be reduced to simple dichotomies of a 'militant' rank and file versus a monolithic and 'moderate' bureaucracy. Rather the picture presented here is of competing interest groups within the membership and multi-layered levels of lay- and full-time officials, whose strategies were the complex outcome of personal attributes, ideological commitments, material status, and organisational loyalties and routines, and which were constructed within the constraints of widely divergent coalfield economies. The complexity of MFGB politics was similarly a product of the diverse experiences of miners within different coalfields and indeed in different communities of the same coalfield.

A final level of political analysis is focussed on the workplace. 'Pit politics', both official and unofficial, also defy any simple equation with stereotypes of militancy and solidarity.[11] The nature of conflicts and accommodations within the labour process varied from seam to seam and pit to pit as well as between coalfields. Equally within one workplace they might change over time in response to changing market conditions and shifts in geology. Their relationship with formal union and party politics, and the tensions between them, varied according to the structures of unionism, the degree of insulation enjoyed by union officials, and the effectiveness of collective bargaining procedures.

The regional chapters seek to elucidate and to explain such diversities which were institutionalised through the structure of the MFGB and the district unions. The contributors differ in their explanatory emphases. Some place significant weight on the labour process and change therein, as in Scotland; others emphasise community patterns especially in coalfields such as Lancashire and Nottinghamshire where many miners did not live in the separate, occupationally homogeneous villages emphasised by an earlier generation of sociologists. Variations of explanation may partly reflect contrasting methodological approaches and disciplinary affiliations; but they also indicate that in differing coalfields, the explanatory emphasis should be located in different places. The centrality of the union for miners could vary accordingly. In occupationally monolithic South Wales, the lodge could be central to communal life; in Lancashire, with its diverse occupational structure, commuting miners and workplace branches, the union was inevitably much more marginal. Once again generalisation is hazardous. However, although there are variations in emphasis and the weighting of respective variables within these analyses of regional and local diversity, there is nevertheless a more general common insistence on examining (in our colleague Duncan Tanner's formulation) 'the means by which social structures and political approaches interacted to turn a community's self-identification and interests into increasingly firm political allegiances'. In their emphasis on the complexity of such interactions our contributors reject both anlyses based on structural reductionism as well as the equally one-dimensional redescriptions practised by historians of 'political discourse'.

The recent emphasis within mining historiography on the diversity of local and regional experiences has been coopted by some 'revisionist' historians to highlight the internal divisions and inherent fragmentation within the working class.[12] While this volume adds to that accumulation of empirical research in challenging the image of miners as *innately* solidaristic, it nevertheless does not abandon the notion that despite this diversity, occupational and class solidarity *could* be constructed. Given our emphases on contingency and diversity, the treatment of Page Arnot's finale is inevitably very different. The construction of the NUM can be seen most effectively as resting on an awareness of district diversities and of the brittleness, not the naturalness of national trade union organisation. District unions were a triumph of collective aspirations over communal particularism and corrosive apathy; at the national level, the problem was repeated with the obstacle not simply district agendas but also officials' power bases. Officials and activists made what they could of the diversities. Equally the formation of the National Coal Board should not be seen as the natural conclusion to a 'forward march'. Labour's 1945 victory was not an 'inevitable' outcome for the party nor for its affiliated unions; the form of nationalisation adopted involved the marginalisation of alternatives debated earlier within mining unions. From the world of Blair and Budge, new questions can be asked of a complex past.

Notes

Place of publication is London unless otherwise stated.

1. R. Page Arnot, *The Miners: years of struggle from 1910 onwards* (1953); *The Miners in Crisis and War, from 1930 onwards* (1961); *The Miners: one union, one industry* (1979); *A History of the Scottish Miners* (1955); *The South Wales Miners, Glowyr de Cymru: a history of the South Wales Miners' Federation* (Cardiff, 1975).
2. R. Harrison (ed.), *Independent Collier: the coalminer as archetypal proletarian reconsidered* (Hassocks, 1978).
3. R. Moore, *Pitmen, Preachers and Politics: the effects of methodism in a Durham mining community* (Cambridge, 1974).
4. R.J. Waller, *The Dukeries Transformed: the social and political of a twentieth-century coalfield* (Oxford, 1983).
5. S. Macintyre, *Little Moscows: communism and working-class militancy in interwar Britain* (1980).

6. A.B. Campbell, *The Lanarkshire Miners: a social history of their trade unions, 1775-1874* (Edinburgh, 1979); D. Gilbert, *Class, Community and Collective Action: social change in two British coalfields, 1850-1926* (Oxford, 1992).
7. H. Francis and D. Smith, *The Fed: a history of the South Wales miners in the twentieth century* (1980).
8. H. Beynon and T. Austrin, *Masters and Servants. Class and Patronage in the Making of a Labour Organisation: the Durham miners and the English political tradition* (1994).
9. P. Davies, *A.J. Cook* (Manchester, 1987), p. 189.
10. R.G. Gregory, *The Miners and British Politics, 1906-1914* (Oxford, 1968).
11. For discussion of the notion of 'pit politics', see P.Gibbon, 'Analysing the British miners' strike of 1984-85', *Economy and Society*, vol. 17, no. 2, 1988.
12. For example, see F.M.L. Thompson, *The Rise of Respectable Society: a social history of Victorian Britain, 1830-1914* (1988), pp. 220-5, 361; and A. Reid, *Social Classes and Social Relations in Britain, 1850-1914* (1992), pp. 28, 68.

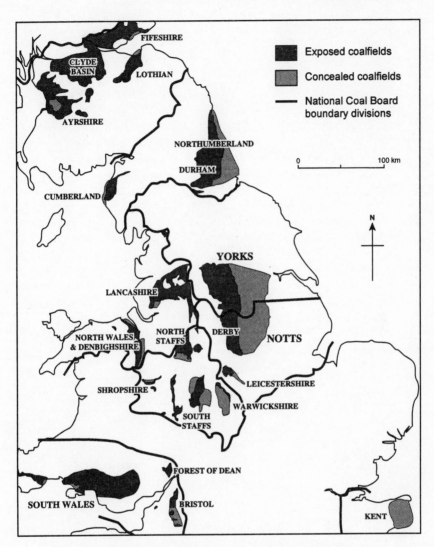

Map 1   The British coalfields at nationalisation in 1947.

PART ONE
National Perspectives

CHAPTER ONE

'A cult of their own': syndicalism and *The Miners' Next Step*[1]

David Egan

In the first days of the new year of 1995, as this is being written, remarkable events are taking place at Tower Colliery near the foot of the Rhigos mountain on the northern outcrop of the South Wales coalfield. On 2 January, led by brass bands and union banners, 239 miners and their families marched in the early morning to take ownership of the only mine to pass into the possession of an employee/management buy-out in the privatisation of the coal industry. In April 1994 its previous owners, British Coal, closed the colliery which it believed to be producing uneconomically mined coal despite the £28 million profit made in the previous three years. This was more than another colliery closure, however. This was the last deep mine in the once mighty South Wales coalfield and it appeared thereby that over 150 years of history, when the valleys of South Wales had become almost synonymous with coal mining, was coming to an end.

The Tower lodge of the National Union of Mineworkers had a proud record of trade union militancy and a highly able and articulate leadership, many of whom had transferred to the colliery from other pits following the spate of colliery closures in the coalfield after the 1984-5 miners' strike. They were able to persuade the men of 'the Tower' and their families to initially fight the closure and refuse the redundancy terms offered. However following pressure by British Coal this decision was to be narrowly reversed and, with other avenues of appeal exhausted, production ceased at Tower on 19 April 1994. The lodge leadership was convinced that Tower was being closed ready for sale in the impending privatisation of the industry. They therefore decided that if they could convince enough of the men and their families to invest their redundancy money they should attempt to purchase the pit as, in the words of the lodge secretary, Tyrone O'Sullivan, the miners 'were the pit's rightful owners'[2]. Over two hundred of the men were persuaded to put £8,000 each into a workers' cooperative and, working from offices provided by the local council in the town of Aberdare, the lodge instigated a remarkably successful campaign to raise additional money by popular subscription.   One of the leaders was to find himself with over £30,000 in five and ten pound notes under his bed as the appeal spiralled in support.   It was clearly necessary to acquire financial management expertise.   After interviewing prospective companies, the miners eventually appointed Price Waterhouse, ironically the very company instructed by the government to sequestrate the miners' union funds in 1984-5.   The management side of the bid was bolstered by the recruitment of former British Coal management including - with further irony - Philip Weekes, as non-executive chairman.   For twelve years he had been area director of the National Coal Board in South Wales when dozens of collieries had been closed, but who retained the respect of the miners who saw him as having been a prisoner of government policy.   In the autumn of 1994 that government announced that the Tower bid had been successful.   On a cold January morning a few months later, as the 'Red Flag' and the 'Internationale' were sung in Welsh and the marching song of the Italian partisans who overthrew Mussolini, 'Bandiera Rossa', rang out across the hillsides, Tyrone O'Sullivan was to reflect that the new period of worker-management of Tower which was about to commence was 'a lot better than the nationalisation of 1947', for this was 'real nationalisation, the workers owning the pit'.[3]

The resonances of this event can be seen to bring echoes from more recent as well as from more distant history.   In the midst of the campaign to save the Tower Colliery, the annual conference of the Labour Party took place in October 1994.   Its new leader Tony Blair announced that he wished to begin a process of reconsideration of the party's constitution, including the famous clause four introduced into the constitution in 1918 at the height of a contemporary debate on nationalisation and industrial democracy.   This clause, which every party member carries on their membership card, has committed the party to 'the common ownership of the means of production, distribution and exchange'.   Under the aegis of a Labour government from 1945-51 this had led to widespread nationalisation, including the coal industry in 1947. Although it was not necessarily the only form of public ownership that clause four would have allowed, the coal industry (in the form of the National Coal Board, NCB) like other nationalised concerns would in future be administered by a 'public corporation' - meaning in essence the state itself. As the Labour Party met in the autumn of 1994, the successor to the NCB, British Coal, was being dismembered ready for the privatisation of the industry. At the forefront of the campaign against privatisation was the president of the NUM, Arthur Scargill, and it would be the same man who at the Labour Party conference would become one of the first siren voices to attack Tony Blair's perceived antagonism to clause four and nationalisation. Yet at one of the lodges of his union, Tower Colliery, his members, who had remained fiercely loyal to Arthur Scargill during the 1984-5 strike and in the difficult times thereafter, were accepting the end of nationalisation of the coal industry and apparently shedding no tears for its legacy as they took ownership of their pit.

The healthy debates and perhaps inconsistencies within the contemporary miners' union on the best form of social ownership of the industry have of course historical echoes which take us back to the first two decades of the present century and which are the main focus of this chapter. Then the South Wales miners acquired a reputation for supporting workers' control of the mines, reputedly influenced by the outlook and policies of syndicalism, a militant socialist ideology given birth to in the French labour movement between 1890 and 1900 and taken up by the Industrial Workers of the World and the Socialist Labour Party in the United States of America. The US movement was to exert a direct influence on Britain through activists such as 'Big Bill' Haywood, who visited South Wales in 1910, and by its leading theoretician, Daniel De Leon, whose ideas were promoted by the Socialist Labour Party set up in Scotland.[4]

Some six miles or so over the Rhigos mountain from Tower Colliery in the midst of what at one time was one of the most famous coal mining areas in the world, the Rhondda Fawr, lies the village of Trealaw. On 13 November 1912 an open debate took place there among miners' leaders on the merits of nationalisation or workers' control as a policy to replace the then private ownership of the industry. This was of course a very different South Wales coalfield to that of 1994-5. The expansion of the coal industry from the four and a half million tons of coal which had been mined annually in the 1840s to a figure of 57 million tons in the peak period of the coalfield's expansion before the 1914-18 war, was as dramatic as these figures suggest.[5] This peak production figure represented nearly 20 per cent of the total production of the British coalfields and the scale of development in South Wales is no better represented than in the previously unexploited river valleys of the Rhondda Fach and Rhondda Fawr where by 1912 there were 53 large collieries. The pell-mell physical and human development of the coalfield struck all contemporaries who could make the comparison as being reminiscent of the settling of the American West. There was a material form to this connection in that the USA became one of the markets for the rich steam coal of South Wales, over half of which was to wind its way down the railway lines of the valleys to the great coal exporting ports of the coast. When the employment provided for 230,000 coalminers and the associated employment in the railways and the docks and the dependency of wives and families on this employment is considered, the domination of coal over the population of 1.7 million people who lived in the South Wales counties of Glamorgan, Carmarthen and Monmouth is clear.

At the heart of this social and economic maelstrom, the crowd which gathered at the Judges' Hall in Trealaw in November 1912 were to hear two Abertillery miners' leaders, George Barker and Edward Gill, speak in favour on the question of 'The nationalisation of mines. Is this in the best interest of the workers?' and to consider contributions against this proposal from the local Maerdy checkweighman, Noah Ablett, and a young miners' agent from the Garw Valley and a future secretary of the Miners' Federation of Great Britain, Frank Hodges.[6] George Barker put forward the practical proposals for nationalisation which were to become the official policy of the MFGB in a campaign which reached its height in the period of the Sankey Commission after the First World War but which was not to come to fruition until the creation of the NCB in 1947. Barker looked to an act of parliament which '... would nationalise the mines ... make the mines and minerals of the United Kingdom the property of the national ... by getting the state to hold and control the whole of the industry'.[7] Ablett castigated this proposal as one that would see the state, even more powerful than the coalowners, exercising control over the miners, their work and their lives. For him, private ownership should be replaced by 'democratic organisation and eventually control of the industries by the workers themselves ... from the bottom upward and not from the top downwards ...'.[8]

Noah Ablett,[9] perhaps one of the most original minds produced by the working class movement of this period, was one of the main authors of the pamphlet *The Miners' Next Step*[10] which was published by the Unofficial Reform Committee (URC) of the South Wales Miners' Federation (SWMF) at the same time as the meeting at Trealaw. The fame, notoriety and indeed eloquence of this tract was to play a significant part in earning a reputation for the strength of syndicalist views among the South Wales miners. It argued for a future policy for the SWMF which would see it 'ultimately take over the mining industry and carry it on in the interest of the workers'.[11] Whilst this could be seen to be a classic statement of syndicalism with an emphasis on trades unionism and industrial, rather than political, action as being the means to a socialist society, only one of the authors of *The Miners' Next Step*, W.F. Hay, ever consistently accepted that he was a syndicalist. Ablett, like so many other supporters of the URC, preferred to refer to himself as an 'industrial unionist'. Such fine distinctions will be explored further in the remainder of this chapter as the nature of syndicalism in South Wales in the period approximately 1910-26 is considered. Having portrayed the main currents in the coalfield which framed the views put forward in *The Miners' Next Step*, an attempt is made to consider to what extent these views were 'syndicalist'. It is suggested that in fact what emerged in South Wales during this period was a more singular response to the changing objective conditions of the coalfield. The appeal of this response is identified as being the way in which it embraced the consciousness and aspirations of the rank and file of the miners. Whilst the appeal of 'syndicalist' influenced ideas was strongest in South Wales in the period up to 1926, it is suggested that they also influenced other coalfields and have a lineage which has become part of the continuing history of mining trades unionism up to modern times.

The life story of one of the 'syndicalists' of South Wales, C.L. Gibbons,[12] a part author of *The Miners' Next Step*, provides a useful backcloth to developments which were to shape the views put forward in the pamphlet. Charlie Gibbons was born in 1888 in London, the son of a stonemason who died when Charlie was eight years old which resulted in him being placed thereafter in a home for destitute children. Beginning work as a farm servant in 1904, he then was employed successively as a dairyman, a messenger boy, a shop assistant and a plumber's mate. In 1907 his adventurous spirit took him on 'the tramp' through the farms of the South West and of South Wales until his journey and his fate brought him to the Rhondda, where at the age of 19 he began work as a collier at the Lewis Merthyr Colliery in the village of Porth. This was an experience very typical of the expansion of the coalfield at this time, where the scale of development had exhausted the migration of farm workers from the Welsh counties and where now immigration came increasingly from the English border counties and even from as far afield as London. The cosmopolitan nature of the South Wales valleys created a crucible of human culture and experience, the effect of which was to play no small part in the emergence of new social ideologies in the coalfield.

Gibbons was initially content to learn the skills of the collier at the Lewis Merthyr and to attend mining classes which he hoped would qualify him to become a mining engineer and a colliery manager. A further twist of fate awaited him, however. On an evening in 1909, his mining class was cancelled and with time to kill he went instead to a debate in a hotel in the adjacent village of Trehafod on the topic of 'working class education'. Here again as a protagonist was the ubiquitous Noah Ablett, confronted on this occasion by the Rhondda miner T.I. Mardy Jones, later a political organiser of the SWMF and the first Labour MP for the neighbouring Pontypridd constituency. Both men had attended Ruskin College, the working class institution in Oxford, on scholarships offered by the SWMF. However, whereas Mardy Jones remained in sympathy with the liberal adult education philosophy offered by Ruskin and associated with the University Extension Movement and the Workers' Educational Association, Ablett had supported a strike of students at the college in 1909 which eventually led to the setting up of a separate institution, the Central Labour College.[13] Ablett and the Ruskin strikers who joined together in the Plebs League supported the cause of independent working class education, believing that the education offered to the worker-students should be for their own class and trade union interests, preparing them to be more effective leaders of these movements.   The debate which Gibbons attended at Trehafod on these issues resulted in a victory for Ablett, mirroring a successful campaign across the coalfield. This eventually persuaded the SWMF to switch its allegiance to the Central Labour College which was established in London. In time the SWMF, along with the National Union of Railwaymen, was to own the college and through the scholarships it offered, a whole generation of militant miners' leaders and other servants of the labour movement were educated there. In the coalfield local classes were organised by the Plebs League and later by the SWMF with the assistance of the Labour College. A less than sympathetic observer pointed out that in one year alone over 300 miners attended such classes in the Rhondda, and it was noted that 'these men are usually among the most intelligent and forceful of the mining population and they are able to impress their ideas on the minds of their comrades both during hours of work and hours of leisure'.[14]

As was the case with the miners who attended Ruskin and the Labour College, these classes, along with the remarkable libraries being built up in the workmen's institutes of the coalfield,[15] exposed young miners, who were 'the first fruits of the spread of popular education',[16] to the welter of socialist thought pulsing through Edwardian Britain. This included the theories of French syndicalism, the industrial unionist views put forward by the Socialist Labour Party of the USA, and the German traditions of Marx, Engels, Kautsky and Dietzgen, often obtained in editions published by the publishing house Kerr and Co. of Chicago. In addition there were the home grown ideas of the Independent Labour Party and Marxist organisations such as the British Socialist Party, the Scottish-based Socialist Labour Party and the locally constituted Rhondda Socialist Society. All of this pressed upon the inquisitive minds of these miner-students, 'the autodidacts of the coalfield' as Stuart Macintyre has called them.[17]

Charlie Gibbons was himself to become one of these autodidacts. The Trehafod debate and the influence which Ablett was now to exercise upon him, saw him abandoning his mining studies to join the regular meetings of the Plebs League at Porth. There he met Will Hay, the one time house painter from Reading and the most staunch and caustic of pure syndicalists; A.J. Cook, later the secretary of the Miners' Federation of Great Britain and renowned demagogue; W.H. Mainwaring, the Clydach miner who would become vice principal of the Labour College, a miners' agent and eventually MP for the Rhondda East constituency; and many other of what the contemporary press were to call the 'advanced men' and 'the syndicalists' of the coalfield. At these meetings 'a wide variety of marxian socialist ideas ... militant trades unionism ... and industrial unionism' were discussed.[19] Gibbons also began to attend meetings of similar groups from across the coalfield which took place at the Aberystwyth Restaurant in Tonypandy on Sunday afternoons. This became the basis of the Unofficial Reform Committee which now began to turn these ideological discussions towards the dramatic events beginning to unfold in the coalfield.

In 1910 the Cambrian Combine dispute began, in which the 12,000 miners employed in four collieries of the Cambrian Company owned by the Liberal MP and coalowner D.A. Thomas (later Lord Rhondda), struck work. Whilst this strike appeared on the surface to be about wage levels, underlying this was a more fundamental defence by the Cambrian miners of the way in which the price for work at the collieries was negotiated and in particular the protection of colliers who worked in difficult or 'abnormal' places. The Cambrian dispute went on into 1911, spilling over in November 1910 into the events in the Mid-Rhondda which have passed into history as the 'Tonypandy riots' and which more significantly in the long term were to transform the South Wales Miners' Federation. In the short term what faced the Cambrian strikers was defeat and a return to work in 1911. But in 1912 the basic cause for which they had fought, a minimum wage, was to be established in principle as a result of the first national strike fought by the Miners' Federation of Great Britain.[20] It was the effect which the Cambrian dispute had on the SWMF which was it true legacy, however.

The SWMF had been formed in 1898 - late in comparison to other British coalfields - as an attempt to federate the longer tradition of district unions.[21] Despite a proud reputation for working class struggle in South Wales, stretching back to the first raising of the red flag at Penderyn (a village very close to the later Tower Colliery) during the Merthyr Rising of 1831 and continuing through the strength of local Chartism in the 1830s and 40s, trades unionism among the South Wales miners had been beset by parochialism and rivalries. These contributed to defeat and union collapse in a number of coalfield disputes including the lockout of 1898, a defeat which preceded the attempt to find greater strength through unity in the foundation of the SWMF. The Lib-Lab leadership of the union, typified by its cautious and populist president, William Abraham, held the federation together by a delicate balancing act which mollified district separatism and local autonomy within the union, whilst conciliating the coalowners. Miners' MPs shared the Liberal benches of the House of Commons with a number of these coalowners until in 1908 the union rank and file voted in favour of affiliation to the Labour Party. This might have seen them switching the benches they henceforth sat on in the Commons, but persuaded no one, least of all the militant miners of the coalfield, that they had changed their political and social outlook. These younger miners, the supporters of the Unofficial Reform Committee and their more moderate allies from the ranks of the Independent Labour Party (ILP) such as Vernon Hartshorn and George Barker, had often come to their socialism (as had Charlie Gibbons) from the more freethinking varieties of religious nonconformity. Within the grip that it exercised over the coalfield, men like Ablett, A.J. Cook and Arthur Horner, were to be deeply affected by movements such as the incandescent religious revival which swept Wales in 1904-5 and by the appeal of the 'new theology' of R.J. Campbell with its stress on the social duties of Christianity.[22] The educational reformer Lord Haldane was to note that the Wales of this period 'suffered from too many ideas rather than too few',[23] and the links between the social messianism of evangelical nonconformity and the 'advanced men' of the Unofficial Reform Committee is striking. Their disillusionment with popular religion and their conversion to socialism saw these young radicals developing, under the influence of independent working class education, the critique of both the SWMF and industrial relations in the coalfield which took shape in *The Miners' Next Step*. The link was a direct one, for as Gibbons notes 'the leaders of the Cambrian Strike Committee were almost to a man members of the Unofficial Reform Committee and also ardent advocates of independent working class education'.[24]

The success of the Unofficial Reform Committee and its appeal though *The Miners' Next Step* to the rank and file militancy which controlled the coalfield in these years, saw its members moving to the fore in the union and replacing the old leadership it so damningly condemned in the pamphlet. The union they would lead would have a very different reputation as industrial discontent spilled over into the years of the First World War and reached boiling point again in the searing social protests and strikes of the postwar years leading up to the General Strike and miners' lockout of 1926. In 1917 this union at a special conference would change its objectives to include 'the entire organisation of all workers employed in and about the collieries in the South Wales and Monmouthshire coalfield with a view to the complete abolition of capitalism'.[25] This was about as unvarnished a statement of industrial unionism and its objectives as it would be possible to conceive. In the more straitened times after the defeat of the miners in the 1921 lockout, the momentum of this ambition led them to conclude that this struggle should take on an international dimension and the SWMF was to the fore in supporting affiliation to the USSR-sponsored Red International of Labour Unions.

Through these momentous years and events, Charlie Gibbons continued to take on experiences apace. In 1911 he won a SWMF scholarship to himself attend the Central Labour College. His time there was interrupted by periods working for the college as a lecturer in Lancashire and it was not until the summer of 1914 that he completed his studies and returned to the Rhondda. His stay was not to be for long, however, for events took him into the British army after the outbreak of the war. The divisions which the war caused in the British labour movement are indicated by the fact that his erstwhile colleague Arthur Cook was to be imprisoned for his anti-war activities. In 1919 Gibbons returned to South Wales where he helped to form the Communist Party of Great Britain and to produce a sequel to *The Miners' Next Step* in the form of the pamphlet *A Plan For The Democratic Control of The Mining Industry*.[26] After various posts in South Wales, inside and outside of the SWMF, Gibbons was in 1924 to take up the remainder of his life's work and his abiding passion as a full-time organiser for the Labour College movement in Scotland. The reason why Gibbons claimed he was forced to join the army in 1914 was because the colliery companies in South Wales refused to employ him because of his association with syndicalist ideas and the Labour College. This gives a good indication both of the strength and of the fear of the ideas of the 'advanced men' in the coalfield four years after they were first set forth in *The Miners' Next Step*.

Were these ideas 'syndicalist' and if not what exactly were they and how can we explain their apparent success in taking hold of South Wales miners and their union? The writers, historians and activists, Sidney and Beatrice Webb, were no enthusiasts for the ideas of syndicalism. Therefore a critique they produced of its theories in 1912 may prove a fairly objective basis for an analysis of *The Miners' Next Step*. The Webbs believed that syndicalism represented 'no hard and fast creed or definite formula, but a medley of thoughts and feelings', but that within this confusion there was a unifying thread of 'acute class consciousness ... of the economic, legal and political subjection' to which the working class was subjected. This ideological catholicism infused nevertheless with a sharp class consciousness can readily be accepted as characteristic of the so-called 'syndicalism' of South Wales, as can their identification of 'disillusionment with orthodox trades unionism' as another key element in its make-up.[27] However the Webbs identify this disillusionment as being a feeling that trades unions 'afford no hope of emancipating the manual workers as a class from their present subjection ... or freeing them from the necessity of passing their working lives under the orders of such owners or their managers and officials'.[28] This was certainly not reflected in the Unofficial Reform Committee or *The Miners' Next Step* which believed that the SWMF could be transformed to become:

> A united industrial organisation ... recognising the war of interest between workers and employers ... constructed on fighting lines ... with a continual agitation to be carried out in favour of increasing the minimum wage and shortening the hours of work, until we have extracted the whole of the employers profits.[29]

This was a form of industrial unionism which saw its dynamic in transforming an existing union, not in superseding it with a new one. Its stress on direct action was, as the Webbs pointed out by extensively quoting *The Miners' Next Step*, typical of syndicalist attitudes, as was the section of the pamphlet which dealt with the future organisation of society after revolutionary trades unionism has used the weapon of the general strike to defeat capitalism:

Our objective begins to take shape before your eyes. Every industry thoroughly organised ... to fight, to gain control of and then to administer that industry. The co-ordination of all industries in a Central Production Board who ... will issue its demands on the different departments of industry, leading to the men themselves to determine under what conditions and how the work should be done. This would mean real democracy in real life, making for real manhood and womanhood. Any other form of democracy is a delusion and a snare.[30]

The 'typicality' was the general vagueness apparent here on how a syndicalist society would actually be administered and a seeming naivety about the existing state allowing these developments to take place without the type of resistance which the authors of *The Miners' Next Step* had seen at first hand in the sending of troops and auxillary police forces to deal with the disturbances in South Wales during the Cambrian Combine and other coalfield disputes in 1910-11. It might be said that this reflects the presence in syndicalism of the final trait which the Webbs identify, and that is 'disillusionment with the parliamentary action advocated by the State Socialists'.[31] However, naive as they may have been about the state, it is not true that the South Wales militants were anti-political, as is often suggested. There was a minority who probably held such views - W.F. Hay and Charlie Gibbons among them. However, *The Miners' Next Step* clearly advocated 'political action, both local and national',[32] and most of the authors and the supporters of the Unofficial Reform Committee either had been or would be associated with the political side of the labour movement. What was true, however, was that they were at least unsympathetic and at times hostile, to the state collectivism of the political wing of the movement. It was a belief in industrial democracy and workers' control which drove these men. To achieve this they wished to work within their union, which they saw as the kernel of a future society based upon these things. For, as Ablett was to put it so tellingly in an oft-cited aphorism, 'it was foolish to swim the river to fill the bucket on the other side'.[33] Clearly for Ablett at least, there was a 'river' between the two 'banks' of industrial and political activity, with politics on the far bank!

The analysis of the Webbs, then, can be used to suggest a number of conclusions about the radical ideas which developed in the South Wales coalfield of this period. If syndicalism is narrowly conceived, then its presence and its extent in South Wales is questionable. If, however, the Webbs' view of syndicalism as 'a medley' is accepted, then the South Wales variety, different as it is to the one depicted by the Webbs, fits this type of characterisation. There was vagueness, inconsistency and even contradiction in the ideas of the South Wales 'advanced men'. W.H. Mainwaring could say 'there was not a syndicalist among us',[34] whereas another part author of *The Miners' Next Step* could say it was 'frankly syndicalist in principle'.[35] It should be remembered these were working men, trade union activists, Labour College students, involved in a quite remarkable attempt to forge a variety of ideological influences upon themselves with the life experience of the coalfield, not simon-pure salaried theorists. It is clear that the tag 'industrial unionist' suits them better than 'syndicalist'. It is also evident that, naive as they may have been about the power and the reactions of the state, they were realists enough to recognise that away from the debates in the Judges' Hall and the Trehafod Hotel, the Labour College lecture rooms and the meetings of SWMF lodges and Unofficial Reform Committees, there was a rank and file of miners they had to win. In attempting to do this they would have to accept an accommodation with more reformist and gradualist views within this SWMF, but this would help to maximise support for the singular vision of the union they proposed. It is recognition of this achievement, rather than an abstract analysis of pure 'syndalism' which gets to the heart of what was taking place in the South Wales coalfield at this time.

What was happening in the coal industry of South Wales during the first two decades of the century was that the conditions of work of rank and file miners were being placed under considerable pressure.[36] The South Wales miners of this period enjoyed a considerable degree of autonomy and control over their work. This is how a miner from Pontardawe in the Swansea Valley expressed this point:

> The industry is free for any man to enter, there being no real apprenticeship. He is paid on piece rates and if not competent ... the union makes no effort to prevent dismissal ... The miner is only a little supervised to see that he is observing the conditions of safety and that he stacks coal properly. On the whole the miner is a greater master of his work than any other worker ... Being paid by piecework ... if he finds he strikes a bad place he may ... approach the manager ... for an allowance ... As to working hours ... as soon as they get finished they can go off. I remember being off sometimes at 10 in the morning.[37]

As well as reflecting the degree of control the collier exercised over his work, the mention of being paid an allowance for working in a 'bad place' where coal was not so easy to cut, indicates the existence of work customs which were as important to the miner as his control over his work. Such customs would vary from pit to pit, but there were widely established ones such as the allowance (usually known as an 'abnormal place' payment) instanced here and others varying from being allowed to take home old pit props for firewood, to being able to leave the pit without management permission to attend the funeral of a fellow miner killed at work. Some of these customs were matters of agreement, others of convention. Some were secret or at least, their existence was not formally admitted by the miners. This included the operation by miners of 'the stint' or 'ca-canny', whereby when working in a seam that was becoming exhausted, miners might agree to regulate production to extend its working life and their employment. This could also be used as a form of pressure upon the coalowners, as what was known as an 'irritant strike' or what would later have been called a 'go slow' and was denounced by the owners as a 'syndicalist' tactic.

The form of trade unionism which had grown up in the coalfield reflected these working conditions of the miner. It was the pit lodge which was the basis and the powerhouse of the SWMF, rather than its district or central organisation, for the miners felt this best enabled them to preserve the work control and customs which they had established at the pit. In the early phases of the development of the coalfield this suited the coalowners as much as the miners, for collieries were in the main owned by companies which had single or small numbers of pits and preferred localised collective bargaining. Thus the lodge developed as the main force in bargaining with the owners over the price lists to be paid to pieceworkers, the rates of wages to be paid to non-pieceworkers, the hours of work above and below ground, and working conditions and allowances. The coming of the SWMF and the conciliation machinery with the Coalowners' Association did little to change this, for it was the way in which the miner prized his work control and his local autonomy which remained the basis of industrial relations in the coalfield. Noah Ablett captured the essence of the miners' attitude on these matters: 'There is the horror of bureaucracy and uniformity commingled with the desire to govern as much as possible the conditions under which one has to live or to put it in the manner of Ibsen - to find oneself by expressing one's individuality ...'.[38] A later leader of the South Wales Area of the National Union of Mineworkers, Dai Dan Evans who was himself strongly influenced by *The Miners' Next Step* has described the effect that local autonomy had on the lodge and the SWMF: '... it tended to build strong independent and versatile thought among the representatives of the men at pit level. It developed a tremendous tradition and possibly accounted for the ultra democratic traditions at the base of the miners' union ...'.[39]

In time, however, Ablett and his fellow members of the Unofficial Reform Committee came to see this autonomy and independence of the miner and his lodge as being as much a weakness as a strength of the SWMF. This was because of the new policies being followed by the coalowners in the first decade of the twentieth century. Although the coalfield was at the peak of its expansion at this time, the coalowners observed two marked tendencies in the economy of the industry which they perceived as a threat to its future profitability. The geology of the South Wales mines and the lack of the successful application of coalcutting machinery meant that the industry was more labour intensive, with higher labour costs than other coalfields. The difficult geology of South Wales, which led to the 'abnormal places' problems described earlier, also meant that the productivity of colliers in South Wales was low and was falling during this period. This was made worse by the effects of the 'Eight Hours Act' of 1908 limiting the length of shifts and, the coalowners believed, by the customs and working practices of the miners such as the use of 'the stint' to limit production. These economic factors played their part in the rationalisation of ownership which was underway in the coalfield during this period and which created the first coal combines, such as the Cambrian Combine Company, which swallowed up former smaller independent concerns. Free, perhaps, of the old ethos of the independent small companies, the combines saw attacking labour costs and working practices in the coalfield as the way to make the industry more profitable. This was done by trying to reduce piecework rates when price lists came up for renewal at colliery level and by attacking customs such as 'the stint' through legal action and dismissal. There was also a concerted attempt to refuse to pay allowances for working in abnormal places and this was the particular background to the Cambrian Combine dispute, the most notable of the legion of disputes, large and small, which rippled across the coalfield from 1906 onwards as the miners responded to these new aggressive policies of the coalowners.   A further illustration of the 'custom-based' nature of these disputes occurred in the Cynon valley where the prosecution of miners for taking home former pit props as firewood, by the Powell Duffryn Company, engendered another long and bitter dispute.[40]   To this day in the valley, timescales are measured by referring for example to events happening 'for the first time since the Block Strike'.

It was from these disputes that the young coalfield militants of the Unofficial Reform Committee began to emerge.   Carrying forward the traditions of independence, work control and lodge autonomy, they found the SWMF and its leadership wanting as the coalowners began an asserted attack upon them.   *The Miners' Next Step* was designed to expose what they saw as the failure of conciliation in the face of this onslaught on their wages and working conditions and to argue that only through adopting a new structure and new policies could this be overcome.   There would be a price to pay, however, for the jealously prized autonomy of the pit and the lodge was seen to have its weaknesses in these new circumstances because, in Ablett's view, '... autonomy divides instead of uniting men, it scatters to waste the wonderful resources of combined solidarity and creates a Babel of interest ...'.   What was needed was a policy of synthesis, which: 'On the one hand embraces the almost innate desire for independence and freedom and on the other the equally intense desire for power'.[41]

This would require the reform of the SWMF into an industrial union under new leadership and with new policies committed to defend what the rank and file miners prized, but equipped to go further and eventually win control of the very industry and its pits for them.   Thus miners' control of their own labour would be extended to become writ large, workers' control of the industry.   This, the message of *The Miners' Next Step*, was in essence the 'syndicalism' of the South Wales militants.   Having taken the rich brew of influences which they had come under and applied them to the objective economic conditions of the coalfield, they came up with their own reasoned, highly articulate and singular response.   Using the life experience of those they sought to give voice to, they attempted to defend what they had which was of worth and to imagine a better life and arrangement of the industry in which they worked. It was neither pure 'syndicalism' nor was it 'bastardised' anything else. In the words of the socialist and feminist Sylvia Pankhurst, who was in close contact with the Unofficial Reform Committee and who noted their arrogance in considering themselves as 'the advanced guard of the workers', what they had fashioned in *The Miners' Next Step* was a 'cult of their own'.[42]

Although it is not possible to trace it in this chapter, it was, however, a cult which was to spread to other coalfields from South Wales and to play a significant part in the militancy and discontent which continued to sweep across the coalfields into the 1920s. In the Northumberland and Durham coalfield, for example, the De Leonist and SLP supporter, George Harvey, and the later national leader of the NUM, Will Lawther, distributed copies of *The Miners' Next Step*. In South Wales this militancy was to persist through the difficult years of the First World War. Although its nature is a matter of some historiographical debate, the coalfield strike of 1915 represented a new highpoint in militancy where the miners of South Wales were seen to have successfully taken on the whole power of a wartime state in achieving a new wage agreement.[43] Such was the continuing spiral of discontent in the coalfield that to protect the desperately needed steamcoal supplies for the navy in 1916, the government took over control of the South Wales mines, a year earlier than the rest of the industry. After the war the ultimately unsuccessful campaign to achieve nationalisation of the industry and the bitter disputes which ravaged the coalfields in 1920, 1921 and in 1926 as the coalowners returned to their policy of driving down wages, saw the ideas of the 'syndicalists' and 'unofficial reformers' to the fore again. Now, in the vocabulary of demonology used by the coalowners and part of the popular press, they were 'bolsheviks' who espoused 'direct action'. In the main the coalfield militants were to find their way into the Communist Party after 1920 (although some, Ablett among them, were to remain aloof) providing an initial strength for that party in South Wales and a tradition it was to draw upon into the future. The Communist Party would now sponsor 'Unofficial Reform Groups' in many of the coalfields in the 1920s which coalesced into the communist-led Minority Movement. It is clear that the defeat of the General Strike and miners' lockout in 1926 dented considerably the confidence in 'direct action' and the power of the miners to take on the might of the state. However, whilst it is also beyond the scope of this chapter to deal with such events, it is possible to argue that the attitudes which developed in South Wales and in other coalfields before the First World War were to re-emerge in the consciousness of the miners and their unions in the 1970s and 1980s, with, of course, varying outcomes. For example, in the circumstances of new unofficial movements which emerged in South Wales and in Yorkshire in the late 1960s and which helped to practice a new militant leadership for the struggles of the 1970s, one South Wales miner recalled the events of 1910-11 in the Rhondda and proudly identified with their ginger group activities.[44]

What can be discerned across the years of this century is a distinctive culture associated with work and trade unionism in the British coalfields which reflects the views and the influences of the South Wales 'cult' of the first decades of the century. It was observed, for example, by sociologists studying a Yorkshire mining community in the 1950s who noted that 'the nature of work... explains in large measure the nature of trades unionism ... the task the miner is called upon to do varies constantly ... this is the reason why unionism has such a powerful appeal'.[45] In the 1980s another sociologist with intimate knowledge of the coalfields was to make the same point in noting that 'the consequence of pit work dominates and persuades all facets of the lives of miners and their families'.[46] Perhaps the connections are best expressed, however, by Will Paynter, a man who was deeply influenced by the traditions he inherited from the coalfield militants of his native Rhondda and, as well as rising to the national leadership of the miners' union, was one of the most percipient of observers of the culture and history of the coalfield. Paynter confesses that:

> It has often been said of me that I was a miner and trades unionist first and a communist second ... I have to admit that it has a good deal of truth in it ... It was true of Arthur Horner and most of the leaders who have lived and worked in the mining valleys of South Wales. Politics took second place to the trade union ...[47]

Paynter believed that this was so because of the uniqueness of the SWMF, although it might be argued that the point he makes here was true of the miners' union across the British coalfields:

> The Fed was a lot more than a trade union; it was a social institution ...
> Its functions became a combination of economic, social and political
> leadership ... It is not surprising, therefore, that this kind of background
> produces a loyalty to the union so strong and primary that the union is
> regarded as a substitute for a political organisation.[48]

It was this reality that Paynter so eloquently describes which was to be the true legacy of the 'syndicalists' of South Wales and the authors of *The Miners' Next Step*. They helped to fashion this union and its philosophy. However their belief in workers' control seemed to have been a casualty in this process, for it would be nationalisation of the mines which would become the policy of the union in Wales and in Britain and which would be welcomed by the Horners and the Paynters when it came in 1947. Perhaps it is to this legacy which, through the quirks of history and fate, the miners of the Tower Colliery now have the right to lay claim. One of the ironies of their situation is that it is the state which has allowed them to do this, rather than to have hindered them. Perhaps in their ability to succeed in their venture, however, they will need to draw upon older traditions and the inspiration they gave to an earlier generation of bold miners' leaders. As their new, non-executive chairman, Philip Weekes, the former NCB man, has observed 'the miners know best how to work the pit'.[49]

Notes

Place of publication is London unless otherwise stated.

1. I am grateful to Nina Fishman and Chris Williams for their assistance in supplying material relevant to this chapter.
2. *Observer*, 1 January 1995. See also the *Guardian*, 3 January 1995 and the *Western Mail*, 3 January 1995.
3. *Guardian*, 3 January 1995.
4. On syndicalism in South Wales see D. Egan, 'The Unofficial Reform Committee and *The Miners' Next Step*', *Llafur*, vol. 2, no. 3, 1978, pp. 64-80; B. Holton, *British Syndicalism 1900-1914* (1976); M.G. Woodhouse, 'Rank and File Movements Amongst the Miners of South Wales 1910-1926', unpublished DPhil thesis, University of Oxford, 1970; D.K. Davies 'The Influence of Syndicalism and Industrial Unionism on the South Wales Coalfield 1898-1921: a study in ideology

and practice', unpublished PhD thesis, University of Wales, 1991.

5. This treatment of the development of the coalfield draws upon my *Coal Society: a history of the South Wales mining valleys 1840-1980* (Llandysul, 1987).

6. The shorthand notes of this debate are to be found in the W.H. Mannering Papers, National Library of Wales, and have been published with an introduction by K.O. Morgan as 'Socialism and syndicalism: the Welsh miners' debate 1912', *Bulletin of the Society for the Study of Labour History*, no. 30, Spring 1975, pp. 22-37.

7. Ibid., p. 26.

8. Ibid., p. 31.

9. D. Egan, 'Noah Ablett 1883-1935', *Llafur*, vol. 4, no. 3, 1986, pp. 11-30.

10. Published at Tonypandy, 1912. Page references in this chapter are to the edition republished in K. Coates (ed.), *Democracy in the Mines* (Nottingham, 1974).

11. Ibid., p. 28.

12. This account of Charlie Gibbons and his life is based on two documents, 'Some facts on which to base public interview of Charles L. Gibbons' c. 1942 and 'Recollections of the movement for independent working class education, 1908-1914', 1959 (National Library of Scotland, Accession 5120, Additional Papers, Box 7, File 5, National Council of Labour Colleges Records). See also Robert Pitt, 'Educator and agitator: Charlie Gibbons 1888-1967', *Llafur*, vol. 5, no. 2, 1988, pp. 72-83.

13. For the story of independent working class education in South Wales see R. Lewis, *Leaders and Teachers* (Cardiff, 1993).

14. *Welsh Outlook*, July 1916, p. 218.

15. H. Francis, 'The origins of the South Wales miners' library', *History Workshop*, no. 2, Autumn 1976.

16. *Welsh Outlook*, ibid.

17. S. Macintyre, *A Proletarian Science: Marxism in Britain, 1917-1933* (1986), p. 38.

18. For Cook, see P. Davies, *A.J. Cook* (Manchester, 1987).

19. C. Gibbons, 'Recollections...'.

20. D.B. Smith, 'Tonypandy 1910: definitions of community', *Past and Present*, no. 87, May 1980.

21. For the history of the SWMF and events in general during this period in South Wales, see H. Francis and D. Smith, *The Fed: a history of the South Wales Miners in the twentieth century* (1980).

22. C.R. Williams, 'The Welsh religious revival, 1904-5', *British Journal of Sociology*, vol. 3, 1952.

23. *Royal Commission on the University of Wales*, 1918, Report and Minutes of Evidence, p. 204.
24. C. Gibbons, 'Recollections...'.
25. University College of Swansea, South Wales Miners' Federation Records, SWMF Special Conference, June 1917.
26. Coates, *Democracy in the Mines*, pp. 105-126.
27. S. and B. Webb, *What Syndicalism Means* (1912), pp. 136-7.
28. Ibid., p. 138.
29. Coates, *Democracy in the Mines*, p. 23.
30. Ibid., p. 30.
31. S. and B. Webb, *What Syndicalism Means*, p. 140.
32. Coates, *Democracy in the Mines*, p. 24.
33. *Merthyr Pioneer*, 10 November 1917.
34. J.A. Cartwright, 'A Study in British Syndicalism: the miners of South Wales 1906-1914', unpublished MSc thesis, University of Wales, 1969, p. 70.
35. C. Gibbons, 'Recollections ...'.
36. See D. Egan, 'Wales at work' in T. Herbert and G.E. Jones (eds), *Wales 1880-1914* (Cardiff, 1988).
37. University College of North Wales, Bangor Mss, Ms 4562, 'Pontardawe 1914-1918' (anonymous, unpublished manuscript) pp. 11-13.
38. London School of Economics, Fabian Research Department Mss, N. Ablett, 'Local autonomy versus centralisation ...' unpublished typescript report, 1913.
39. University College of Swansea, South Wales Area NUM Records, D.D. Evans, 'Change in character of the union' undated (c. late 1950s), unpublished typescript memorandum.
40. See M. Barclay, '"The slaves of the lamp": the Aberdare miners' strike 1910', *Llafur*, vol. 2, no. 3, 1978.
41. N. Ablett, 'Local autonomy versus centralisation...'.
42. S. Pankhurst, *The Home Front* (1932), p. 163.
43. See A. Mor O'Brien, 'Patriotism on trial: the strike of the South Wales miners, July 1915', *Welsh History Review*, vol. 12, 1984-5, pp. 76-104.
44. Francis and Smith, *The Fed*, pp. 462-5.
45. N. Dennis, F. Henriques and C. Slaughter, *Coal is Our Life: an analysis of a Yorkshire mining community*, (2nd edn, 1969), p. 84.
46. V.L. Allen, *The Militancy of British Miners* (Shipley, 1981), p. 62.
47. W. Paynter, *My Generation* (1972), p. 109.
48. Ibid., p. 110.
49. *Observer*, 1 January 1995.

CHAPTER TWO

'All or nowt':
the politics of the MFGB

David Howell

Thus Hugh Dalton characterised the Miners' Federation's style in the summer of 1942.[1] As President of the Board of Trade he had just experienced a bruising battle over the reorganisation of the coal industry. A Labour minister within the Churchill coalition he had faced pressure from Conservative backbenchers, many of whom saw the issue as symbolic, a test of encroaching 'socialist' influence. In contrast, miners' leaders and many Labour Members believed that the proper response by a Labour minister had to be state ownership. For the protagonists the case of coal summoned up images of past battles; it was a test of political identity. The resulting compromise involved a cumbersome apparatus of dual control which strengthened government powers over production, but maintained private ownership. A scheme for coal rationing was effectively abandoned. The Miners' Federation of Great Britain (MFGB) endorsed the deal as the best available and most of its sponsored MPs supported the arrangement.[2] In this context Dalton's suggestion of inflexibility requires clarification. This product of Eton and Kings sat for a County Durham seat and enjoyed a close relationship with the local miners' leadership. Here was the image of miners as a reliable support for the party leadership, a loyalist ballast. Yet there were other images of miners' as sectional and inflexible. If Labour leaders could idealise the Durham miners as 'the salt of the earth',[3] they could also cast A.J. Cook and later radicals as destructive militants who threatened any conception of orderly progress. The diverse images raise important issues about the complex relationship between the MFGB and the Labour Party.

The complexities begin with the structure of the MFGB. Most fundamental was its federalism. From its formation in 1889 the

Federation had taken almost two decades to absorb all the district organisations. The effective national organisation was limited; only in 1919 did the general secretaryship become a full-time post. There were three significant institutions. The executive always included representatives from the larger coalfields, along with a rotation of men from the smaller districts. Total membership was around twenty and members reported back to their districts. Constitutionally the executive was subject to a delegate conference with a membership approaching two hundred. District delegations were composed according to a variety of formulae, but typically were combinations of district officials and some working miners. The annual conference met in July. It concentrated mainly on industrial issues, but some time was allocated to political questions. Industrial crises precipitated special conferences. Conference sovereignty was circumscribed by the third institution, the national ballot, employed on industrial issues such as the approval of wage offers or the initiation or termination of strikes.

The portrait suggests a balance of expertise and popular sentiment with officials and executive members giving guidance to delegates whose decisions had prior status, but whose positions sometimes faced the test of a ballot. This image explains the Webbs' commendation of the early Federation structure as a valuable solution to the problem of trade union government.[4] But the judgement is incomplete. Except in the periodic use of the national ballot and the election of the general secretary, the preferences of members were mediated through district unions. The districts sent their men to the MFGB executive; district conferences determined policies which could be used, sometimes at the discretion, or with the interpretation of district officials, to mandate delegations to MFGB conferences. The bulk of funds collected by district unions remained there with only a pittance going to the Federation.

The consequence was that the Federation often seemed more a collection of disparate unions than a national body. Frequently men sat on its executive or in its conference as ambassadors from coalfields rather than as participants in a collective enterprise. Coalfield chauvinisms emerged at moments of stress. Each district union had its own history - usually longer than the Federation's - its own myths and symbols, and ethos. Against these fissiparous tendencies there was the fact of Federation, an institutional acknowledgement of the desirability of national organisation and action. Such aspirations had to combat not just district identities, but diverse economic conditions and expectations. Maintenance of the MFGB's unity was an art built around the recognition yet limitation of difference.

The district identities typically incorporated political characteristics. Economic experiences within districts had complex relationships with the formal political allegiances of district unions. In part the complexity can be explored through the changing pattern of MFGB factionalism. Prior to 1908, the Federation had divided between Liberals and advocates of affiliation to the Labour Party. The residues of the controversy survived formal affiliation on New Year's Day 1909, but gradually a new alignment began to emerge. Initially this reflected a divergence between advocates of industrial caution and a close relationship with the Labour Party - and those influenced by sentiments of 'direct action'. The character of the Federation left was affected along with other trade union lefts by the formation of the Communist Party and subsequently of the Minority Movement. The transition from the language of 'direct action' to Communist Party membership or sympathies was complex. But by the mid-twenties a pattern of factionalism had emerged that dominated the Federation and subsequently the National Union of Mineworkers for decades. The left was a coalition of communists and those sympathisers, such as S.O. Davies, who remained within the Labour Party. The right included the bulk of district officials and emphasised a 'realistic' defence of miners' interests.

The balance of forces ebbed and flowed with the specific issue, the state of the industry, the skills and follies of individuals and the policy of the Third International. In general the 1926 disaster strengthened the right who fought with vigour and vehemence against post-lockout communist challenges. Left hopes of advance in Durham and Lancashire were largely unfulfilled; in Fife and in Lanarkshire contending factions embarked on a mutually ruinous civil war. South Walian communists retained in contrast a degree of legitimacy. The bitterness reached its zenith in the 'third period'; by the late thirties the MFGB had a more institutionalised pattern of factionalism with the more astute figures in each camp appreciating the need for a *modus vivendi*.

In some cases the affinity between local industrial experiences and political identities seemed straightforward. Relatively prosperous Nottinghamshire had two miners' MPs in the mid-twenties, George Spencer ultra-respectable and militantly anti-communist, and Frank Varley, a thoughtful exponent of industrial and political moderation. The large Yorkshire district with its relative economic strength was a bastion of orthodox Labour politics, but there were significant stylistic differences between the Notts leadership, and the abrasive Herbert Smith and most of his lieutenants. The impoverishment of the Durham coalfield proved compatible with robust Labour loyalism, albeit with a significant cultural shift as the nonconformists James Robson and Peter Lee were succeeded by the secular Will Lawther and Sam Watson. Similarly depressed South Wales often demanded a 'forward' industrial policy; the relative legitimacy of the Communist Party was indicated by the election of Arthur Horner as South Wales president in 1936. Poor conditions in Lancashire meant that its spokesman often articulated a tough line on wages and hours but radical political initiatives were resisted by the local leadership.

The formal political positions of districts sometimes masked internal divisions. In South Wales, several officials had scant sympathy with the more radical district policies. Tom Richards was a venerable and venerated survivor from the old Liberal dominance of mining union politics, and remained active, latterly as Federation president until 1931. Vernon Hartshorn, from the subsequent Independent Labour generation, epitomised key strands in the party-union relationship - trade union official, MP, cabinet minister. In 1927 he played a significant part in the expulsion of communists from his Divisional Labour Party. The characteristic South Wales miners' Member was more James Griffiths, the conciliator from Carmarthenshire or the ultra-respectable loyalist Charles Edwards than Aneurin Bevan or S.O. Davies.[5]

MFGB political policies came out of a complex web of institutional structures, district loyalties, economic priorities and political factionalism. They were articulated by the Federation's officials and were coloured by these individuals' political characteristics. Several national leaders shared a similar pedigree - membership of the ILP, a long career in their coalfield unions and then national eminence. As officials they were loyal to the Labour Party and sought to balance Federation priorities against a wider political agenda. This profile was perhaps the dominant one, represented by Robert Smillie,

Herbert Smith and Ebby Edwards. A variant on the theme was provided by Will Lawther whose political apprenticeship had been more radical but who by the late 1930s fitted this pattern. Joseph Jones was more firmly a partisan of the right, whilst in divergent styles, Tom Richards, Peter Lee and Thomas Ashton were survivors from an earlier Federation politics.

In contrast successive general secretaries fitted no such moulds. Frank Hodges went from radical prodigy to chauvinistic anti-communist, to the status of classic renegade; A.J. Cook, his rhetoric often hiding the pragmatism that came from his syndicalist roots, was as much a victim of the rigid factionalism of the late twenties as of the 1926 defeat. Yet these exceptions during their years as Federation officials played significant roles as articulators of Federation priorities within the Labour Party and to Labour governments.

The most significant formal Federation presence within the Labour Party structure was at the party conference. Until the 1926 defeat and the subsequent decline in membership the Federation affiliation overshadowed all others. For the 1925 conference it affiliated on a membership of 800,000 and had a delegation of 186. Five years later the affiliation had been halved and the size of the delegation was down to 80.[6] The MFGB always took one seat in the trade union section of the party's national executive; in some years in the twenties it secured two.

This massive presence did not lead to overt domination of conference; but the MFGB mattered when votes were cast. Federation delegates typically restricted their interventions to issues of concern to them as miners, but their vote mattered on all issues. Sometimes the MFGB had an unambiguous policy, but often there was little or no guidance from Federation decisions. Officials could be targets for lobbying. In 1927 MacDonald, keen to reverse the previous year's setback on birth control, wrote to the miners' Member Stephen Walsh - 'I hope you will keep a very sharp eye upon how the miners' vote is to be cast at Blackpool. I hear there are all sorts of tricks going to be played upon you, if they can be brought off'.[7]

Often influential figures within the conference delegation were able to obtain what they wanted. It seems that the delegation had little discussion of several issues; indeed the size of the group militated against this. Shortage of time frequently seems to have prevented discussion of the final conference agenda at the district level, and there was no sense in which many delegates could be regarded as representatives.[8] Increasingly the Federation vote seems to have been cast on the basis of loyalty to the party leadership, in part because industrial vulnerability after 1926 seemed to highlight the necessity of a credible political alternative.

One dimension of this search for political influence was the sponsorship of parliamentary candidates. This strategy had its first success in 1874 and became more viable with the expansion of the county franchise in 1884. By the time of the MFGB's affiliation to the Labour Party, the Federation had a credible parliamentary presence. Two Lancashire Members belonged to the Parliamentary Labour Party; the remainder sat as Liberals. The formal affiliation led to most MFGB Members taking the Labour whip, but often this was a prudential decision and had no personal ideological significance. Nevertheless following the general election of 1918 the PLP contained a bloc of Members sponsored by the MFGB who could best be characterised as Labour loyalist. This group expanded, and as former Liberals gave way to the next generation, became politically homogeneous. By the mid-1920s the character and scale of the miners' parliamentary presence was relatively stable. In the general election of 1924, the Labour Party won 151 seats; 40 had Members sponsored by the MFGB. Significantly when the membership of the PLP grew to 287 in 1929, the number of MFGB sponsored Members grew by just one. The Federation had come to dominate a bloc of seats that could be relied on in all but the most cataclysmic of elections. Even in 1931 with the party reduced to 46 seats the MFGB had 23 success; in 1935 the number was restored to 34.[9]

Many miners' MPs intervened in parliamentary debates and party discussions only on coal questions. Some spoke with eloquence on the sufferings of their constituents; in the last months of the 1926 dispute, their speeches often sparkled with anger as habitually cautious men recounted the activities of police and coalowners. Such interventions were the product of crisis; often miners' Members had entered parliament in middle age after long service as checkweighman and perhaps as full-time official. George Warne, elected for Wansbeck in 1922, was unusual in coming direct from coalface to Commons.   Increasingly selection as a sponsored candidate became a consolation prize for those who failed to secure a top post in their district union; typically selection meant a job for life. The deselection of Evan Davies of Ebbw Vale in favour of the 31 year old Aneurin Bevan in 1929 was a singular event; significantly the decisive choice occurred within the miners' union and not within the Divisional Labour Party.[10]   Miners' MPs sometimes continued to act as agents responsible for a group of collieries in their own coalfield. Agent-MPs could return there only at weekends or in parliamentary recesses. A Notts official recalled how in the 1920s the return of Spencer and Varley meant that 'all hell was let loose in the Office between Friday night and Monday morning'.[11] Such moonlighting provided abundant scope for leftwing critics to attack officials for drawing excessive salaries and for incompetence.

The rule-governed careers of most miners' Members were hardly conducive to iconoclasm. A few could be characterised as on the left, most prominently Aneurin Bevan but also two 1930s entrants to parliament, S.O. Davies and Alex Sloan. In the 1920s George Barker was sometimes a dissenting voice whilst Will Lawther brought a left reputation if not practice to the 1929 parliament. One strand in the dominant pattern was captured in characteristically supercilious style by Beatrice Webb in a portrait of the Fife miners' MP, Willie Adamson:

> ... a typical British proletarian in body and mind with an instinctive suspicion of all intellectuals or enthusiasts ... a total abstainer ... domesticated and pious ... He had pushed his way up from hewer to checkweighman, from checkweighman to district agent, from miners' agent to miners' MP by industry and trustworthiness and the habit of keeping himself to himself, making no enemies and never giving himself away.[12]

But if such figures were often prone to the bureaucratic conservatism noted by Michels, often they could point to significant records of creativity in the construction of trade union and political organisation. Whatever their personal predilections as they become men of local standing, one consequence of this status was that they articulated the grievances and priorities of their constituents. One claim brought against the deselected Evan Davies was his blatant disregard of this relationship.

As a political identity was gradually established for miners'
Members in the complex transition from Liberalism to Labour
loyalism, this involved limitations on the activities of sponsored MPs.
George Spencer had risen through the Nottinghamshire Miners'
Association becoming president in 1912 and a sponsored MP in
1918. Very much the respectable, punctilious trade union official,
he acquired a formidable reputation for his skill on compensation
cases. Politically and industrially there was little to distinguish him
from his fellow Notts official and MP Frank Varley. But in October
1926, as Notts' resistance crumbled, the NMA's authority began to
disintegrate. Spencer's negotiation of return-to-work terms at a
group of collieries produced his expulsion from a MFGB conference.
With the subsequent formation of the Nottinghamshire Miners'
Industrial Union (the so-called 'Spencer Union'), the breach took an
organisational form. Spencer's political career effectively ended as
the dominoes fell in quick succession - the end of his MFGB
sponsorship, disowning by his divisional party, opposition from the
party's national executive and the PLP decision to remove the whip.

A Derbyshire miners' MP, Frank Lee queried the wisdom of the
exclusion. MacDonald's response focussed on the constitutionality
of the proceedings:

> The unfortunate thing is that the Labour Party organisation has to act in
> certain ways in accordance with the provisions of its Constitution, and the
> action of Spencer's local people and of the Miners' Federation has given the
> Party no option whatever.

The party leader made his own position clear: 'it is very hard that
men who have served us faithfully, building up the Party for a great
many years, should be turned out because some person or some
movement has come along which has brought destruction near to
us'.[13] The significance of Spencer's exclusion is clarified by the fate
of his colleague, Frank Varley. His crucial difference from Spencer
was that he remained with the official union. The dividing line came
over organisational loyalty rather than political values.

The basic objective behind the sponsorship of Members, and the
making of political policy was to secure results on issues where the
MFGB had an interest. Lodges affiliated to local parties, union
members were active on local authorities. In Durham and in South
Wales they helped to construct political machines that exercised

formidable powers of patronage. But essentially the MFGB was concerned to influence national government. The Federation's early agenda had contained a demand for the eight hour day by legislation. The achievement of this measure in 1908 gave credibility to the strategy. Four years later, legislation on the minimum wage saw the PLP acting for the first time as the articulator of a Federation policy - for the celebrated 'five and the two' (that is, five shillings per day for underground workers and two shillings for boys).[14] Under Robert Smillie's presidency, symbolic of a broader political and generational change, the Federation began to take more seriously the objective of a publicly owned coal industry. Experience of wartime state control and the expectations raised by the Sankey Commission provided the MFGB with a political agenda that lasted until 1947.

The first Labour government offered an introduction to the problems of reconciling Federation priorities with the exigencies of parliamentary arithmetic, perceptions of the economically feasible and the wider concerns of organised labour. MacDonald included three miners in his cabinet - Adamson at the Scottish Office, Stephen Walsh at the War Office and Hartshorn at the Post Office. Only three miners held junior posts but the MFGB was well-represented in the Whips' Office. In 1924, its competence was reckoned to be limited partly on account of the illness of the Chief Whip, Ben Spoor. But Beatrice Webb saw little merit in his assistants: 'the dull-headed miners (the senior Fred Hall, a notorious old slacker) who are subordinate to him, receive but do not earn over £1000 a year as Household Officers'.[15] A patronising image of miners' MPs as intellectually limited and lacking parliamentary involvement was becoming established.

The most critical ministerial posts for the MFGB were the President of the Board of Trade, and within the same Department, the Minister for Mines. The senior post went to Sidney Webb, Member for a Durham mining constituency, and backed in his election campaign by the local lodges of the Durham Miners' Association. The appointment to the second post proved acrimonious. Two Scottish miners' Members wrote critically to MacDonald about the choice of the Glasgow-based trade union official and ILPer Emmanuel Shinwell. James Welsh, a MacDonaldite loyalist suggested that the appointment should go to someone who understood the industry:

That has been our chief complaint for years against Liberal and Conservative administrations ... With the coming of Labour to office; it was expected that we'd be able to get an intelligent discussion on mining questions ... instead of listening to the permanent officials speaking through the figurehead of the Government.[16]

Here was a significant issue that went beyond the specific appointment - how should a Labour government respond to the priorities of a major union? Welsh's case, modestly presented was at odds with MacDonald's philosophy of government. The underlying principle was elaborated by him during the 1926 dispute; it can be found also in his earlier critique of syndicalism and in his response to the 1931 crisis:

Nor do I like the fear of doing something of which the Miners' Federation, may not approve. So soon as a Parliamentary Party subordinates itself to the edicts of any non Parliamentary body, it ceases to be responsible. It must consider public opinion and the conditions under which it has to work, but its decisions must be taken on broader grounds than those held by any outside body. Its duty is not to take orders, but to consider advice. The political organ in society, to me, must ever be the supreme organ and its responsibility belongs to itself.[17]

The 1924 government had already encountered this problem; and its negotiations with the MFGB must be placed within this context. The government's early weeks saw stoppages by the Associated Society of Locomotive Engineers and Firemen, by dockers and by London tramway workers. The first dispute intensified inter-union animosities; the other two were demonstrations of a robust strategy adopted by the Transport Workers' leader Ernest Bevin. The government responded to the tramway strike by proclaiming, but not activating, a state of emergency. J.A. Hobson, the Radical economist, deplored the forcing of sectional demands at 'the expense of the Community of Labour'. Bevin's response was characteristic: 'What is described as separatist policy is the seizing of opportunity ... we must not lose sight of the fact that governments may come and governments may go, but the workers' fight for betterment of conditions must go on all the time'.[18]

Although there was potential for discord between the MFGB and the government, it was realised only rarely during 1924. The sheer novelty of a Labour government produced a supportive response by most miners' leaders and the condition of the coal industry showed some improvement. The French occupation of the Ruhr in January 1923 facilitated a rising demand for British coal, and many miners' wages rose slowly. Nevertheless when the Labour government took office, wages per shift in South Wales, Lancashire and North Staffordshire were at the minima permitted by the agreement of 1921. The government's formation had been preceded by a decisive MFGB ballot vote to terminate that agreement.

Negotiations between the MFGB and the coalowners began only in mid-March and Shinwell and MacDonald immediately became involved.[19] The Federation had adopted a dual strategy. They hoped to achieve improved terms through industrial bargaining, but they also had some optimism about political action. A Yorkshire miners' Member, John Guest, had secured parliamentary time to introduce a bill amending the 1912 Minimum Wage Act. However a week before the scheduled date, the Federation executive met the miners' MPs and found MacDonald, Shinwell and Spoor also present. MacDonald explained that the exigencies of the parliamentary timetable meant the loss of Private Members' time and Guest's bill was an unavoidable casualty. Ministers were also pessimistic about the necessary lobby support from beyond the PLP; even if the bill secured a second reading, it could be irretrievably damaged in committee. Such admonitions applied equally to any ministerial bill on the topic, and despite pressure from both the MFGB, and the PLP, there was no subsequent government initiative. Most miners' officials reacted with understanding to the government's case. Their responses occurred just as the government was moving to declare a state of emergency in the tramway dispute. The parliamentary position was clear; there was no point in securing damaged legislation and there was a general feeling that the government's position should not be jeopardised: 'we are a very important section of the Labour movement, but we are not the Labour movement ... we have the right to take into consideration, if for nothing else, out of pure comradeship, the rest of the men in the movement ...'.[20]

Ministers were eager that the dispute should be resolved as a purely industrial question. Shinwell was active as an intermediary and floated the prospect of a Court of Inquiry. The owners 'final' offer was rejected by a Federation conference, a decision endorsed only narrowly in a subsequent ballot. There followed the Buckmaster

Inquiry into wages in the industry.   Its remit was not to make recommendations, but to produce a reasoned assessment of the points at issue.   The MFGB represented its findings as broadly supportive of the Federation case.   Subsequent negotiations produced small concessions by the owners and the Federation then settled.[21]

Whether the owners were more flexible because of the fact of a Labour government is debatable.   Once the inquiry had been established, the government stayed on the sidelines.   More stress should be placed perhaps on the brief upturn in the industry's fortunes, and the owners' awareness that the MFGB lacked the industrial strength to sustain a strike.   The narrow ballot vote against the March offer was illuminating.   Although the final improvement on the 1921 agreement was limited, it made a fine propaganda point that the advance had occurred under a Labour government.   Plausibly this was their government in a way no predecessor could have claimed.   Yet as Smith praised the government at the Federation's annual conference, the industry's brief upswing was ending.[22]   With the resolution of the Ruhr crisis, markets began to contract and profits were squeezed.   For any economically orthodox government, the implications were sombre.   Loss of office in October 1924 meant that Labour avoided responsibility for a ministerial response to the coming crisis.

The government's minority status meant any attempt to pursue an agenda of public ownership could only be symbolic.   In May 1924, two miners' Members, George Hall and Frank Varley, introduced a Nationalisation of Mines Bill.   Given the state of the parties in parliament, this could only be a propaganda gesture.   The proposals included a Mining Council - a chairman and ten members to be nominated by the government, and ten to be nominated by the MFGB.   Such a proposal highlighted one legacy of the debates over industrial democracy and worker's control which had preoccupied sections of the Federation between 1911 and the early 1920s.   Defeat of the bill was inevitable, but 168 Members backed the bill on second reading demonstrating the predictable strength of PLP opinion.[23]

The most robust exchanges between ministers and Federation officials came just a week before the government's parliamentary defeat.   The Dawes Plan for Reparations might have been lauded as evidence of the government's diplomatic skills, but the Federation leadership was perturbed about the implications for the British coal industry. The indictment of the Minority Movement was hyperbolic - 'No greater insult ever came from Baldwin or Lloyd George to the most powerful industrial organisation in this land' - but discontent was felt by those who were firm Labour loyalists. MacDonald's perception of the argument was coloured by his distaste for the recently elected MFGB General Secretary, A.J. Cook:

> A disappointing interview with the Miners who unfortunately have now got one of the vainest asses in Christendom as Secretary. I gave him a trouncing much to the delight of most of his delegates. The poor miner, facing as he does a serious crisis in his industry, has a man at their head utterly incompetent for his job and with enough vanity to go round the whole of our empire. Some of the wiser heads and the capable young fellows present were at no pains to hide their feelings.[24]

This early round in a long-running obsession missed the point. The MFGB's misgivings were articulated, not just by Cook, but with characteristic vigour by Herbert Smith. Significantly his criticisms concerned procedure as much as policy. The Dawes Report had been adopted by the government without consultation with the MFGB - 'we would not have expected it from the Tory or the Liberal Government'. The crucial question was one of governmental priority. Smith indicted Sidney Webb: 'he simply says what a Tory would do, "I am in". I want to say while he is in, he must represent the people that put him in ...'. The MFGB president's response to MacDonald contrasted with his public panegyrics - 'I used to understand you, but I do not understand you now'.[25]

Tensions between the party leadership and much of the Federation diminished with the advent of the Baldwin government and the industry's deepening crisis. The feud between MacDonald and Cook continued through 'Red Friday', '1926', and the acrimonious postmortems; but another strand in the Labour Party-MFGB relationship was an attempt to construct a more considered policy for the industry. The policy's development occurred in the context of the Samuel Commission, industrial defeat and the strengthened post-1926 commitment of most trade unions to the MacDonald leadership. Faced with industrial weakness, the hope was for electoral victory and a responsive administration.

In March 1929 MFGB officials met MacDonald and some of his parliamentary colleagues to discuss references to the coal industry in the party's forthcoming election manifesto. MacDonald emphasised that there would be no nationalisation measure in the first parliamentary session; instead attention would be given to the repeal of the 1926 Eight Hours Act. A subsequent exchange of letters between Cook and the Parliamentary Labour Party (PLP) secretary, Scott Lindsay seemed to produce an unambiguous commitment on hours.[26] Yet the 1929 Labour government once again found itself dependent on Liberal support. Moreover ministers faced constraints other than the parliamentary. The industry's condition was much worse than in 1924 and most ministers' endorsement of orthodox economic prescriptions meant that scope for manoeuvre was limited. This time the President of the Board of Trade was Willie Graham, a close colleague of Philip Snowden. Cautious, non-adversarial and capable of taking infinite pains, he was much more involved in coal questions than had been Webb.[27] His first colleague as Minister for Mines was Ben Turner, an 'elder statesman' from the trade union movement. He was generally reckoned to have been unsuccessful, and was replaced in mid-1930 by Shinwell.

The new government moved rapidly on the hours question; within days the Federation executive met a team of ministers and MacDonald reiterated the pledge to reduce hours to the pre-1926 level. But another meeting on 19 July 1929 proved more ambiguous. Ministers had spoken to the coalowners who had claimed that the planned reduction of the underground working day by one hour would entail an average increase in costs of two shillings a ton; the consequence would be widespread closures. The only solution would be significant wage cuts. MacDonald asked the officials for their response; Cook, aware of the Federation's industrial weakness emphasised the organisation's political dependence: 'we don't want the Labour government to be pulled down at the moment there is too much to do'. Tom Richards, from another political tradition put it graphically: 'the only hope of getting out of hell, or in any way mitigating the position at all is at the present time with the Labour Government'.[28] Nevertheless the Federation annual conference, meeting soon after the encounter with MacDonald, pledged the MFGB to the repeal of the 1926 Act.[29] The response of ministers became apparent only in mid-October. The initial reduction should be half an hour, not one hour. Further changes would depend on the state of the industry. In some coalfields, most notably Yorkshire where the underground day was already seven and a half hours, the proposal offered nothing. The ministerial announcement produced an immediate critical response. Smith suggested that ministers were 'simply playing the game that the other side want to be played'; Cook emphasised the breaking of the electoral pledge.[30]

The government's prognosis was that the half hour reduction need not involve any wage reductions, but for ministers this was an expectation, not a policy. From its first meeting, the cabinet committee responsible for preparing the draft bill had been clear on the limits of governmental responsibility: '... the question of wages was one for negotiation between the parties ... the government saw no source from which wages could be paid other than the proceeds of the industry itself'.[31] Government attempts to persuade the coalowners to negotiate nationally had produced no response. All that Turner could offer was the hope of an attitudinal shift that ignored dominant perceptions of economic necessity:

> It is desirable that a new atmosphere be created so that the two sides may face the question of wage agreements in a more helpful mood than occurred in 1926. The 'New Atmosphere' can be engendered best ... if we get the two parties arguing in one room together, and if the dogmatic spirit is less displayed by the chief parties in the coalfield.[32]

When a Federation conference met in early November, Yorkshire opposed any deviation from the policy of one hour's reduction without prior consultation in the districts. The outcome was an open division with the Yorkshire delegation walking out of the conference, and Herbert Smith quitting the chair and resigning as national president. The Federation executive responded with a resolution which abandoned the previous policy, whilst proclaiming commitment to it. This was carried by thirteen votes to three and the proposal was then debated in the districts.[33] Subsequently a Federation conference endorsed the retreat with opposition from Yorkshire and the Forest of Dean. MacDonald's reaction to this disunity was typically lugubrious:

> The terrible tragedy of the coal situation is that neither side in conference with each other or with the Government will face the facts and relate them to a policy. What chances have been missed! Owners, men and Government might have come to an agreement to put life into the trade; owners refused to try. Men and Government might have done it, Herbert would not help,

but had one remark for all points - 'Give us 7 hours now'.[34]

The bill covered not just the hours question but complex proposals for amalgamations and marketing which were intended to promote a stronger industry. The second reading in December 1929 came soon after a major ministerial embarrassment over unemployment insurance; the bill's prospects were entangled in the byzantine parliamentary relationship between the Labour and Liberal Parties. In part this involved broader strategic concerns; in part it centred on Liberal concern that colliery amalgamations would not be property facilitated by the bill's proposals. The second reading passed only by eight votes. Whatever the bill's limitations, for Labour loyalists it became a symbol of the government's willingness to survive, an aspiration aided by an eventual concordat with the Liberals.[35]

The Federation executive liaised with miners' MPs on the bill; loyal support should be given to the government despite MFGB criticisms of the bill's contents. The tactic was buttressed by the thorough loyalism of almost all miners' Members, and their antipathy towards the administration's leftwing critics. In committee, James Maxton of the ILP left moved an amendment that the proposed Coal Mines National Industrial Board fix minimum wages for all grades, provided that any minimum was not less than the highest rate for that grade in the district. The initiative must be located in the growing alienation of the ILP left MPs from the government; it was linked to the ILP 'Living Wage' policy and also to Federation concern that wage levels should be protected with the pending cut in hours. Turner's ministerial response was thoroughly orthodox. A living wage could be best secured through effective trade union organisation. A more acrimonious rebuff was given by the miners' Member Duncan Graham:

> the groups who have put forward this Amendment might take it for granted that the Miners' Federation know their own business and do not require to be told by experts outside the mines what they ought to do ... we have come to an honourable understanding with the Government and the miners are supporting the Government ...[36]

When the bill had passed its Commons third reading Willie Graham was strongly appreciative to MacDonald of backbench support:

THE POLITICS OF THE MFGB 51

I should like to pay tribute to the loyalty of our rank and file, and particularly to the Miners' Members ... In my numerous meetings with them they have had only one desire - to be absolutely loyal to you as Prime Minister, to me as Minister in Charge of the Bill, and to the Movement ...[37]

The Lords, with coalowners prominent in debate, precipitated a new crisis for the MFGB and the government. The coalowner, Lord Gainsford, successfully moved an amendment in committee permitting the option of a spreadover on hours.[38] Instead of a straight half hour cut in the daily maximum, the Gainsford amendment allowed the option of a ninety hour fortnight. This could be presented as the equivalent of six shifts of seven and a half hours in each week. The consequences varied between districts depending on local customs including the extent of Saturday shifts. In several districts this would mean in effect the continuation of the eight hour day. Turner felt that the amendment was critical: 'The House of Lords seems to have knocked the Coal Bill into bits ... I do hope that we shall stick to the hours and not allow the spreadover, it has the opposition of practically every miners' Member'.[39] Vernon Hartshorn was emphatic: 'we would infinitely prefer to have this Bill defeated ...'; Shinwell admitted that in the existing economic predicament, for many miners, the spreadover would not be a choice, as the alternative offered would be wage cuts in a situation of weak trade unionism.[40]

The Lords' insistence on the amendment produced a crisis meeting between Federation officials, miners' Members and Willie Graham. The minister insisted that the bill still contained much of value. The parliamentary time expended on the bill represented a substantial investment and abandonment would damage further a government already battered by rising unemployment. The government proposed that the Lords' amendment be itself amended so that a spreadover could be introduced in any district only with the agreement of both owners and the MFGB. The Federation executive were pressurised into a quick decision. No conference was called and the executive decided, apparently by a vote of ten to nine, to accept the government's proposal.[41]

The act came into force on 1 December 1930. All districts hitherto working an eight hour day required a new agreement, thereby raising the issues of wages and the spreadover. District unions had to face their own weaknesses. The government's refusal to become involved in negotiation meant that coalfield unions were forced on to their own resources. With a world depression superimposed on the industry's long term crisis these were few. Whatever the MFGB's principled position, miners were ill-equipped to embark on any stoppage in defence of existing wage standards. The earlier expectation of ministers that a seven and a half hour day was compatible with previous wage levels was exposed as a pious hope. As an experienced district official expressed it: 'If there has to be no reduction and no fight, what is left to the districts. The only way to keep working is to agree to the spreadover'.[42]

An initial Federation stand against the approval of spreadover applications led to chaos as in some coalfields the option was simply adopted. Federation discussions with MacDonald, Graham and Shinwell produced unappealing suggestions: the amendment of the act to remove the MFGB's veto, the prosecution of those acting illegally or MacDonald's suggestion that the Federation accept spreadovers for three months to allow some improvement in the industry. The last proposal went to the districts who accepted it by a very narrow margin. Once again the MFGB had conceded ground to a government whose economic strategy was built around the hope of a trade revival.[43]

In early 1931 such a hope was ludicrous and the truce solved nothing. South Wales miners embarked on a strike which they lacked the resources to maintain. When the MFGB met in conference in March, Tom Richards, voiced the disillusion of even cautious officials:

> if we had a shred of reputation - risking it by urging a disgruntled body of men to accept this, accept that, and accept the other, because it was a Labour Government, believing they were trying to assist us, or believing they were sincere in their attempt to reorganise the industry and that ultimately we should have better conditions. Gentlemen: all that has gone.[44]

Cook was more outspoken in private to MacDonald. The general secretary had been criticised often in Federation conferences for giving the government the benefit of the doubt. The spreadover and the South Wales strike revived the language of 1926:

> I am terribly disappointed at the shabby way our men have been treated in face of the attacks of the coal owners especially in South Wales. I did think a Labour Government would defend its own Mines Act and put up a fight

against the coalowners attacking the mineworkers - but no, we are left to
battle alone against the most vicious set of capitalists existing in this country.
We have had nothing but lavish promises from a Labour Government which
makes it difficult and impossible for some of us to defend in future.[45]

The Eight Hours Act of 1926 was due to expire in July 1931.
Unless the government renewed it, the maximum working day would
be reduced automatically to the seven hours of the 1919 settlement.
If the half hour reduction of 1930 had produced the choice of
spreadover or wage cut, then July 1931 suggested an even worse
prospect. The Federation response was to reject any more
authorisations of spreadovers and to seek an amendment of the 1912
Minimum Wage Act. This initiative involved collaboration on the
drafting of a bill between executive members and some miners' MPs.
But the strategy had to confront the established ministerial view that
the government should not become entangled in wage fixing. These
sentiments had been expressed forcibly by Tom Shaw of the Textile
Workers at an informal ministerial discussion early in 1931:

If the Government enforced this minimum wage the pits would be closed and
the Government would have to maintain the displaced miners. Even if
unification of the mines were arrived at, the mines would still be subject to
the competitive prices of the Continent. It was impossible to graft small
pieces of Socialism onto a non-Socialist system.[46]

Similar concerns were voiced by his ministers. Willie Graham
objected to politicians becoming saddled with trade union
responsibilities: 'the Miners' Federation were not prepared to accept
responsibility for the decisions which would have to be taken; and
were determined to impose on the Government the responsibility for
the decisions and any odium that might attach to them'. Shinwell
dismissed the miners' draft bill as 'quite impracticable'.[47] Protracted
negotiations achieved little with ministers claiming repeatedly that the
combination of a seven hour day and minimum wage legislation
would produce mass closures. Some miners' officials were hostile;
in contrast Ebby Edwards both a miners' Member and an
increasingly significant figure in the Federation demonstrated an
awareness of the competing pressures:

In existing circumstances our Conference would naturally reject the offer of
the owners and call upon the Government to do something. We shall have

to be very careful what we ask them to do. To put it frankly, speaking for the Federation, I do not want to ask the Government for more than it can deliver because I can see that immediately we do that, and we don't deliver ... you have a conflict between the industrial and political movements and a situation which will be neither good for you nor good for us.[48]

MacDonald sometimes was supercilious about the Federation's spokesmen - 'what we are to do with people of that mentality is a great problem'.[49]

Predictably the government delivered little - no reversion to the seven hour day, no new minimum wage legislation. Instead the seven and a half hour day would be continued for twelve months together with the maintenance of the existing minimum rates. The Federation executive eventually accepted the proposals by eleven votes to six and conference delegates endorsed them by a majority of less than two to one. Ministers were all aware of the offer's unattractiveness:

the greatest efforts must be made to persuade the Executive to command the Government's proposals to their Delegate Conference ... In particular it would be necessary to ask the Executive to put the strongest pressure on the Members of Parliament representing mining constituencies, in order to secure their undivided support during the passage of the Bill.[50]

When the bill was debated, the strategy was evident in the comments of one miners' Member: 'my instructions are contained in a telegram from the Yorkshire Miners ... who while expressing their disappointment at the result of the negotiations find themselves unable to do other than support the passage of the Bill'. Edwards identified the bill as 'merely a truce'. Jennie Lee, from a mining family and on the ILP left, acknowledged the industrial reality: 'we know the alternative ... a conflict would be a calamity'.[51]

The subsequent disintegration of the government and the defection of leading ministers gave a retrospective colouring to this history of hopes and disillusion. But the treatment of the miners was not a consequence of a government dominated by leaders who became renegades. This would be a misleadingly teleological view of the government's record. The disintegration was not implicit in earlier ministerial actions and inactions. Moreover, the pessimism about economic possibilities, the refusal to become involved in wage bargaining, the concern not to be seen as the political instrument of

a major union - such sentiments were not specific to MacDonald and
the other defectors. They were articulated by Webb and Graham,
Shinwell and Turner. The complexities of the relationship must be
situated at a specific moment in the party's development and in the
industry's fortune, but they also illuminate broader themes about the
relationship between the political and industrial sides of the labour
movement.

Dalton's 1942 comment managed to combine condescension and
error: 'The miners' leadership this time has been good. They have
learnt the lesson that their traditional policy of "all or nowt" always
ends in nowt'.[52] In fact the MFGB between the wars had been
remarkably flexible in its relationships with Labour politicians, but
it had received little in return. Political leaders often felt constrained
not just by parliamentary arithmetic and perceptions of the
economically feasible, but also by the view that the party should
serve a national or communal interest rather than a sectional one.
Within such parameters Labour politicians might welcome miners'
MPs as docile lobby fodder and seek the backing of district unions
in their local party activities; but they also feared the MFGB as a
sectional, obstinate and potentially disruptive force. The record of
the 1945 administration with the public ownership of the industry,
accompanied by fuel scarcity and the impact of the Cold War on
trade union politics, seemed to exorcise these spectres; but from
1964, the old order returned. Relationships between the NUM and
the Wilson and Callaghan administrations - and subsequently the
party leadership in the years of Thatcherism - had striking parallels
with the world of MacDonald and Cook, Willie Graham and Herbert
Smith.

Notes

Place of publication is London unless otherwise stated.

1. Dalton Diary, 12 June 1942, in Ben Pimlott (ed.), *The Second World
    War Diary of Hugh Dalton 1940-1945* (1986), p. 457.
2. See *HCDeb* 5th Series, vol. 380, cols. 1078-1214 and 1268-1350 (10-
    11 June 1942).
3. A comment made by Douglas Jay (subsequently Lord Jay) to the
    author, July 1969.

4. S. and B. Webb, *Industrial Democracy*, (1901), pp. 43-6.
5. See W. David 'The Labour Party and the "exclusion" of the communists; the case of the Ogmore Divisional Labour Party in the 1920s', *Llafur*, vol. 3, no. 4, 1983, pp. 5-15. For James Griffiths see his autobiography *Pages from Memory* (1969). Griffiths held office in both the Attlee and Wilson administrations. He was MP for Llanelli 1936-1970. Charles Edwards MP for Bedwelty 1918-1950.
6. Figures taken from *Labour Party Conference Reports*.
7. PRO, 30/69, File 1172, MacDonald Papers, Ramsay MacDonald to Stephen Walsh, 22 September 1927.
8. For a demonstration of the problems see the report of Gordon MacDonald MP on the 1930 Party Conference to the Lancashire Miners' Conference, 1 November 1930, Lancashire and Chesire Miners' Federation Records, 1930. See also the *Miner*, 1 October 1927; also on that year's TUC a letter from William Allan, ibid., 17 September 1927.
9. For lists of sponsored Members see *Labour Party Conference Reports*.
10. J.G. Jones, 'Evan Davies and Ebbw Vale: a note', *Llafur*, vol. 3, no. 3, 1982, pp. 93-9.
11. The comment is by Herbert Booth and is cited in A.R. Griffin, *The Miners of Nottinghamshire 1914-1944* (1962), p. 239.
12. M. Cole (ed.), *Beatrice Webb Diaries 1912-1924* (1952), p. 142.
13. MacDonald Papers, File 1172, Frank Lee to Ramsay MacDonald, 22 February 1927 and MacDonald's reply 24 February 1927.
14. *HCDeb* 5th Series, vol. 35, cols. 2239-2310 (22 March 1912).
15. M. Cole (ed.), *Beatrice Webb's Diaries 1924-1932* (1956), p. 13.
16. MacDonald Papers, File 1169, James Welsh to Ramsay MacDonald, 26 January 1924; ibid., File 1168, letter from Duncan Graham to MacDonald 4 January 1924. 1168.
17. PRO 30/69, MacDonald Diary, 4 July 1926.
18. For material see, H.A. Clegg, *A History of British Trade Unions Since 1887 vol. II 1911-1933*, (Oxford, 1985), pp. 369-77; A. Bullock, *The Life and Times of Ernest Bevin, volume one, Trade Union Leader 1881-1940* (1960), pp. 236-47. The Hobson and Bevin comments are in Clegg, *History*, p. 373 and Bullock, *Bevin*, pp. 243-4, respectively. Original locations are *New Leader*, 4th April 1924, and the *Record* (Transport and General Workers' Union) April 1924.
19. The discussion can be traced in Miners' Federation of Great Britain Records for 1924 especially the special conferences of 13 and 14 and 26 March and Executive Committee minutes for 14, 21 and 22 March.
20. E. Hough of Yorkshire, MFGB Special Conference, 26 March 1924, p. 32.

THE POLITICS OF THE MFGB 57

21. MFGB Special Conference, 29 May 1924. Also *Report by a Court of Inquiry concerning the wage position in the coal mining industry* (Cmnd. 2129, 1924).
22. MFGB Annual Conference 1924, pp. 17-22.
23. See *HCDeb* 5th Series, vol. 173, cols. 1715-98 (16 May 1924).
24. MacDonald diary, 1 October 1924.
25. PRO PREM 1.37.
26. For texts of letters between Cook and Scott Lindsay, see MFGB Annual Conference, 1929, Appendix XIII, pp. 276-7.
27. For Willie Graham see T.N. Graham, *Willie Graham* (1948).
28. See Cook's account, MFGB Annual Conference, 1929, pp. 65-9. The judgement about the need for a Labour government is at p. 69 and Richard's comment is at p. 87. The conference debate on the hours question is pp. 62-110.
29. For the text of the resolution see ibid., pp. 109-10.
30. See MFGB, Coal Mines Bill, Reports of meetings with H.M. Government (1930). Smith's comment is at p. 5; Cook's at p. 8 (both 16 October 1929). For the cabinet decision on the same date see PRO CAB 23/62.
31. PRO CAB 27/395, First meeting of Cabinet Committee on preparation of Coal Mines Bill, 18 July 1929.
32. John Rylands University of Manchester Library, MacDonald Collection, Ben Turner to Ramsay MacDonald, 9 August 1929.
33. For the Executive vote see report of John McGurk to Lancashire Special Conference, 16 November 1929, Lancashire and Cheshire Miners' Federation Records, 1929. For the Yorkshire walkout see MFGB Special Conference, 7 November 1929, pp. 80-1.
34. MacDonald Papers, File 559, Ramsay MacDonald to Joseph Jones, 15 November 1929.
35. *HCDeb* 5th Series, vol. 233, cols. 1245-1357 and 1661-1778 (17 and 19 December 1929).
36. Ibid., vol. 235, cols. 294-295 (11 February 1930).
37. MacDonald Papers, File 1175, Willie Graham to Ramsay MacDonald, 4 April 1930.
38. *House of Lords Debates*.
39. MacDonald Papers, File 1175, Ben Turner to Ramsay MacDonald 24 May 1930.
40. Commons consideration of the Lords position on the spreadover is in *HCDeb* 5th Series, vol. 239, cols. 2317-36 and vol. 241, cols. 561-5888 (15 June and 9 July 1930); Hartshorn's comment is in vol. 239, col. 2329 and Shinwell's in vol. 241 at col. 564.
41. For MFGB responses, see Minutes of Executive Committee 4 June

1930 and Report of Executive Committee dated June 1930, but covering that controversy including the July discussions also at pp. 79-88. For the Executive vote of ten to nine, see report of John McGurk to the Lancashire Conference of 9 August 1930, Lancashire and Cheshire Miners' Federation Records 1930.

42. The comment was by Harry Twist of Lancashire, see MFGB Special Conference, 20 November 1930, p. 42.

43. See ibid., p. 82 for decision against approval of spreadover applications from districts, and Special Conference 4 December 1930 for Richard's resumé of discussions with Ministers at pp. 96-100. For District responses to MacDonald's proposal, see Appendix 3 to Minutes of Executive Committee, 16 December 1930. The vote was 271 to 265. An accompanying estimate showed the total numbers working on each side and indicated the MFGB's organisational weaknesses - the balance was 884,622 against 330,214.

44. MFGB Special Conference, 19 March 1930.

45. MacDonald Papers, File 674, A.J. Cook to Ramsay MacDonald, 9 January 1931.

46. An account of the discussion provided for MacDonald is in ibid., File 248.

47. For these comments see PRO CAB 27/450, Minutes of Cabinet Committee established 5 April 1931 to deal with The Coal Situation. Graham's remark is in Minutes for 20 April 1931, Shinwell's comment was made on 22 April.

48. Ibid., Meeting of 25 June 1931, p. 16.

49. MacDonald Papers, File 1176, Ramsay MacDonald to Lord Sankey, 4 May 1931.

50. PRO CAB 27/450, Cabinet Committee Meeting 2 July 1931.

51. *HCDeb* 5th Series, Vol. 251; for the Yorkshire comment see Tom Williams at Col. 1789, Edward's comment is at Col. 1768 and Jennie Lee's at Col. 1778 (6 July 1931).

52. See reference at note 1.

CHAPTER THREE

The Labour Party and electoral politics in the coalfields

Duncan Tanner

Introduction

Surprisingly little has been written on the Labour Party's electoral domination of the coalfields. The inevitability of Labour's forward march, and of the miners' dominant and unproblematic role in that process, was simply assumed. After the miners' unions committed themselves to the Labour Party, historians observed, its victory in the coalfields became inevitable. Trade unions, the most tangible representation of a burgeoning class consciousness, were responsible for Labour's birth and expansion. The miners were the most radical, the most political, union within the labour movement. They dominated whole communities. Their employment conditions created solidarity. Employer paternalism and variations in the prosperity of particular coalfields could delay political change but not halt it. There was thus little to discuss or explain once Labour was established as the main party of the left in 1918.[1]

Newer emphases originate from two distinct spheres. Electoral historians, anxious to challenge a reductionism which saw trade union expansion and 'social class' as a sufficient explanation of electoral change, have argued for a more sophisticated examination of electoral politics.[2] Rather than seeing the miners as the advance guard of a general working class movement, they see them as a distinct group with an unusually pronounced Labour bias which requires special explanation. Recent coalfield historians have also emphasised the variety of social experiences within and between coalfields, suggesting that older simplifications and explanations of 'militancy' collapse under more careful scrutiny.[3]

It is argued here that Labour's domination of the coalfields was achieved gradually and in a far from uniform manner. Emphasis is placed on the means by which social structures and political approaches interacted to turn a community's self-identification and interests into increasingly firm political allegiances. The chapter shows that Labour was unable to produce anything like the same response in more socially diverse areas. A re-examination of Labour's electoral progress in the coalfields can thus enhance our increasingly complex awareness of the coalfields' diverse structures and histories. But it can also contribute to a growing reappraisal of Labour's strengths and weaknesses as a political force in the interwar years,[4] and play a part in the developing challenge to conventional treatments of electoral politics in the first half of the twentieth century.[5] Although political scientists and sociologists have long suggested that Labour support has been higher in mining than in non-mining areas, there is no substantial body of 'revisionist' secondary material on Labour's expansion in the coalfields which this chapter can merely summarise.[6] The extent, impact and chronology of Labour's expansion in the coalfield has not been the subject of detailed analyisis.[7] Given this fact, and the diversity of coalfield experiences documented in section two below, the following pages offer a tentative interpretation, rather than a detailed study. The chapter builds on recent work and draws attention to significant statistical and other information on the nature of Labour's support. It uses such information to suggest that a conceptual change is necessary in order to explain the overall pattern of Labour's electoral position in the coalfields between 1910 and 1947.

Labour's electoral performance in the coalfields

The electoral importance of the coalfields in this period can hardly be overstated. Miners were a large occupational grouping. They constituted more than 30 per cent of the electorate in 40 constituencies before 1918 and 66 thereafter. In a further 16 constituencies before 1914 and 17 thereafter they constituted 20-30 per cent of the electorate.[8] In some of these 'semi-mining' seats, like Doncaster or Wansbeck, miners inhabited and dominated discrete areas of more diverse constituencies.[9] Moreover there were further seats where only a small proportion of the total electorate was employed in mining, but where whole wards or villages were dominated by the coal industry. This is not to suggest that all miners inhabited such communities. There were substantial numbers of miners living alongside non-miners in English and Welsh towns and cities near to coalfields and in diverse and smaller Scottish communities.[10] Nonetheless the mining workforce was sufficiently numerous and concentrated to be a considerable electoral force.

This occupational concentration was an important factor in the early development of working class representation in the coalfields. The earliest miners' MPs were Lib-Labs, accepted by Liberal associations because of the miners' domination of particular seats. After the affiliation of the MFGB to the Labour Party in 1908, most Lib-Lab seats were redesignated 'Labour' from the election in January 1910 (although in a small number the MPs refused to take the Labour whip). In the 1910 election, 14 of Labour's 42 MPs represented mining-dominated seats and a further two were sponsored by the miners' unions. However historians have only recently begun to examine the process by which particular mining communities developed specifically Labour allegiances in the decades before the First World War. In areas like the Rhondda, the miners' candidates elected after the 1884 Reform Act may have taken the Liberal whip, but miners themselves had less and less to do with the Liberal Party. Their allegiance to Liberalism was increasingly doubtful. As new mining settlements were established after 1885, the process of community formation and community campaigning was led by the young and more radical Labour miners moving into these areas.[11] Pockets of support, in which Labour made steady progress in local government as the voice of these new community's values and needs, were thus established. In a few instances, most notably the Labour-held coalfield seats of Chester-le-Street and West Fife, powerful local Labour organisations were established even before 1908, and subsequently made rapid progress.[12]

Despite this, coalfield Labour parties were not known for their strong political organisation. Political activity did increase a little following the MFGB's affiliation, pressure from the Labour Party and the minimum wage strike of 1911-12. Local Labour parties were established or extended, municipal activity was expanded[13] and union organisers engaged in some political work.

Yet even in the 'advanced' coalfields many miners remained

apathetic and some lodges declined to affiliate to local Labour parties. Attempts to establish Labour organisations in coalfields where Lib-Lab sentiment remained strong - in the Midlands in particular - were unsuccessful. In the Scottish coalfield, frequent electoral campaigns produced only limited support.[14]

In electoral terms, however, a gap was already opening between Labour's position in the coalfield seats and that in more socially mixed working class constituencies. Between 1910 and 1914, Labour made substantial progress in the coalfields. In Lancashire Labour had largely overtaken the Liberals by 1914, with substantial municipal successes, especially in the mining areas of Wigan and Leigh.[15] Labour strongholds became stronger and new footholds were established in the weaker areas. In Yorkshire, the North East and South Wales, support was increasing. Nonetheless even here the Liberals were overhauled in just a handful of constituencies. Labour was even weaker in many of the remaining coalfields. The Midlands coalfields were electoral wastelands, while sectarian divisions in Scotland were still a considerable obstacle.[16]

This position changed after the war. As Tables 3.1 and 3.2 indicate, the 1918 election initiated a period in which Labour dominated the coalfield constituencies. It won most of the coalfields seats at every election except 1918 and 1931. In 1929 and 1945 scarcely any of the mining and semi-mining divisions were *not* held by Labour. In some seats Labour's majority was so enormous that all other parties were insignificant. Whilst Labour performed well in non-mining seats, especially in 1929 and 1945, the coalfields stand apart as a uniquely pro-Labour bloc.

The significance of this last point cannot be overstated. Even in the 1918 election, called by the Coalition government almost before the sound of gunfire had faded, Labour won nearly half of the constituencies where miners were a major element. Coalfield constituencies returned nearly 60 per cent of Labour's MPs in 1918, and were responsible for Labour becoming the official party of opposition after the election. Whilst Labour gained seats in other areas where it had pre-war roots and expanded even where it had been weaker, its progress in mining areas was exceptional.[17] Turner concludes his elaborate statistical analysis of the 1918 election thus: 'Labour's voting strength in 1918 rested upon the mining seats, even more than on working class seats in industrial and other towns'. He adds with justice (but limited evidence) that this was not a transient phenomenon: 'Throughout the interwar years Labour's national share of the vote was grounded not just on trade unionists, but more specifically on special groups of trade unionists, particularly miners'.[18]

By the early 1920s, Labour was polling far better in coalfield seats than in nearby seats with a more diverse but largely working class electorate. The Liberals inability even to field candidates in many coalfield seats could explain some of this disparity. Yet even where the Liberals remained semi-active, the difference is still apparent. Table 3.3 shows that in Yorkshire, there was a consistently large difference (of perhaps 10-15 per cent) between Labour's performance in mining constituencies and that in adjacent semi-mining and predominantly working class seats. It also suggests that this margin was less substantial in 1929 (Labour's best interwar election performance) than in 1923. This data is only suggestive. The mining and semi-mining seats referred to in the table are not necessarily typical and the sample is small.[19] The varying voting patterns of the non-mining elements in such seats could distort the comparisons. However, as the 'mining' category excludes those seats with the highest concentration of miners, the table may actually understate the difference between Labour support in these areas and non-mining constituencies. The pro-Labour bias in mining seats became more pronounced in the 1930s. With the exception of several Scottish and a few other mining seats, Labour regained and sometimes extended its coalfield support after the debacle of 1931. The same cannot be said of the party's performance in more diverse working class seats as Tables 3.4 and 3.5 indicate. In 1931, Labour support in predominantly working class Lancashire and Yorkshire constituencies fell by up to 20 per cent *more* than that in nearby coalfield seats.[20] The party's subsequent recovery in 1935 was also far more pronounced in the coalfields than in other seats. As Turner suggested, Labour probably remained disproportionately strong in mining seats throughout the interwar years.

Labour's strength in the coalfields allowed it to break through in 1918 and survive as a major political force in 1931. Without its coalfield base, its position would have been much weaker. It may have been forced to become a very different political party. The

Table 3.1 Labour electoral performance (%) in mining constituencies, 1910-1945

ENGLAND	%Mining	1910J	1918	1922	1923	1924	1929	1931	1935	1945
Cumbria,										
Whitehaven	37.9	28.8	45.6	45.3	53	47.2	46.8	46.7	48.9	61.1
Derbyshire,										
Belper	34.8	-	-	38.9	31.5	41.8	43	39.8	48.9	52.9
Chesterfield	33.2	59.1	-	-	25.9	39.7	54.1	42.5	51	62.8
Clay Cross	62.3	-	45.9	57.9	56	64.4	80.2	64.6	74.6	82.1
Ilkeston	51.4	-	45.2	40	42.1	44.9	59	50	64.3	66.8
North-East	54.6	57.6	28.6	33.9	39.5	44.9	54.6	47.5	57.2	65.6
Durham,										
Barnard Castle	44.6	56.7	42.8	49.3	55.1	49.2	42	44.7	49.8	58.3
Bishop Auckland	50.7	27.9	50.6	53.7	51.2	55.1	55.8	48.6	62.3	64.1
Blaydon	53.6	-	41.6	53.9	67.9	62.6	59.1	49.3	62.3	71.7
Chester-le-Street	56.6	64.8	unop.	68.5	74.7	71	69.8	60.6	71	76.8

contd

Consett	55.4	-	**32.8**	46.5	52	55.9	56.5	**47**	unop.	70.1
Durham	58.5	-	**49.4**	55.2	56.8	54.9	56.8	49.6	59.1	66.2
Houghton-le-Spring	53.6	-	36.4	51.9	59.3	57.8	57.1	**47**	57.2	66.7
Seaham	71.4	-	**41.3**	59.9	71	65.5	72.5	43.7	68.2	80.1
Sedgefield	33.7	-	**36.8**	43.6	**50**	**47.3**	47.7	41.2	52.3	63.8
Spennymoor	62.2	-	**46.5**	50.3	65.7	63	71.8	56.2	71.2	69.9
Gloucestershire, Forest of Dean	33.6	-	62.8	52.4	60.9	53.1	52.1	**47.3**	57.6	65.2
Lancashire, Farnworth	34.2	-	**40.8**	45.6	57.2	47.5	52.2	**46.5**	51.7	66.1
Ince	57.8	60.6	87	67.7	73.5	70	73.8	63.4	72.6	74.4
Newton	30.3	52.7	55	55.6	59.9	56	60.5	**49.4**	58.5	62
Westhoughton	43.3	56.8	63.9	55.4	60.3	55.8	61.4	53.5	60.4	64.9
Leigh	46.9	**24.7**	**46.4**	45	43	51.5	57	52.3	unop.	69.8
ST. HELENS	30.6	53.3	57.1	58.7	55.5	55.8	58.6	**47.6**	53.7	66.2

contd

WIGAN	42.3	52.8	48	56.5	57.6	57.6	58.5	51.1	61.3	68.2
Leicestershire, Bosworth	33.2	-	33.6	31.8	28.9	31.5	37	32	40.8	55.6
Northumberland, Wansbeck	45.3	-	43.1	45.2	56.8	52.9	54.5	41.8	49.2	60
MORPETH	58.2	-	34.3	48.3	64.2	56.8	61.3	48.7	59.2	73.2
Nottinghamshire, Broxtowe	52.9	-	55.2	50.8	54.5	55.4	59.1	51.9	63	72
Mansfield	56.3	-	43.6	48	57.8	59	58.6	55.8	68	75.1
Staffordshire, Cannock	45.2	-	-	36.8	41.4	51.9	54.2	45.4	51	62.6
Leek	30.1	-	51.7	50.8	53.6	51.7	58.5	48.6	57.4	67.2
Lichfield	30.1	-	36.4	46.8	48.5	46.2	42.6	37.2	46.2	55.2
NEWCASTLE-UNDER-LYME	37.3	-	-	60.2	65.6	57.7	69.9	unop.	unop.	66.2
Warwickshire, Nuneaton	40.3	50.8	25.8	32.5	29.1	31.3	44.4	37.7	48.4	58.4

contd

Yorkshire,

Don Valley	41.8	-	**24.5**	47	60.4	53.9	73.3	58.6	68.9	71.7
Hemsworth	65.4	-	55.5	63.2	70.1	69.3	79.9	70.5	80.1	81.4
Normanton	62.7	72.2	unop.	73.3	78	unop.	83.1	69.6	81.4	84.3
Rother Valley	56.1	-	55.1	unop.	68.6	65.3	76.3	62.3	72	75.2
Rotherwell	45.8	-	46.4	62.8	66	61.8	61.7	52.9	64.5	74
Wenworth	66.5	-	59.8	unop.	unop.	unop.	75.1	68.8	82.1	83.6
BARNSLEY	43.7	-	-	55.1	48	51.7	53.8	**49.1**	58.9	72.9

WALES

Denbighshire,

Wrexham	42.6	-	**23.7**	35.8	39	**44.4**	46.4	**47.9**	56.3	56

Glamorganshire,

Caerphilly	65.6	-	54.8	57.2	58.7	59	57.9	67.6	76.3	80.2
Gower	33.1	78.6	54.8	54.2	59.1	57.2	54	53.4	66.8	68.5

contd

Neath	44.6	-	**35.2**	59.5	62.3	unop.	60.2	64	unop.	79.2
Ogmore	63.6	-	unop.	55.8	unop.	unop.	56.7	61	unop.	76.4
Pontypridd	55.1	-	**42.8**	47.2	54.9	55.9	53.1	58.3	unop.	68.6
MERTHYR, ABERDARE	61.2*	-	**21.4**	57.2	58.2	61.6	64.6	unop.	unop.	84.3
MERTHYR, MERTHYR	61.2	-	**47.3**	53	60.1	59.8	59.6	69.4	68	81.4
RHONDDA, EAST	74.4*	78.2*	unop.	55	71.9	unop.	50.2	68.1	67.8	48.4
RHONDDA, WEST	74.4	78.2	unop.	62.1	65.4	unop.	65.1	84.3	unop.	unop.
Monmouthshire,										
Abertillery	73		unop.	unop.	unop.	unop.	64.5	unop.	unop.	86.6
Bedwellty	67		53.6	63	67.6	unop.	79	unop.	unop.	82.1
Ebbw Vale	55.6		unop.	65.4	65.6	unop.	60.3	unop.	77.8	80.1
Pontypool	47.5		39	40.6	50.6	52.6	51.5	56.3	67.9	77.3
SCOTLAND										
Ayrshire, South	40.2	-	37.3	55.6	55.9	50.4	58.1	**45.2**	57.6	61.3
Fife, West	51.9	**36.7**	**72.6**	unop.	65.4	70.9	60	**35.8**	**35.7**	**37.3**

contd

DUNFERMLINE	32.3	-	**32.8**	50.4	53.6	57.9	58.5	**42.1**	52.3	64.7
Lanarkshire, Bothwell	48.2	-	**49.1**	57	60.2	56.3	55.2	**43.5**	60.3	65.8
Hamilton	46	-	42.1	57.6	58.4	60.8	67.1	53.9	65.7	73.5
Lanark	36.8	-	**31**	**45**	50.5	**43.5**	48.7	**36.4**	**35**	52.8
Northern	37.3	-	**34.1**	47.3	50.5	**46.1**	55.9	**44.7**	**14.6**	59.6
Rutherglen	32.9	-	**40.9**	55.1	54.5	52.1	52.2	**43.2**	**49.3**	59.6
Linlithgowshire	36.4	-	**40.3**	46.4	50.9	**48.9**	51.6	**45.3**	54.1	64.1
Midlothian, North	31.7	-	-	**38.3**	45.3	**44.8**	**37.5**	**27.7**	**37.1**	**45.7**
Stirling, West	30.1	-	**28.7**	52.4	51.9	**49.3**	56.7	**46.7**	55.1	54.4

Source: F.W.S. Craig, *British parliamentary election results 1885-1918* (1974) and *1918-49* (1983); M. Kinnear, *The British voter, An atlas and survey*, (2nd edn, 1981).

Notes: Results in bold are Labour defeats. Seats identified in block capitals are borough constituencies. 'Mining constituency' defined as a seat with 30% or more of the male population employed/occupied as miners in 1921. 1910J is the figure for the election in January 1910.

* Figures are for the borough as a whole.

Table 3.2 Labour electoral performance in semi-mining constituencies 1910-45[1]

ENGLAND	%Mining	1910J	1918	1922	1923	1924	1929	1931	1935	1945
Cumberland, Workington	27.5	-	51.5	54.7	56.5	55.6	65.2	54.9	unop.	72.5
Durham, South Shields	23.6	-	**24.8**	**39.7**	**40.7**	**42.1**	42.2	**40.2**	48.1	59.4
WALLSEND	28.1	-	**34**	46.8	55.5	52.4	49.6	**41.4**	**47.4**	60.1
Northumberland, Hexham	27.3	-	26.2	24.2	-	22.7	28.7	26.9	37.5	**41.8**
Nottinghamshire, Bassetlaw	25.8	-	-	**44.8**	28.3	**41**	58.7	33.4	51.3	62.8
Somerset, Frome	27.6	-	**43.9**	48.8	54.4	47.2	45.5	41.7	**43.9**	55.1
Yorkshire, Doncaster	28.5	-	**25**	46.5	60.6	52.7	56	**45.1**	57.6	70.2
Penistone	23	-	-	**33.7**	**33.5**	**38.5**	45.2	**35.6**	53.5	65.8

contd

Pontefract	23.6	-	**37.1**	38.9	45.3	**48.7**	47.8	**44.6**	53.4	60.6
ROTHERHAM	23.9	-	**38.1**	**49**	53.9	54.6	60.4	**49.2**	67.5	74.2

WALES

Brecon & Radnor	23.7	-	-	**32.6**	-	**30.5**	33.7	**40.2**	**47.4**	46.8
Carmarthenshire, Carmarthen	22.5	-	-	-	24.8	**31.5**	38.2	**36.4**	**36.4**	47.4
Llanelli	27.8	-	**46.9**	59.3	55.1	52.9	55.4	**65.3**	unop.	81.1
Glamorganshire, Aberavon	26.8	-	**35.7**	46.6	55.6	53.1	55.9	**58.4**	unop.	72.5

SCOTLAND

Fife, Kirkcaldy	26.4	-	-	**48.6**	54.4	52.7	59.6	**43.1**	56.3	45
Midlothian, South	29	-	**39.4**	36	43	40.8	45.5	**34.5**	**47.2**	55.8
Stirling, East	23.8	-	**32.8**	42	51.1	52.6	53.2	**40.1**	42.1	62.9

1. Seats with 20-30% of the adult male population employed in mining.

Source: as for Table 3.1. Results in bold and block capitals as for Table 3.1.

Table 3.3 Labour electoral performance in mining, semi-mining and predominantly working class constituencies in Yorkshire, 1923 and 1929 (comparable contests only)

1923	Mining[1]	Semi-mining[2]	Predominantly working class[3]
Labour	48	39.4	34.41
Liberal	26	27.75	35.53
Conservative	26	32.85	30.05
1929	Mining[1]	Semi-mining[2]	Predominantly working class[3]
Labour	53.8	46.5	40.48
Liberal	30.8	25.7	28.84
Conservative	15.4	27.8	30.68

1. Barnsley.
2. Penistone and Pontefract.
3. Huddersfield, Cleveland, Colne Valley, Shipley, Sowerby.

Table 3.4 Labour electoral performance in Yorkshire, mining, semi-mining and predominantly* working class constituencies, 1931-35**

Mining constituencies	%Mining	1931	1935
BARNSLEY	43.7	49.1	58.9
Don Valley	41.8	58.6	68.9
Hemsworth	65.4	70.5	80.1
Normanton	62.7	69.6	81.4
Rother Valley	56.1	62.3	72
Rotherwell	45.8	52.9	64.5
Wentworth	66.5	68.8	82.1
Semi-mining	**%Mining**	**1931**	**1935**
ROTHERHAM	23.9	49.2	67.5
Doncaster	28.5	45.1	57.6
Penistone	23	-	53.5
Pontefract	23.6	44.6	53.4
Predominantly working class		**1931**	**1935**
BATLEY AND MORLEY		38.8	53.6
HUDDERSFIELD		29.9	39.2
Cleveland		39.6	47.3
Elland		34.8	47.8
Keighley		-	50.5
Shipley		34.5	-
Sowerby		31.7	46.2
Spen Valley		35.4	49.2

* Constituencies with less than 20% adult males in middle class occupations.
** Labour v Conservative contests only.

Table 3.5 Labour electoral performance in Lancashire mining and other predominantly working class constituencies 1931-35*

Mining constituencies	%Mining	1931	1935
ST. HELENS	30.6	47.6	53.7
WIGAN	42.3	51.1	61.3
Ince	57.8	63.4	72.6
Leigh	46.9	52.3	-
Newton	30.3	49.4	58.5
Westhoughton	43.3	53.5	60.4
Predominantly working class		1931	1935
ACCRINGTON		37.1	45.8
ASHTON		-	50.2
BARROW		43.2	49.7
BLACKBURN		31.6	47.8
BOLTON		31.7	42.8
BURNLEY		-	53.6
BURY		29.7	-
ECCLES		38.2	47.3
NELSON		42.3	54.5
OLDHAM		35.2	-
PRESTON		35.3	46.4
WARRINGTON		43.8	49.3
Heywood and Radcliffe		28.5	39.5
Widnes		37.9	44

* Only results in Conservative v Labour contests recorded.

following section charts, and tries to explain, the creation of Labour's most loyal heartland.

Social structure and political strategy

Labour's expansion in the coalfields was not the inevitable outcome of an emergent class culture, of industrial conflict, trade union expansion or the essential solidarity created by the underground labour process, as historians once assumed and still sometimes argue. Labour's electoral domination of the coalfields was not concurrent with the emergence of class divisions (and industrial unrest) before the First World War, and it was far from uniform thereafter. Whilst Labour captured most coalfield seats from 1918 onwards, the rate, extent and reasons for this progress varied substantially. Evidently, the distribution and scale of Labour's 'core' vote was in part conditioned by the structural characteristics and dynamics of particular coalfield settlements, including the position of women within those communities, the attitudes of other industrial workers, and changes in community relations as a result of economic and social restructuring. Yet structural factors alone can not explain the level of Labour support. Appropriate local political strategies were necessary to realise support, especially when initial political allegiances were being formulated. National political orientations were also significant in expanding support beyond the party's established electoral 'core'. Labour first swept to triumphant success in the election of 1929, when an almost uniformly dramatic increase in the level of its support across the coalfields swept all opposition aside. Although Labour maintained much of this support in 1931 and 1935, there was no further and comparable landslide until 1945, when again it swept to triumphant success as part of a national electoral tide. Explanations of Labour's electoral expansion should consequently address the significant *political* characteristics of these two periods, as well as the features noted above.

The social construction of constituencies had an obvious impact on the pattern of electoral results. In seats with a higher percentage of enfranchised miners (like Hemsworth, Normanton and Wentworth in Yorkshire or many of the South Wales constituencies) Labour polls of over 60 per cent were common by 1922. There was limited scope for further expansion. At the other extreme, however, Labour was much less successful in seats where less than a third of the electorate were employed in mining, especially if a good percentage of the remainder were employed in agriculture - as in Wansbeck, Hexham, Lichfield and many of the Scottish seats - rather than in manufacturing.[21] However, the presence of unionised workers was not itself a guarantee of support. There were manufacturing areas, including some unionised manufacturing areas, where Labour consistently did badly. It may also have been circumstances within particular unionised sectors of the economy which encouraged Labour voting, rather than the fact of unionisation itself. This is an area where assumption is more dominant than evidence. More attention has been paid to showing that sectarian division in some parts of Scotland and in Lancashire was a factor in minimising the level of community solidarity and hence Labour support. Where local politicians could appeal on religious lines, it was difficult to establish the cultural roots which made Labour so popular elsewhere.[22]

There were other and more complex respects in which the structure of communities influenced the pattern of Labour support. In Nottinghamshire, communities established and controlled by companies were far less likely to generate independent political sentiments. In other parts of the same coalfield, mining families enjoyed access to a diverse range of occupations and cultural outlets, and sometimes commuted to pits from distant settlements. Those living in such circumstances were less likely to develop an industrial radicalism than the inhabitants of 'closed' settlements, where the pressure to conform to local norms reinforced shared experiences and values. In the Lothians miners were also less than fully integrated with, and established within, the rather mixed local community. Through consultation and discussion of industrial matters, and by providing facilities to a workforce of locally born, second or third generation miners, capital was less alienated from labour than in other areas.[23] In all three instances Labour support was correspondingly lower for much of this period.

Whilst the mining village (and increasingly, the mining town) were common, especially in the North East, Yorkshire and South Wales, it was not unusual even in these areas to find miners living in larger industrial centres. Sunderland, South Shields, Doncaster, Rotherham,

Morley and Merthyr all contained miners who commuted to work.[24] In Lancashire this was even more common, whilst in smaller and expanding coalfields (notably those of Kent and North Wales) commuting was parallelled by the development of pit villages and company towns.[25] Again, there is some evidence that this was accompanied by lower levels of support for the Labour Party.[26] It was difficult enough in the 1920s to construct a political appeal which was acceptable to a disparate community which contained only a minority of miners. In the 1930s it probably became harder. We know that in some non-mining areas unemployment and a paternalist renaissance provided a fertile environment for Tory politicians. It is possible that similar circumstances were apparent on the fringes of the coalfields and even in the coalfields themselves.[27]

Other hitherto neglected structural characteristics could also be significant. The establishment of 'miners' council estates in Kent and elsewhere, and the coalowners' retreat (in many areas) from the provision of housing, influenced the nature of mining communities. The expansion of urban council estates into coalfield seats significantly altered some constituencies. Such developments could foster solidarities; they could increase Labour support by encouraging a sense of class unity or simply by altering the numerical balance of power in a seat. They could also create tensions within and between the older and newer communities. The impact of suburban development in non-mining areas was far from uniform and there is no reason to assume that the coalfields were any different.[28]

The age structure of coalfield communities may also have been influential. Inhabitants of newer settlements, younger families with different housing and social needs and fewer established community political norms, were more easily converted to Labour's political creed. Of course, the political impact of generational changes should not be exaggerated. It is unusual to see more than limited political change from one generation to the next, except in circumstances similar to those noted above. The young were also less likely to vote than older voters and many did not qualify for the municipal franchise even after 1918.[29]

Without wishing to endorse sociological theories which emphasise the impact of geographical isolation, the centrality of the union to the community and the religious and occupational unity of coalfields, such factors certainly made it easier for Labour to become the

accepted voice of coalfield communities. It was easier to represent
the economic interests of communities whose whole livelihood was
dependent on a single industry's prosperity. It was easier to create
a sense of pride in the unique political unity of these areas, to portray
Labour as the voice of morality and natural justice, when
communities shared so much and the dominant 'external' culture
seemed critical and alien.[30] It was easier to manufacture a language
of class which was locally meaningful.

Labour in the coalfields, 1918-45

Many Labour victories in 1918 occurred in seats where the party had
already established its roots in the community. War had further
enhanced the party's credibility. Colliers felt they had contributed
massively to the war effort. They had accepted reasonable wage
increases, increased production, volunteered for the front in vast
numbers.[31] They had made their patriotic sacrifice and felt betrayed
by profiteering coalowners. Labour represented the miners'
patriotism and their sense of moral superiority over, and distance
from, the affluent.[32] The party had also developed a more practical
image. Nationalisation of the coal industry became a more prominent
and credible feature of Labour's programme in 1918-20.
Government regulation and control of the coalfield during the war
suggested that state involvement could work. More uniform wage
rates improved prospects, especially for those working in
unproductive or dangerous pits. The unions wanted recognition of
coal's position in the economy, and an opportunity to create a more
productive and rational industry free from managerial oppression.
Labour offered communities the possibility of security and
independence through a new definition of what was economically
right.[33] The increased involvement of the miners' unions in Labour
politics, their formation of local parties and sponsorship of
candidates, seemed to lend credence and respectability to Labour's
cause.[34] This new respectability and social salience helps to explain
Labour's victories in areas where it had previously enjoyed little
support - in Somerset, for example, and in Staffordshire.[35] Labour
was helped by the Liberals' demise as a credible alternative and by
the allocation of the 'coupon' in 1918 (which meant that a number of

'patriotic' Labour miners were not opposed by a Coalition candidate.)[36]

Despite these successes some unions, and some miners, were unenthusiastic about the Labour Party in 1918, not least because of Labour's 'socialist' image.[37] However, in the immediate postwar years miners' unions, local coalfield Labour parties and the national leadership took steps to consolidate the recently established bridgehead. In Yorkshire, Derbyshire and Durham, for example, political levies were increased. As a result more organisers and election agents were employed and increased financial assistance was given to union members standing in local elections.[38] Local parties attempted to affiliate more union branches and to increase their representation on public bodies.[39] In the 1919 municipal elections many succeeded. Labour gained political control in a number of coalfield settlements. In semi-mining seats, it was generally the mining villages and wards which produced the most substantial Labour support (although some remained resistant to change).[40]

Miners placed their weight behind the Labour Party, standing as candidates in local contests, publicly stating their position and generally establishing Labour's credibility as *the* miners' party.[41] 'Union', 'community', 'Labour' and often 'religious' leaders became one and the same. Union fiefdoms were established. In Barnsley, for example, it was not only the leading union officials, Joseph Jones and Herbert Smith, who were municipal candidates - by 1927 the East ward was represented by Smith and two of his relatives (both active in the union). This was not unusual.[42] Most coalfield Labour parties contained few politically active miners and even fewer individual members. The local secretary, agent, and sometimes MP, played vital roles. Individual membership and union involvement only increased substantially in the 1930s.[43] With political success the community functions of Labour and union leaders expanded still further. Labour's status and respectability was correspondingly enhanced.

Labour's stance at the national level also contributed to its expansion. By deliberately emphasising the importance of nationalisation in 1918, Labour was publicly supporting the miners' unions and defending the future of coalfield communities. A massive literature and propaganda campaign was subsequently conducted across the country.[44] It was matched, however, by an anti-Labour campaign which portrayed nationalisation as a means to increase wages at the expense of the consumer. Labour and the MFGB counter-attacked,[45] but the public did not necessarily accept their arguments. What miners saw as a progressive and morally justified policy was not necessarily endorsed outside the coalfields.

If the 'public' saw the miners' interests as very different from their own, then Labour clearly faced a serious problem in supporting the latter rather than the former. This problem was particularly acute because the mining 'block', though large, was not securely 'Labour' whilst the Liberals remained a political force. As Tables 3.1 and 3.2 show, the vast majority of coalfield seats had fallen to Labour by 1922. However in many such seats Labour's majority was substantially lower than classic assumptions about miners' politics might lead one to expect. There were also a number of constituencies, particularly in the Midlands and Scottish coalfields, and where miners were a less substantial part of the electorate, where Labour was unsuccessful. Labour's position was not secure; nor was its further expansion guaranteed.

Social conditions were certainly less favourable in some coalfields and in semi-mining seats containing a mixture of occupational groups. But the problem here was similar to that in the country as a whole. If Labour acted to represent the perceived interests and views of miners, it could alienate the remainder of the population. Where miners were just one of several powerful groups in an area, and in a local Labour party, any attempt to adopt the approach successful in coalfield dominated seats created problems. In Derbyshire, for example, Labour officials stated emphatically that they were 'not going to be dictated to by the miners'. The miners' union in turn identified a clique within the party, an amalgam of 'trade unions and individual Labour Party members banded together in opposition to any step the Miners' Association might take'. Mutual suspicion was common. In South Shields similar tensions led to lodge complaints that Labour officials were 'pouring contemptuous and scurrilous odium upon Trade Unionists and particularly miners'.[46] When the Staffordshire miners declined to lend financial support to Labour parties in Lichfield and Nuneaton, as funds were allegedly too limited, Labour's election agent produced contrary figures to suggest that this was just 'the same old tale'.[47] It was often suggested that miners used their potential financial contribution and other forms of pressure to get nominees accepted as candidates, and concentrated money and support only on seats where they could dictate the political approach.[48]

In these circumstances, Labour parties sometimes abandoned attempts to select miners as candidates. Some attempted to increase individual membership or shifted the balance of campaigning towards 'new' issues - either focussing on a broader range of industrial groups or on issues such as housing, education and 'welfare' matters generally. Some established constituency newspapers as a means to reach a broader audience.[49]

This reorientation may have been part of a broader shift within Labour politics during the 1920s. Savage has suggested that such a change took place in southern Britain, that it coincided with an increase of women members, and could have been matched by an increase in support from women voters.[50] It should not be assumed that similar developments were absent from the coalfields. Networks of women's committees appeared in a number of coalfield seats and women were often a majority in Labour's individual membership.[51] They consequently dominated some local Labour parties and were represented on some divisional executives.[52] Yet the impression that coalfield politics were dominated by the masculine values of life underground is not without substance. Women seldom obtained leading positions in coalfield Labour parties, which invariably declined to discuss issues such as birth control.[53]

Yet it would be misleading to see Labour politics in the coalfields as a simple choice between a union-dominated 'Labourism' and a 'welfarism' advocated by 'new' elements within the party. By 1925, Labour was the leading party on a vast array of local bodies. It had to be concerned with 'welfare' issues, and often wanted to address such matters. Many Labour local authorities prided themselves on the contribution which they made to alleviating the housing problem.[54] Labour county councils, in Durham and South Wales at least, funded more free places at grammar schools than most local authorities. Labour's political appeal undeniably expanded in the 1920s; why it did so, and how its local government policies contributed to this, remains unclear.[55]

Whether as a result of a broader approach, better organisation, or simply changing circumstances, Labour made further and substantial electoral progress between 1923 and 1929. In the municipal elections of 1927 voter enthusiasm generated a substantial nationwide swing towards Labour. In Labour-dominated mining areas turnout sometimes reached 70 per cent. In 1928 further successes established one-party domination across whole areas of the coalfields. Again turnout was often high.[56] In Monmouth, Glamorgan, Yorkshire and Durham, Labour gained between six and eight seats on the county council. It achieved total, or near total domination of a vast array of urban councils and boards of guardians - 'breaking all previous records' in parts of County Durham, 'sweeping' the Afon Valley and establishing an unassailable domination elsewhere. However Labour also made massive progress in the Midlands, hitherto a weaker area. In Nottinghamshire it gained seats in 'radical' centres like Mansfield, but also in Eastwood and Hucknell, where Gilbert has shown that social conditions were less favourable.[57] Labour also established an even tighter hold over mining areas in constituencies like Nuneaton.[58]

Gains made in municipal contests were reflected in the 1929 parliamentary election. Labour won all but one of the coalfield seats, and almost all of those with a smaller mining element. In seats where Labour had made early progress its vote reached proportions hardly surpassed even in 1945. The most dramatic and significant shift, however, was in the Midlands. As Table 3.6 indicates, Labour added between 14 and 18 per cent to its vote, even when faced with Liberal opposition in areas with a strong Liberal tradition. Labour's position was no longer threatened by a Liberal revival.

In the circumstances of 1929 such victories seem unsurprising. In 1927-9 unemployment and short-time working was growing. Pits were being closed. Rationalisation did little to remedy the position. Often it made matters worse. Prosperity and security were threatened. Union action could only minimise the damage.[59] Labour did not promise easy solutions. It did not have to. Its main policy proposals, nationalisation and rationalisation, were not so much policies which gained support as expressions of Labour's commitment and a community's hopes. As in 1918, intervention by the state seemed the only means of providing a future. Labour seemed the only party which might be trusted to help.[60] The party's triumph in 1929 was wholly predictable.

Labour's victory in 1929 was not based solely on miners' votes, even in coalfield seats. The election was preceded by attempts to expand the party's machinery and broaden its electoral base.

Table 3.6 Electoral trends in selected seats, Midlands
coalfields, 1923-29

A. Derbyshire

	1923	1929	Change
LABOUR	34.3	52.57	+18.27
LIBERAL	34.46	21.61	-12.85
CONSERVATIVE	31.24	25.81	-5.43

Seats covered: Belper, Chesterfield, Ilkeston, North-East

B. Other Midlands constituencies

	1923	1929	Change
LABOUR	34.58	48.74	+14.16
LIBERAL	33.95	24.04	-9.91
CONSERVATIVE	31.47	27.22	-4.25

Seats covered: Staffs, Cannock, Warwicks, Nuneaton

Municipal election results seem to indicate a degree of success.[61] Rossiter's work suggests that non-miners in coalfield seats were more likely to vote Labour in 1929 than they had been in 1923, whilst in both elections they were more firmly committed to the Labour Party than voters outside the coalfields.[62] The party also benefited from the spread of working class council estates into coalfield seats which bordered cities - a process which continued into the 1930s.[63] Although there is still evidence of mutual tensions and suspicion between miners and non-miners, there was also public sympathy for the miners' plight in 1929 (evident in the formation of the Prince of Wales fund). The strength of Labour's position in 1929 needs to be recognised. Labour's approach to the economy, and its growing concern with health, education, housing and economic reconstruction, helped the party assemble a broader political appeal.[64] By the 1920s Labour was beginning to develop a concrete programme. It advocated 'sane' long term changes in the economic and social structure of Britain through rationalisation, nationalisation or state involvement. Leaders spoke of social rights and social duties, of a new social relationship between the individual and the state. Despite this, 1929 is often seen as a 'negative' or 'fragile' victory, while the programme of the second Labour government has been seen as a dismal failure.[65] Yet the party's *aims* were not proven inadequate by its period in office; it was simply overwhelmed by a massive economic crisis which made its essentially long term programme an inappropriate response to a short term crisis. As a result of the damage done in 1931, Labour's national electoral progress was deferred for almost 15 years.

Nonetheless a recovery, and a partial reorientation, did occur in the 1930s. This chapter can only outline some of these developments. In a number of coalfield seats, party membership reached record levels in the 1930s; in Doncaster it almost doubled between 1929 and 1937, when it was five times greater than in 1921; elsewhere union officials became more actively involved in Labour politics.[66] Organisation was improved in the weaker sections of constituencies.[67] If things were difficult immediately after 1931, subsequent years brought substantial improvements.

As the figures in Tables 3.1 and 3.2 indicated, in 1935 Labour often polled better than in 1929. Coalfield seats became even more strongly Labour, at a time when other working class seats did not.

Whilst some local lodges continued to assert their control over local politics, even when the mining population was falling,[68] other Labour parties in coalfield seats selected candidates with a potentially broader appeal.[69] Several parties came to recognise that those in public employment, and those who lived on council estates, were likely supporters of a party which wished to improve collective facilities and services.[70] It is difficult to determine the extent of these changes or their impact on Labour's position by 1939. Whilst the expansion of council estates added to Labour's support in some places, this progress may have slowed after 1935.[71] However, it is clear that by 1939 Labour had recreated and extended parts of the political appeal - and the electoral base - which it had erected ten years earlier. Whether Labour's collectivist thrust had a negative impact on its attempts to mobilise support outside the heavy industrial areas is an important possibility which cannot be addressed here.

In 1945 Labour triumphed across Britain. Public hopes for the viability of collective provision as a means of recreating a better version of the past were considerably enhanced.[72] The imbalance between Labour support in coalfield and non-coalfield areas was reduced, even though Labour achieved enormous majorities in the coalfield seats. 1945 cemented the almost legendary electoral relationship between the Labour Party and the mining areas of Britain. The nationwide approach which Labour had started to develop in 1929 was extended and reinforced by new experiences and a more concrete vision. This time, however, the party was able to turn (some) of its aims and visions into concrete policies, and to have a marked impact on the coal industry and its communities.

Notes

Place of publication is London unless otherwise stated.

1. See R. Gregory, *The Miners and British Politics 1906-14* (Oxford, 1968). There is little analysis of domestic Labour politics in most union histories, e.g. R. Page Arnot, *The Miners: years of struggle* (1953); W.R. Garside, *The Durham Miners 1919-60* (1971), ch. 8; H. Francis and D. Smith, *The Fed* (1980).

2. D.M. Tanner, *Political Change and the Labour Party 1900-18* (Cambridge, 1990), esp. pp. 10-16, 419-21, 441; J. Turner, *British*

Politics and the Great War (1992), ch.11. See also my 'Class voting and radical politics: the electoral expansion of the Labour Party 1910-31', in M. Taylor and J. Lawrence (eds), *Party, State and Society: electoral behaviour in modern Britain* (Scolar, forthcoming) and J. Turner, 'Sex, age and the Labour vote in the 1920s', *History and Computing II* (Manchester, 1989).

3. A.B. Campbell, *The Lanarkshire Miners* (Edinburgh, 1979) and 'Communism in the Scottish coalfields, 1920-36: a comparative analysis of implantation and rejection', *Tijdschrift voor Sociale Geschiedenis*, vol. 18, 1992; D. Gilbert, *Class, Community and Collective action* (Oxford, 1992); I.M. Zweiniger-Bargielowska, 'Miners' militancy: a study of four South Wales collieries during the middle of the twentieth century', *Welsh History Review*, vol. 16, 1992.

4. See, for example, A. McKinlay and R.J. Morris (eds), *The ILP on Clydeside* (Manchester, 1991) and D.M. Tanner, 'British and European socialism', *Journal of 20th Century British History* (forthcoming).

5. This includes works which place more emphasis on social structures and 'class' experience than does the following analysis, e.g. M. Savage, *The Dynamics of Working Class Politics* (Cambridge, 1987), and his 'Urban history and social class: two paradigms', *Urban History*, vol. 20, 1993.

6. W.L. Miller *Electoral Dynamics in Britain since 1918* (1977), pp. 88, 214; D. Butler and D. Stokes *Political Change in Britain* (2nd edn, 1974), pp. 130-4.

7. Although see the statistical study by D.J. Rossiter, 'The Miners' Sphere of Influence: an attempt to quantify electoral behaviour in mining areas between the wars', unpublished PhD thesis, University of Sheffield, 1980.

8. Gregory, *Miners*, pp. 198-201; M. Kinnear, *The British Voter. An atlas and survey since 1885* (2nd edn, 1981), pp. 116-8 and calculations from the Census.

9. K. Teanby, '"Not Equal to the Demand": major concerns of the Doncaster Divisional Labour Party', unpublished MPhil thesis, University of Sheffield, 1983, pp. 3-17; J. Quinn, 'Wansbeck Labour Party', introduction to the Wansbeck Labour Party records in the E.P. Microform series 'Origins and development of the Labour Party at local level', pp. 1-5. All local party records cited below are from this collection, available at the British Library of Political and Economic Science (BLPES) and other archives, unless otherwise stated.

10. See references at n.30 below.

11. C.M. Williams, 'Democratic Rhondda: politics and society

1850-1955', unpublished PhD thesis, University of Wales (Cardiff), 1991, chs 2-3; Gilbert, *Class, Community and Collective Action*, pp. 110-122; V.G. Hall 'Aspects of the Political and Social History of Ashington, a Northumberland Coal Mining Community 1870-1914', unpublished PhD thesis, University of London, 1993, pp. 211-78, 312-23.

12. D. Howell, *British Workers and the Independent Labour Party 1888-1906* (Manchester, 1983), pp. 46-9; *Northern Democrat*, July 1910; *Forward*, 5 October 1912.

13. Williams (thesis) pp. 253-5; Tanner, *Political Change*, pp. 203-4, 216-22.

14. Tanner, ibid., pp. 22-4; BLPES, Francis Johnson Ms, 1913/74, Keir Hardie to A. Henderson, 7 May 1913 (South Ayr); I.G.C. Hutchison, *A Political History of Scotland* (Edinburgh, 1986), p. 255.

15. Comments on municipal results and annual report, *Wigan Observer*, 11 June 1914; Leigh DLP *Annual report and balance sheet* 1915.

16. Tanner, *Political Change*, pp. 205-26 for the evidence to this effect. See also Campbell, Chapter 6 in this volume, below.

17. Tanner, ibid., pp. 412-15.

18. Turner, *Great War*, pp. 424, 435.

19. The 'predominantly working class' category excludes constituencies in cities which were divided into several parliamentary divisions. Such constituencies *might* have contained a largely working class population, but census information on occupational types is only available for the whole boroughs.

20. Chosen because both counties contained large numbers of mining and predominantly working class constituencies.

21. In Lanark, for example, even individual wards contained a mixed population (see *Electoral register 1918-19*, which lists the occupations of voters).

22. See, for example, *Hamilton Advertiser*, 19 April 1919, 15 April 1922, noting municipal success of Roman Catholic candidates and protestant clergymen.

23. R. Waller, *The Dukeries Transformed. The social and political development of a 20th century coalfield* (Oxford, 1983), pp. 132-7, 291-3; Gilbert, *Class, Community, Collective Action*, ch. 5; P.M. Bonsall, 'The Somerset and Lothian Miners 1919-c.1947: changing attitudes to pit work in the twentieth century', unpublished PhD thesis, University of Warwick, 1991, pp. 15-20, 50, 115, 144-5, 175, 222.

24. C. Baylies, *The History of the Yorkshire Miners 1881-1918* (1993), pp. 1, 5, 21; R.G. Neville, 'The Yorkshire Miners 1881-1926: a study in labour and social history', unpublished PhD thesis, University of

Leeds, 1974, pp. 811-12; Gregory, *Miners*, p. 200.

25. W. Johnson, 'The Development of the Kent Coalfield, 1890-1946', unpublished PhD thesis, University of Kent, 1972, pp. 181, 234, 238, 410-35; G.G. Lerry, *Collieries of Denbighshire* (2nd edn, Wrexham, 1968), pp. 65, 75.

26. Compare, for example, municipal reports, *Dover Standard*, 4 November, 1927 and details of later successes in Kent, Johnson ibid., pp. 400-1; R. Eatwell, 'Wrexham Labour Party', p. 14.

27. As suggested by Savage, *Dynamics of Working Class Politics*, pp. 180-4.

28. Johnson (thesis), pp. 234-8. For differing views on the social impact of council estates, see, for example, J. Turnball, 'Housing Tenure and Social Structure: impact of interwar housing change in Carlisle, 1917-1939', unpublished PhD thesis, University of Lancaster, 1992, esp. pp. 403-11; A.J. Olechnowicz 'Economic and Social Development of Inter-war County Municipal Housing Settlements', unpublished DPhil thesis, University of Oxford, 1991, esp. pp. 105-17. For the encroachment of council estates into coalfield seats, below p. 85.

29. Hall (thesis), pp. 323-34. Cf. D. Hopkin, 'The rise of Labour: Llanelli 1890-1922', in G.H. Jenkins and J.B. Smith (eds), *Politics and Society in Wales 1840-1922* (Cardiff, 1988), pp. 173-7.

30. For the coalfield culture which created this value system see, for example, D. Smith, *Aneurin Bevan and the World of South Wales* (Cardiff, 1993), ch. 8. Miners often (and rightly) felt their lifestyle was derided and under attack from 'outsiders'. See, for example, allegations of theft, violence and absenteeism in mining areas, *Barnsley Independent*, 16 and 30 May 1925. See also miners' opinions on their unfair treatment by outside authorities, Johnson (thesis), p. 437. For broader parallells, C. Wrigley, *Lloyd George and the Challenge of Labour. The postwar coalition 1918-22* (1990) and R.I. McKibbin, 'Class and conventional wisdom: the Conservative party and the "public" in interwar Britain', in his *Ideologies of Class* (Oxford, 1990).

31. J.J. Lawson, *A Man's Life* (1946), ch. 22.

32. A.R. Griffin, *A History of the Nottingham Miners' Union* (1962), pp. 22-3, Durham Miners' Association *Monthly Circular*, January 1916, March 1918; A. Mor O'Brien, 'Patriotism on trial: the strike of the South Wales miners, July 1915', *Welsh History Review*, vol. 12, 1984, pp. 92-5.

33. B. Supple, *The History of the British Coal Industry*, vol. 4 (Oxford, 1987), pp. 82-6, 110, 121-3, and R.H. Tawney, *The Nationalisation*

of the Coal Industry (1919). For local examples of campaign speeches, see *Wrexham Advertiser*, 30 November, 1918 (I owe this reference to Sally Venn).

34. Tanner, *Political Change*, pp. 396-7, 400-1, 465, for details of union involvement. For the miners' domination of constituency parties in Durham, see material in the Shotton Collection, Durham County Record Office (CRO). See also Hutchison, *Political History of Scotland*, p. 298.

35. Bonsall (thesis), chs. 3-4; *Leek Times*, 4 January 1919.

36. Tanner, *Political Change*, pp. 378-82, 404-8; Turner, *Great War*, pp. 409-12.

37. For example, railway and steelworkers withdrawing from Labour politics in Llanelli (Hopkin, 'Llanelli 1890-1922', p. 179) and miners clashing with ILP supporters in Scotland (Hutchison, *Political History of Scotland*, pp. 282-3).

38. Neville (thesis) pp. 780-89; J.E. Williams, *The Derbyshire Miners* (1962), pp. 808-9; H. Beynon and T. Austrin, *Masters and Servants* (1994), pp. 253-6.

39. For example, Houghton-le-Spring LP Annual Report 1919; Williams (thesis), pp. 244, 265-6; Hopkin, 'Llanelli 1890-1922', p. 172. Intentions were not always realised. See Williams, ibid., p. 256; Hamilton LP Minutes 1918-20 passim; Durham CRO, Shotton Collection, Durham LP Annual Report and Blaydon LP Annual Report 1920; Penistone LP Minutes, 22 October 1922-20 January 1923.

40. Bonsall (thesis), p. 140; Quinn, 'Wansbeck Labour Party', pp. 5-7; Teanby (thesis), p. 72.

41. For example, *Dover Standard*, 1 November 1919; *Morpeth Herald*, 1 April 1920 (Ashington and Newbiggin); *Barnsley Independent*, 3 November 1923.

42. *Barnsley Independent*, 5 November 1927. For similar circumstances in Durham and North and South Wales, Beynon and Austrin, *Class and Patronage*, chs. 8, 12; Gilbert, *Class, Community and Collective Action*, pp. 126-9; S. Venn, 'Labour Politics in North East Wales: a study of the North Wales Miners Association', Unpublished MA thesis, University of Wales, 1994, pp. 26-7, 51-4.

43. D. Clark, 'South Shields Labour Party', p. 10; B. John, 'Pontypridd Labour Party', pp. 5-6; and more generally, C. Howard, '"Expectations born to death": local Labour Party expansion in the 1920s', in J. Winter (ed.), *The Working Class in Modern British History* (Cambridge, 1983).

44. Ramsay MacDonald, 'Outlook', *Socialist Review*, October-November 1919, p. 312; C.Howard, 'Henderson, MacDonald and Leadership in

the Labour Party 1914-22', unpublished PhD thesis, University of Cambridge, 1978, p. 227. For Labour views on nationalisation, D.M. Tanner, 'The Labour Party and 1918', unpublished paper delivered to Conference on the History of the Labour Party, Warwick University 1994.

45. Labour Party, *Mines for the Nation* (1920), esp. sections by Money and Webb, and *New Statesman*, 2 August 1919.

46. Williams, *Derbyshire Miners*, p. 811; South Shields LP Minutes, 3 August 1924. For tensions between miners and local Labour parties in Kent, Johnson (thesis), p. 401.

47. Warwick CRO, W. Lewis Ms, H. Celey to W. Lewis (Nuneaton election agent) 19 October 1923.

48. For example, Penistone LP Minutes, 20 January 1923, 24 May 1924; Doncaster LP Minutes, 2 December 1922; Eatwell, 'Wrexham Labour Party', p. 7.

49. Selection conference of Rennie Smith, Penistone LP Minutes, 28 April 1923; W.Lewis to F.Smith, for example, 25 November 1929; Nuneaton agents' report, 3 February 1934. A miners' candidate was rejected in Lothian as 'it would tend to prejudice the electorate in the non-mining districts of the constituency and therefore be unadvisable', (Bonsall thesis, pp. 225-6).

50. Savage, *Working Class Politics*, pp. 171-9, 195-7.

51. E.g. Hamilton LP Womens' Section Minutes, 1923-27; Wansbeck DLP Womens' Section records. Wansbeck had 15 womens' sections by 1926, South Shields 5 by 1929. For County Durham, Beynon and Austrin, *Masters and Servants*, pp. 258-9.

52. Hamilton LP Minutes, 27 May 1926; Teanby (thesis), pp. 51, 57; Quinn, 'Wansbeck LP', p. 6 and also DLP Minutes, 26 April 1924, 26 June-21 August 1926, showing pressure for consideration of womens' interests. Even where women were not politically strong, Labour was sometimes willing to support measures such as the formation of maternity and child welfare committees (for example, Pontypridd Trades Council Minutes, 30 April 1919).

53. Williams (thesis), pp. 331-4; South Shields LP Minutes, 12 April 1924; Doncaster LP Minutes, 6 June 1928. Typically, women were 'asked to undertake the work of opening the rooms and lighting fires for meetings and locking up after meetings' (ibid., 14 January 1920). In Penistone women were not represented on the EC; in South Shields they had one representative. For limited recruitment of women in Scotland, Hutchison, *Political History of Scotland*, p. 295.

54. As in *Stanley and Chester-le-Street News*, 24 March 1927. For Labour campaigns and surveys on housing needs, see, for example, *Nuneaton*

Observer, 21 November 1919; R. Eatwell, 'Wrexham Labour Party', p. 8; Williams, *Derbyshire Miners*, p. 782. For the impact of housebuilding in County Durham see R. Ryder, 'Council house building in County Durham, 1900-39: the local implementation of national policy', in M. Daunton (ed.), *Councillors and Tenants: local authority housing in English cities, 1919-39* (Leicester, 1984).

55. R. Barker, *Education and Politics 1900-51* (1972), p. 56. Allocation of housing, treatment of rent arrears and attitudes to poor relief are areas where Labour's policy could assist its position, although favouring some could alienate others: Bonsall (thesis), pp. 141-4; C. Williams, '"An able administrator of capitalism"? The Labour Party in the Rhondda, 1917-21', *Llafur*, vol. 4, no. 4, 1987, pp. 25-6, 27; B. Williamson, *Class, Culture and Community* (1982), pp. 206-7.

56. *Stanley and Chester-le-Street News*, 7 April 1927; *Miner*, 10, 17 March, 14 April 1928. Organisers complained at the 'low' turnout of 59 per cent in Hamilton (*Hamilton Advertiser*, 8 November 1928.)

57. *Miner*, esp. 10 March, 7 April 1928. Party records contain numerous similar cases, for example, Wansbeck Agents' report 1928.

58. For example, the accumulation of support in 'Red' Stockingford. (*Nuneaton Observer*, 6 April 1928, 2 Nov. 1928.)

59. For the general position, Supple, *Coal Industry*, pp. 445-56. For particular local difficulties between 1926 and 1929, see, for example, *Manchester Guardian*, 23 January, 27 May 1929 (St Helens, Bishop Auckland); C.P.Griffin, '"Three days down the pit and three days pay": underemployment in the East Midlands coalfields between the wars', *International Review of Social History*, vol. 38, 1993.

60. Reports on constituency campaigns, for example, *The Times*, 28 May 1929.

61. As in Mansfield (*Manchester Guardian*, 24 May 1929), and Nuneaton (for example, *Nuneaton Observer*, 4 November 1927; F. Smith to W.Lewis, 16 October 1928, 3 January 1929).

62. Rossiter (thesis) pp. 171-2, 176 and Table 5.24.

63. See, for example, *Manchester Guardian*, 27 May, 1 June 1929 (Ormskirk); J.A. Chandler, 'Penistone Labour Party', pp. 2, 4.

64. These observations on Labour politics in the 1920s are partially elaborated in Tanner, 'British and European socialism'.

65. A.Thorpe, *The British General Election of 1931* (Oxford, 1991), pp. 9-10, 30, 32; R.Skidelsky, *Politicians and the Slump* (1967).

66. Teanby (thesis), pp. 24, 27, 29; John, 'Pontypridd Trades Council', p. 6. See also e.g. P.Wyncoll, *The Nottingham Labour Movement 1880-1939* (1985), pp. 234-5; Williamson, *Class, Culture and Community*, p. 204.

67. Penistone LP Minutes, 14 April 1934, 13 April 1935; Hamilton LP Minutes, 12 March, 21 April 1933, 29 June 1934. In South Shields miners gave more support to the Labour Party: see D. Clark, *We Do Not Want the Earth. The history of South Shields Labour Party* (Whitley Bay, 1992), p. 73.
68. W. Hamish Fraser, 'Hamilton Labour Party 1918-51', p. 4.
69. Teanby (thesis), pp. 88-90. See also Garside, *Durham Miners*, p. 347, noting selection of non-miners at Seaham and Barnard Castle.
70. For example, Nuneaton agent's Report to the executive committee 1934, noting Coventry council estates in the division as a source of strength, and Penistone LP Minutes, 25 January 1936 (AGM).
71. See, for example, evidence of support in Sheffield council estates within the Penistone division, Penistone LP Minutes, 18 January 1933, but for indications that levels of support on council estates first grew and then fell back in Carlisle, see Turnball (thesis), p. 132, 415-6.
72. Miller, *Electoral Dynamics*, p. 214; T. Mason and P. Thompson, '"Reflections on a revolution"? The political mood in wartime Britain', in N. Tiratsoo (ed.), *The Attlee Years* (1991); I. Zweiniger-Bargielowska, 'South Wales miners' attitudes towards nationalisation: an essay in oral history', *Llafur*, vol. 6, no. 3, 1994.

CHAPTER FOUR

Heroes and anti-heroes: communists in the coalfields

Nina Fishman

The significance of communism amongst miners is usually approached through a dense cultural undergrowth. Assumptions abound about both in popular, political and academic mythologies. Pre-1914 reputations of coalfield militancy, particularly in South Wales, provided the prism through which communist miners' activities were viewed. Red images were reinforced in the 1920s by the epic strikes and lockouts and throughout the 1930s and 40s commentators were confident that coalminers were susceptible to communism.

The available evidence presents a more complicated picture. The Communist Party of Great Britain (CPGB) made few recruits amongst miners after 1926. Officials at King Street, the party's London headquarters, found the low mining membership frustrating and inexplicable. The economic depression was acute in South Wales, the North East and most of the Scottish coalfields. Revolutionary fruit ought to have been ripe for picking. Local communists were wearily berated with serious neglect of their party duties. The annual propaganda campaigns organised from King Street placed special emphasis on South Wales and Scotland in the expectation of making a breakthrough in these coalfields. Communist Party membership rose slowly from 1933 but the increase was largely confined to conurbations where engineering was expanding, West London and the Midlands. Communist membership rose in engineering unions; it remained low in the coalfields, even where communists were elected to full-time and lay union positions in mining unions, mainly in South Wales and Scotland.

This profile stands in stark contrast to the MFGB's Labour Party persona. Duncan Tanner points out the critical contribution made by coalmining electorates to Labour's increased parliamentary representation after 1918.[1] Constituencies dominated by mining communities remained loyal citadels of Labour even in the aftermath of the 1931 split. David Howell has shown that most miners' MPs and the miners' delegations at Labour conference evinced little interest in issues outside coalmining. Their votes were increasingly cast with the national executive committee and the parliamentary leadership.[2]

The two volumes of Page Arnot's official history of the MFGB dealing with this period were published in 1953 and 1961.[3] Arnot was a prominent communist intellectual commissioned to write the history of a union which unquestioningly supported Labour. He had been associated with mining unions since the 1920s and knew well the self-portrait which the MFGB leadership constructed of itself in the 1930s. It continued to be exhibited for public consumption throughout the Cold War. Arnot made minor adjustments and subtle retouchings, but he faithfully preserved the sense and underlying coherence of the leadership's version.

This chapter analyses the picture which Arnot presented of a united union leadership untroubled by political conflict. In reproducing the self-image which the MFGB leadership projected, he had to omit or obscure relevant evidence. Nevertheless his description is accurate in many respects. The unity which the MFGB took such care to present to the public gaze was genuine. With the exception of the late 1920s, political differences within the MFGB were subordinated to the perceived need to present a united and effective front to the coalowners. From 1933, MFGB officers abandoned attempts to isolate and marginalise communists on the union's executive. Indeed they relied on communist support and talent to help restore the MFGB's strength and morale which had been so severely weakened by the events of 1926.

The CPGB was founded in 1920. (For readability, I have adopted the abbreviation used by communists and describe the British Communist Party as 'the party'.) The new revolutionary party contained a small number of miners. The British Socialist Party (BSP) was its principal constituent, and its members were concentrated in London and Manchester.[4] Some leaders of the South Wales Miners' Unofficial Reform Committee who were still active joined the party. Many of their younger protegés, including Arthur

Horner and Arthur Cook, were eager recruits. The veteran Noah Ablett viewed the new bolshevik state with considerable trepidation.[5] Most British communists were more impressed by the democratic side of the October revolution than the Leninist prescriptions which followed. They did not study the implications of democratic centralism nor the dictatorship of the proletariat. After the party had undergone its 'bolshevisation' and emerged in a more Leninist mould in 1922-3, most ordinary party members, including miners, found little reason to alter their pre-war attitudes towards either the class struggle or unions.

From 1910, activists had travelled from South Wales spreading the militant 'syndicalist' word to other coalfields. They were well received, especially in Scotland, by miners who were industrial unionists or in the BSP. Miners' reform movements were established in emulation of the South Walian model. Members hoped to persuade their unions to adopt militant policies and to get reform candidates elected to union office. It is not known how many miners associated with reform movements joined the party.[6] But enough mining activists became communists to fuel high hopes that a fresh militant upsurge would gather momentum in coalmining.

The party's first formal intervention in mining occurred in March 1921. The various reform movements and caucuses came together to found a 'revolutionary' organisation, the National Miners' Reform Movement. Non-communist activists evidently acquiesced in this initiative. This may well have been because the new 'revolutionary' organisation's activities differed very little from its predecessors. The movement soon became became part of another 'revolutionary' organisation, the National Shop Stewards' and Workers' Committee Movement (NSSWCM). The NSSWCM was the product of a party-inspired merger between the Amalgamation Committee Movement, a loose reform movement in the engineering industry which had flourished before 1914, and the wartime, syndicalist Shop Stewards' National Council.[7]

Predictably the most vigorous sections of the reform movement were South Wales and Scotland. Leftwing mining activists continued to direct their activities towards influencing the district mining unions and the MFGB. They were both loyally and militantly attached to their respective unions. A unified national miners' union remained an essential aim. Economic demands had been somewhat modified in recognition of coalmining's parlous position. Instead of an increase, the movement called for no wage cuts. It still adhered to the call for an hour's reduction in the working day to six hours. In fact, the only addition to the earlier reform aims was the demand for the MFGB's affiliation to the Moscow-based Red International of Labour Unions (RILU). Reform movement supporters persuaded the South Wales Miners' Federation (the Fed) to propose a motion in favour of MFGB affiliation to RILU. It was overwhelmingly defeated at the 1922 conference by 118,00 votes to 883,000.[8]

The modest successes and undoubted vigour of the Miners' Reform Movement were not replicated by the engineering shop stewards' section of the NSSWCM. Workplace union organisation and 'rank and file' militancy did not recover in engineering until the mid-1930s, however the sanguine young engineers were undeterred. In 1923, the Comintern decreed a fresh drive towards world revolution, including the thorough bolshevisation of communist parties. In Britain, bolshevisation entailed dumping the stillborn NSSWCM. A fresh attempt was made to tap trade union militancy for revolutionary ends with the launch of the National Minority Movement (NMM) with Harry Pollitt, the charismatic hero of the party's bolshevisation, as its honorary secretary. The National Miners' Reform Movement was extricated from the shell of the NSSWCM. It simply changed its name in January 1924 and re-emerged as the Miners' Minority Movement (MMM). A paper, *The Mineworker* was published and a national organiser from South Wales, Nat Watkins, acquired.[9] In view of the demoralisation in engineering unions, Martin's judgement is unsurprising that mining unions 'provided the largest body of support' for the NMM.[10]

The MMM played a major role in the election for general secretary of the MFGB in 1924. The victor, Arthur Cook, had left the party in 1921, but remained a close friend of Arthur Horner and an enthusiastic Minority Movement supporter.[11] Macfarlane summarised the MMM's energetic and self-confident campaigns:

> South Wales was the stronghold ... Welsh missionaries were sent out from there to other coalfields ... Arthur Horner turned down the unanimous nomination of the Rhondda Minority Movement to stand for the post of Miners' agent [of the Fed] ... in order to devote more time to building up the Minority Movement. During the spring and summer of 1924 conferences ... were held in Lancashire, Cheshire and

Nottingham. The Northumberland Miners' Minority Movement was established and meetings addressed by A.J. Cook were arranged by the Yorkshire Miners' Minority Movement. By August 1925, there were over 200 Miners' Minority Movement groups in the country and on the eve of the General Strike, sixteen lodges with 14,500 members were affiliated.[12]

The miners used the Minority Movement to mobilise support from other unions. When the Samuel Commission's compromise report surfaced in the spring of 1926, the NMM organised a national conference with 883 delegates, representing more than one million workers. Horner proposed the resolution which was carried by acclamation. It called on unions to establish a centralised, solid, and militant organisation 'to repel the [employers'] attack and to secure the demands of every section of the workers'.[13] The resolution faithfully reflected Communist Party policy.[14] However, after the General Strike, leading communists argued the party should have seized the opportunity presented by the Trades Union Congress (TUC) General Council's retreat. If the party had called upon workers to repudiate the 'reformist' union leadership, it could have led millions in total war against the bourgeois state. Trotsky had criticised the British party in the same vein.[15]

The validity of this critique cannot be examined here. It did not form the basis of party policy during the long months of the lockout. The party and the NMM called on the miners to stand firm behind the MFGB and exhorted the rest of the trade union movement to support them. During the summer and autumn of 1926, the augmented forces of the Communist Party and the Minority Movement were mobilised to their fullest extent. They gathered vital financial support and kept the spirit of resistance alive in the coalfields.

Historians have paid insufficient attention to the part which the party played in maintaining miners' morale. It is evidently inconvenient to observe that a small, 'renegade' organisation was important in events at the heart of labour mythology. During 1926, party membership doubled from 5,000 to 10,000; most of the recruits were miners.[16] They joined pragmatically. Party membership seemed the most effective means of ensuring victory. Communist activists did not stress revolution, but rather portrayed the party as a stiffening agent, working alongside mining unions. In July 1926 the MFGB executive recommended the Bishops' proposals as the basis of a compromise to end the lockout. The party and MMM campaigned vigorously against them, opposing the MFGB executive for the first time. The executive's proposals were narrowly rejected in what Arnot describes as a 'District vote' by a majority of 34,614. The two largest districts, South Wales and Yorkshire, cast their votes against the executive.[17]

The party and the MMM kept thwarting the MFGB executive's attempts to manoeuvre into an expeditious retreat. The dwindling number of miners who voted in successive union ballots recorded majorities against recommended compromises. By the end of November one-third of miners were back at work, including large numbers from the hitherto solid Durham and South Wales coalfields. Each day thousands more gave up the fight.[18] The MFGB executive eventually resorted to fiat and instructed district unions to negotiate settlements to end the dispute. The party leadership forbore to challenge their expedient manoeuvre, recognising there was nothing to be gained but martyrdom from continuing the struggle. Coalfield casualties were legion. Many victimised miners never worked again in their coalfields. Men and women who became communists in good faith in the summer left the party disillusioned by the winter. Many miners finished with trade unionism altogether, concluding that the efficacy of collective action had been proved false. The district unions all suffered membership haemorrhages, with varying degrees of seriousness.

The party leadership turned sharply leftwards except for Johnny Campbell, whose outstanding intellect and keen political sense had already propelled him to a prominent role in the formation of party policy. Against his advice, policy prescriptions now violated the party's pre-General Strike assumption about the importance of trade union unity in the face of attack. Horner attacked unions' 'reformism' and invoked *The Miners' Next Step* in his call for one miners' union with a fighting rank and file structure.[19] This approach met with apathetic, even negative responses and party membership declined further as union conferences, including that of the MFGB, declared the party and the Minority Movement responsible for the 1926 defeats. This scapegoating was not repudiated by either organised or unorganised rank and file workers.[20]

These developments induced Pollitt and Horner to move back

towards the centre and they joined Campbell in arguing that communists should help rebuild existing unions. Pollitt and Campbell became the chief pragmatists at King Street. They faced a difficult task because their more realistic assessment was not universally accepted inside the party. In February 1928 they encountered another obstacle. The Comintern declared a new line, 'class against class', in response to political conflict in the Soviet Communist Party. Affiliated communist parties were instructed to lead workers in repudiating 'reformist' trade unions, which were now labelled 'social fascist'.

Pollitt and Campbell engaged in political manoeuvres aimed at damage limitation. But the cadres in the Young Communist League (YCL) had no doubts about the Comintern's new line. Comintern influence parachuted them into power at the party centre. However, the reign of these erstwhile revolutionaries, Bill Rust, Wally Tapsell, Johnny Mahon and Ernie Woolley, lasted only 16 months from May 1929 to August 1930.[21] The Young Turks failed to overwhelm the pragmatists inside the party. Pollitt and Campbell were supported by outspoken party members who were veteran union activists and who were deeply hostile to calls to found new revolutionary unions.[22]

The Young Turks' expectations centred on coalmining. They argued that miners' demoralisation could be swiftly reversed if communists applied sufficient amounts of bolshevik determination. When Horner disagreed, they forced him to resign as MMM secretary. They launched offensives against Horner and other South Walians at the party congresses held in January and December 1929 because they refused to form a rival red union to the Fed. At the second congress, the refuseniks also had to contend with the example of the newly formed revolutionary union, the United Mineworkers of Scotland (UMS). Horner held them at bay.[23]

Many party members, including mining activists, accepted the political imperative to form red unions. The dearth of results belied their convictions. Despite constant encouragement from the Young Turks, no mining activists in England and Wales emulated the UMS and led members out of their lodges to form revolutionary unions. When the Comintern embarked on elaborate manoeuvres to move back from the extreme left, Pollitt and Campbell were in an excellent position to take advantage of the situation. The Comintern judged it expedient to undertake an appaisal of the British party at the end of

1930 and found that the party had lost influence in the working class. They condemned the CPGB for falling into a 'left sectarian error'. While Pollitt and Campbell urged members to resume activity in 'reformist' unions, they took great care not to move outside the strictures of the newly modified 'class against class' line. Their message was welcomed by many party activists who had never given up trade union work, but they encountered determined resistance from leadership cadres, including Palme Dutt. The *Daily Worker* published a pre-congress discussion in the autumn of 1932 which was full of the conflict about 'reformist' unions and Dutt eventually decided to retreat. At the 12th party congress in December, there was no opposition from the floor to Pollitt's and Campbell's arguments.

The obvious question was how the post-congress position on 'reformist' unions differed from the approach prevailing before 'class against class'. It was only asked in South Wales, where conflict over this issue had escalated to the point of civil war within the party. In January 1931, Horner refused to accept instructions from the South Wales party leadership to lead an unofficial strike to repudiate the compromise which the Fed executive had negotiated in an official strike. He was accused by the Young Turks of flouting 'class against class' and wilfully creating a renegade line, 'Hornerism'.

To extricate Horner, the Comintern summonsed him to Moscow to put his case. In the autumn Horner returned, absolved of the serious charge of ideological deviation but pronounced guilty of a tactical error. He dutifully performed a ritual *mea culpa*, and then resumed his previous behaviour exercising greater circumspection.[24] The congress resolution on trade union work was a patent repetition of Horner's venial sin. Pollitt and Campbell evaded the issue during 1933 by pouring lavish quantities of ideological glue over the obvious and clear similarities and Horner was able to use the cover they provided to great advantage.

Pollitt and Campbell worked hard to persuade all party members to concentrate on activity in 'reformist' unions. In 1933, they closed down the Miners' Minority Movement without any public explanation. They had little choice. The Young Turks and their supporters had traded on the MMM's high reputation amongst miners earned in 1926 and had used MMM platforms to denounce the mining unions as irredeemably social fascist. Consequently, the

MMM had lost all credibility as a reform movement which could lobby mining unions to adopt more militant policies. The MMM's disappearance meant that leftwing activists lacked a vehicle for their union activities. The 12th party congress had declared rank and file movements to be the new transmission belt to revolution and Pollitt urged delegates to go forth and multiply them.[25] Horner duly presided over the establishment of the South Wales Miners' Rank and File Movement, became editor of its paper and then steered the movement's forces into rebuilding the Fed. He also used it to canvas support for his election as an agent in the Fed's anthracite area. Though miners' rank and file movements appeared in other coalfields, they apparently did little more than raise the leftwing standard in lodge meetings.[26]

The strong identity of interests inside the MFGB's leftwing underlies the transience of the miners' rank and file movements. There was a clear consensus that the first priority must be redressing the weak position of the official mining unions. Giving precedence to unofficial groupings whose aim was to influence the unions was illogical when the unions themselves were demoralised and in some cases in imminent danger of collapse. In many mining communities in South Wales, the North East and Lanarkshire, there were more unemployed than working miners. It was a natural transition for victimised communist miners to engage in full-time unemployed agitation. They believed that the hunger marches would precipitate a revolutionary situation and awaited the day with eager anticipation. But by 1933 the explosive mood in the depressed coalfields had been contained. From the late 1920s, an increasing number of young men and women had emigrated to the profitable pits in Yorkshire, the East Midlands and Kent, and the expanding manufacturing sectors in Birmingham, Oxford and London. Coal production in the depressed coalfields eventually recovered due to the national economic recovery and the impact of the statutory marketing scheme imposed by the 1930 Coal Mines Act. More miners were re-employed in consequence.

Substantial numbers of unemployed miners remained. However, their state benefits were administered liberally by Labour local authorities in mining communities, which included some communist councillors in South Wales and Scotland. The National government's attempt to rationalise unemployment benefit in 1934 was successfully

countered by a *de facto* united front in which all mining union activists participated. By 1935 even the most sanguine communists could observe that the situation had stabilised in the depressed coalfields, and that no revolution was imminent. Moreover, the Communist International had officially postponed revolution in August 1935 at its 7th world congress. Making common cause with social democrats inside 'reformist unions' was now the prime task of all communists. The British party's 13th congress in February 1935 had already agreed that the urgent priority was to rebuild trade union strength.[27] In South Wales, Nottinghamshire and Scotland, the legacy of the 1920s made this task very problematic. The existence of rival unions made it easier for coalowners to impose substantial changes in working conditions. Many miners lost their belief in efficacy of solidarity. They opted out of the culture of union loyalism and became 'nons'.

The Fed and the Nottinghamshire Mineworkers' Association (NMA) both organised periodic recruiting campaigns but these yielded few members. In 1934 Horner scored a dramatic victory at the Emlyn colliery, adjoining his agent's territory and which had a large number of unwilling members of the 'scab' union, the South Wales Miners' Industrial Union (SWMIU).[28] Horner patiently prepared the ground. The election of a veteran communist, Ianto Evans, as checkweighman was effected and a reliable core of Fed members were assembled underground. When the time was judged ripe, they led a strike which inevitably involved the question of recognition. It involved 900 men and lasted nine weeks. The men returned to work having won both material concessions and recognition for the Fed.[29] The CPGB paper, the *Daily Worker*, commented:

> No small measure of the credit is due to Comrade Arthur Horner, who
> ... threw himself wholeheartedly into the struggle and when it was
> decided to retreat temporarily, no other man could have persuaded the
> strikers of the advisability of this step and maintain their confidence and
> keep up their morale.[30]

The bitter legacy of internal conflict from 1926 and 'class against class' was effaced by the unexpected victory. The Fed's new officers, particularly Jim Griffiths, recognised the union had to fight to survive and were prepared to work with party activists under

Horner's tutelage. The Fed executive selected Taff-Merthyr colliery, one of the 'scab' union's main strongholds, as the next target. Their decision was influenced by a myriad of personal connections, which were also intertwined with the local Communist Party networks. They seconded Horner from his agent's job to organise the campaign on the recommendation of Ness Edwards, the agent for Taff Merthyr who appreciated Horner's superior abilities for the job.[31]

The Fed's fight against the 'scab' union was helped by the more favourable economic circumstances in the coalfield. But the decisive factor was Horner's generalship. Following a youthful vocation as a Baptist preacher, Horner learned the difficult art of holding an audience's attention whilst making complex arguments intelligible. He acquired the essential kernel of evangelising: rousing powerful emotions and then linking them to a collective resolution to take a positive moral course of action. Horner would have been an outstanding preacher. He became an exceptional communist.

In the milieu of South Walian socialism, miners' leaders developed theory in order to affect practical reality. Horner was schooled to become a man of action. As a thinking Marxist, he was depressed but never fatalistic about the monumental defeats of 1926 and after. Horner eventually found time for reflection during a 15 month gaol sentence in 1932 when he found Clausewitz's classic on war in the prison library and read it 'with very great interest'.

> I realised that here were some of the principles which we in the trade union movement had got to apply if ever we were to win. Clausewitz taught that if you enter into active struggle you can succeed only if you adopt the principle of inflicting the greatest degree of damage on your opponents, with the least possible hurt to your own forces ... We had to mobilise our forces with the same care as a successful general. We had to use the strike weapon carefully ... In all the situations I have found myself in since then I have never started a struggle which I did not think we had a good chance of winning ...[32]

Horner's organising capacity included a flair for leading the attack under fire. Like all gifted generals, he turned the particular social and cultural features of his terrain to good account. He drew on union activists' commitment and inspired others to achieve impressive concentrations of force. He also relied on local communists' willingness to risk martyrdom in the tightest spots. Horner learned not only to organise and lead an attack, he also became an adept in leading the difficult manoeuvres of compromise and retreat. This skill was vital in dealing with communists and other veteran activists socialised into the moral imperative of 'no surrender' on matters of trade union principle. Their militant culture was reinforced by adrenalin in the heat of battle. He patiently reasoned with them and, in spite of their desire to go on fighting, they believed him when he declared that he would lead another charge if it had any chance of gaining ground.

Nevertheless there was a continuing undercurrent of hostility to his alleged tendency to 'turn tail under fire'. Horner's antagonists included the same communists who denounced 'Hornerism' and protested when he refused to use the Rank and File Movement to prolong official strikes unofficially. Men who had been induced by his charismatic oratory and good faith to follow him backwards could regret their decision in the cold light of day after a negotiated settlement had been effected, their conviction that more could have been gained by standing firm reinforced each time events were rehearsed at subsequent lodge and party meetings.

Horner superintended a series of protracted and epic battles against the SWMIU with continuing support from the Fed executive. His method was to de-stabilise the 'scab' union through painstaking preparation on the inside, precipitate an escalating dispute and then deploy large numbers of supporting forces on the pit-top. He reluctantly concluded that the SWMIU could not be forced into total surrender. Nevertheless, by the end of 1935, the Fed had turned the tide against it. The 'scab' union continued to function in an attenuated fashion, but it no longer threatened the Fed's survival.[33]

When Jim Griffiths was elected to parliament, Horner was the favourite in the contest to choose his successor as Fed president. In May 1936, he won the election with a massive majority. The *Daily Worker* was jubilant:

> 50,000 Welsh miners cannot be wrong. His election is the reply ... to all who oppose the affiliation of the Communist Party to the Labour Party. It is a clear call to the TUC General Council to drop once and for all the policy of class collaboration and industrial peace and the attacks on militants in the trade union movement.[34]

The coalowners were not alarmed by the prospect of Horner leading the Fed. During the strikes against their recognition of the SWMIU, they found that he was a man with whom they could do business. In 1937, they signed a wide ranging agreement with Horner which conceded substantial wage increases in return for rationalising industrial relations at pit level, including a comprehensive conciliation structure. Idris Cox was moved to defend Horner against attacks by the *Daily Herald* that he had betrayed the rank and file:

> There must ... be some system of negotiation, and particularly in an industry like mining where a hundred and one disputes crop up every day. If strike action is the only answer to every dispute ... there would never be any work in the mines. Trotsky's theory of permanent revolution would live again in the theory of 'permanent strike action'![35]

Horner's enhanced authority extended from the Fed to the MFGB executive. As one of the larger districts, South Wales representatives wielded substantial influence. Horner also brought his intellectual ability and negotiating acumen to bear on the executive's often tortuous and difficult deliberations. The effective weight of his presence reinforced the existing relationship between communist and Labour activists inside the MFGB. The relationship was not merely a marriage of convenience. There was also a shared identity of basic outlook.

At MFGB executive meetings and delegate conferences, no rightwing miners' leader attempted to counter the passionate oratory of South Walian communists nor that of the leftwing representatives from Durham, Sammy Watson and Will Lawther. Watson's and Lawther's refusal to become communists may have been partly opportunist. Advancement inside the Durham Miners' Association (DMA) was predicated on conspicuous Labour loyalism. But they also disagreed fundamentally with subordinating their socialist politics to Comintern discipline. Nevertheless they approached their world of economic struggle with the coalowners and viewed the outside world of increasingly sinister forces in the same way as their communist colleagues. Their moral abhorrence of a system which reduced their members' families to grinding poverty was as deep as Horner's, and also strongly reinforced in Watson's case by a close reading of Marx.

During the 1930s the MFGB adopted an increasingly leftwing orientation in trade union politics. Besides South Wales and

Durham, the left bloc often included delegates from Derbyshire, Kent, Nottinghamshire, Somerset, the Forest of Dean, Northumberland and Cumberland.   Most left delegates were not communists, but they agreed with with much of the Communist Party's 'real united front' political agenda.   Both left activists and communists put forward motions at lodge level which travelled up the union hierarchy to MFGB annual conference and the TUC.   They supported formal inclusion of the CPGB in a united front, opposed fascism and demanded that the government sell arms to republican Spain.   At the 1937 MFGB Conference, both the Fed and the DMA proposed real united front motions which argued for the Communist Party to assume a legitimate role in the labour movement, alongside trade union leaders and the Labour Party.   W. Pearson spoke for the DMA:

> I want to give credit where it is due, and it is this. I find we have in many of our branches, thirty six delegates attending our Council, who are members of the Communist Party, and I also find that they are the most disciplined in our movement, and have worked very hard for a number of years in fighting the cause of the worker ...

He concluded by saying that although the Soviet Union was a dictatorship, delegates should not forget what it had done in 1926.[36] The Durham motion was narrowly rejected on a card vote by 284,000 to 259,000, with South Wales, Cumberland and the Forest of Dean supporting it.[37] At the 1938 TUC, the MFGB proposed a motion of strong support for the Spanish Republican government. Will Paynter, a protege of Horner, spoke in favour of the motion. He had recently returned from Spain where he had been political commissar to the British battalion of the International Brigade. His speech moved delegates to tears and they voted unanimously in favour of the motion against the advice of the General Council.[38] At the TUC, miners' delegates frequently were allied with the AEU and smaller unions with enduring leftwing traditions.

The relationship between Labour and communist miners can be clearly observed during the 1935-6 national wages dispute.   King Street felt the party had an important role nationally, and they played it with timing and tact.   During the MFGB's national strike ballot, the *Daily Worker* urged union activists to work harder in inspiring the rank and file and ensuring a good turnout.   Learning the miners' case was a priority for party members outside the coalfields. They were expected to mobilise support for the MFGB in trades councils, trade union branches, cooperative guilds, and local Labour parties.[39]

The *Daily Worker* was conspicuously reticent in considering the executive's motives in calling the strike ballot. Its speculations about a strike were confined to vague rhetorical assurances about its probability and assertions that not merely the miners, but the whole working class would come together in a national, militant upsurge. On the eve of the MFGB special conference which was to decide whether or not to hold a national strike ballot, the *Daily Worker* leader column declared:

> From below the movement is growing for joint action of the workers. At this moment, when the miners, engineers and railwaymen are putting forward demands for wage increases, the National Miners' Conference can make a big advance towards united trade union action for those common demands. There can be no doubt that such a lead will have a response never before equalled in the trade union movement of this country.[40]

The CPGB's clearly visible place on the left flank of the MFGB forces extended the freedom of manoeuvre of the MFGB national officers. Edwards, Jones and Lawther were well aware of the respect and gratitude which miners felt towards the party for its role in 1926. Soviet gold and the party's unstinting support during the lockout were viewed as debts of honour by many rank and file miners. There is impressionistic evidence that the enthusiastic endorsement which Pollitt and the *Daily Worker* gave to the MFGB leadership impressed veteran lodge officials and mining activists along the entire political spectrum. MFGB officers never seriously contemplated using the majority in the national strike ballot to actually call a strike. The coalowners could marshal superior financial resources; they would strongly resist a national strike with its echoes of 1926. Although public opinion was strongly sympathetic to the miners, if the threat of a strike became a reality, public support would fracture, leaving those in favour of the miners a passionate minority.

In November 1935 the *Daily Worker* reported the result of the ballot, a majority of nearly fourteen to one in favour of strike action, without comment.[41] The MFGB officers had to extract the maximum moral and political effect from the overwhelming majority for a strike. In order to make such tactical use of the ballot result, the threat of a strike had to appear seriously credible. The *Daily Worker's* sanguine assumptions were very apposite. On 15 January 1936, it enthused:

> The coalowners and the National Government are scared to death of a national strike. They realise that the miners would be bound to win. This is why they are working night and day to get a settlement without a national strike ... The miners must stand firm. The delegates to the national conference must be mandated to vote for handing in strike notices without further delay. Preparations must go ahead for successful strike action.[42]

On 24 January, the MFGB delegate conference voted to accept the executive's recommendation to accept the settlement negotiated by the national officers. The Fed president, Jim Griffiths, failed to convince conference to hold a ballot vote on the settlement. Ebby Edwards' conference speech included a tribute to the Communist Party' for the work they did on behalf of the campaign of the miners'.[43] The *Daily Worker's* conference report contained an oblique criticism of the compromise, but there was also an element of implied self-criticism. Next time, leftwing activists had to ensure that the rank and file's willingness to fight was satisfied.[44]

However, the party centre did not give practical priority to building the rank and file's self-confidence. King Street continued to stress the need to strengthen the official trade union movement. An incident soon occurred which tested communist miners' commitment to their unions. As part of the January 1936 settlement, the coalowners agreed to the formation of joint national consultative machinery for the first time since 1926. For MFGB officers, this was a crucial step towards national wage bargaining. However the Nottinghamshire coalowners refused to participate. The only effective means which the MFGB possessed of putting pressure on the owners was the Nottinghamshire Miners' Association. But the NMA remained weak with no prospect of dislodging the breakaway Nottinghamshire Miners' Industrial Union (NMIU). In South Wales, the Fed's recent battles had made vital breaches in the 'scab' union's defences. Activists wondered whether the Fed's example could be emulated by the NMA. In July 1936 Ebby Edwards observed at the

MFGB conference:

> Nottinghamshire cannot be won unless the people themselves are prepared to fight. Let us be frank because some of us have been there weeks, and know the difficulty. Nottinghamshire holds the key position in the industry ... and yet they are one of the weakest links in the Federation.[45]

Communist mining activists took the initiative. When they gained the requisite support on the ground, the MFGB officers did what was required of them. The decision about where to stage the battle was probably taken during the national wages dispute. Horner and Pollitt were touring the coalfields and stopped to visit Sheffield with its complement of mining activists including the Kane brothers, Mick and Jock, who had worked at the Harworth colliery in Nottinghamshire in the early 1930s. Harworth was chosen for its terrain and the quality of its troops.[46] Mick Kane found work at the colliery in early 1936. In June he was elected chairman of Harworth NMA lodge. He rallied miners around the NMA building on the strong union loyalism of the Durham emigrants working in the pit. David Gilbert considers the Harworth strike in detail elsewhere in this volume.[47] Here, we should focus on the CPGB's multi-faceted role. Vital contributions were made by the party centre, Arthur Horner on the MFGB executive, the communist activists in the NMA Harworth lodge, mining activists and party officials in Sheffield, and mining activists in the other coalfields.

From its inception in November 1936, Horner was publicly adamant that the Harworth strike would have to be settled by compromise. He was fearful that the Harworth officers, by taking up a principled position, would become enmired in a battle of attrition from which it would be impossible to retreat in good order. Horner's advice was not initially heeded either by the party activists in Harworth or King Street. Jones and Edwards agreed with Horner. However their combined powers of persuasion failed to contain the situation. The bitter and protracted strike inspired miners and elicited deep feelings. Against all the odds, a national ballot produced a decisive majority in favour of striking over Harworth. Nevertheless the MFGB was operating from a position of comparative weakness. The MFGB officials used the majority to apply moral and political pressure without serious intention of unleashing it.

The party centre had campaigned vigorously for a 'yes' vote in the miners' ballot, certain that a national strike would result. When the MFGB officials failed to call one, no charge of class traitor was made against them either by the *Daily Worker* or communist mining activists. King Street had faced up to Horner's warning that the 'scab' union would emerge victorious unless the Harworth strikers accepted retreat and compromise. The *Daily Worker* acquiesced whilst the MFGB's negotiators tried to extract better terms from the Harworth owners and the NMIU. The strike achieved the MFGB officers' aim. The NMIU disappeared by fusing with the NMA into a new MFGB-affiliated union. This result would have been impossible without the determination of the Durham emigrants, capable leadership at the pit, and Horner's dextrous, energetic manoeuvrings. But the settlement also consigned most of the strikers to martyrdom. MFGB negotiators were unable to extract guarantees against victimisation, the issue which caused miners to vote for a national strike.

The settlement conceded most of the demands which NMIU secretary George Spencer made in return for agreeing to fusion. NMA officials resented having to sit alongside Spencer and serve under former NMIU officials. Whereas Horner had bribed the leaders of the SWMIU to discreetly disappear from the union scene, Spencer and his lieutenants were taken back into the fold. These results were profoundly disturbing for activists for whom the principles of trade unionism were inviolable. In the aftermath of the strike, the party centre took great care to cover its own left flank. Rhetoric and considerable sophistry were deployed to assuage activists who felt the MFGB leadership had turned coat and sold out the strikers. In the national wages dispute, mining activists had willingly colluded in the rhetorical claims being made by the party and MFGB about rank and file militancy. They could see little evidence of this fighting spirit in their coalfields and concluded that a national strike was improbable. The Harworth strike was different. Mining activists were genuinely fired up and prepared for a national battle. The risks were much greater, both for the party and the MFGB. The *Daily Worker* threw a thick ideological smokescreen over the compromise. It allowed activists to engage in wilful self-deception. The strike was painted as a triumphal victory and the strikers became proletarian heroes. Mick Kane was awarded the signal honour of election to the party executive at the 14th party congress.

The close relationship between communists and Labour activists in the MFGB leadership was substantially unaffected by the vicissitudes of war. From October 1939 until 22 June 1941, the party opposed the war for being imperialist. In practice, the party centre moved back towards the position adopted at the outbreak of war in September. This was fighting the war on two fronts: the foreign front against Hitler and fascism and the domestic front against the undemocratic Chamberlain government and employers.[48]

Communist miners succeeded in getting an anti-war motion passed in Scotland.[49] They were assisted by low union density and the decay of union life at branch level. In South Wales, many mining activists wanted the Fed to take the same principled stand. The party centre, (temporarily without Pollitt and Campbell who had opposed the anti-war line), encouraged them, even though it placed Arthur Horner in a virtually impossible position. The agitation inside the Fed pulled Horner in opposing directions. His commitment to communism induced him to make tortuous declarations against war in general. But he remained passionately opposed to fascism. His job as president of the Fed required him to actively participate in the war effort which he did with visible enthusiasm.

Communist anti-war activists were reinforced in their campaign to get Horner off the fence by the Fed's MPs, notably Aneurin Bevan, W.H. Mainwaring and Ted Williams. The tenacity with which they pursued this issue appears to be only partially based upon their own political convictions. Their personal feelings about Horner were probably also involved. They felt that the war should be their finest hour and not his. They envied his charismatic following in the coalfield and hoped to use this opportunity to dislodge him from what they felt to be his plaster sainthood.

Horner confounded his antagonists. He conducted the debate on the anti-war motion with scrupulous fairness throughout. He insisted on holding two coalfield conferences so that delegates could be mandated on the question. Then, having made a token genuflection against the war, he maintained a silence befitting the neutrality of his position as presiding officer. The anti-war motion was rejected by a substantial majority. The result was acknowledged by the party centre with deep irritation.[50]

Nevertheless the difference between Scotland and South Wales was minimal for it would appear that Scottish mining activists never intended their anti-war motion to be other than rhetorical since no action was taken on it. Throughout the coalfields, communists were no exception to union activists' acquiescence in the war against fascism. They concentrated on fortifying the unions' position in the balance of class forces. Communist activists made no attempt to rekindle the revolutionary spirit of mining syndicalists in the 1914-18 war.

The Soviet Union's entry into the war in June 1941 made little impact on communist miners' activities. They were undoubtedly keen that the USSR should defeat Hitler. But they did little to translate their commitment to the Socialist Fatherland into practice. The government sponsored the creation of pit production committees in emulation of engineering joint production committees. Despite the public commitment from communist union leaders like Horner and Abe Moffat, the committees made little difference to labour problems in coalmining. Compared to engineering, there were few changes in either miners' methods of work or pit-level collective bargaining. The wartime demand for coal was not met by new production techniques nor any influx of labour from outside the coalfields. One of the main reasons that productivity in the coalfields stubbornly failed to show any increase during the war was the advancing age of working miners. Men who had not worked since the 1920s went back down the pits. As in shipbuilding, a sceptical conservativism was the typical response to suggestions for new divisions of labour and other changes in the production process.[51]

There is a stark contrast between the steady stream of productionist propaganda aimed at miners emanating from the party and the outbreaks of unofficial strikes which occurred from 1942 onwards. But the *Daily Worker* and the central leadership refrained from condemning the strikes outright. They stressed the need for miners to receive better wages and working conditions. The strikes were not condoned, but placed sympathetically in context. Party members holding full-time and lay offices in mining unions took up uncompromising positions against the strikes. They wanted to help the war effort, but they also saw themselves as having responsibilities as union leaders in the nationalised industry which they hoped would emerge after the war. This sense of proportion fuelled Abe Moffat's outspoken condemnations of the rash of unofficial strikes in Lanarkshire. Horner's response to the young miners' strikes is full of the sense of socialist destiny betrayed. Jock Kane was voted out of lodge office for opposing unofficial strikes in Yorkshire. It is less clear how the 'rank and file' communists in the coalfields viewed the strikes. We have observed the opposition from some communists before the war to Horner's policies in the Fed. The ideological glue applied liberally by King Street and the positive results Horner achieved neutralised their reaction. They stayed in the party because communism was as essential to their own identity as it was to Horner's. In 1944, a few reached breaking point, being viscerally incapable of condemning young miners for going on strike.

Allied victory in the European war was followed by the Labour general election victory in the summer of 1945. The nationalisation of coal is considered in another chapter in this book. We should note here Horner's crucial role in achieving unification of the district unions into the National Union of Mineworkers (NUM) and his subsequent election as NUM general secretary in 1946. The close relationship between communist and Labour activists in the MFGB leadership was seamlessly transferred to the NUM. Its durability was severely tested at the outset of the Cold War yet the relationship survived intact and underpinned the union's commitment to the success of the National Coal Board.

Notes

Place of publication is London unless otherwise stated.

1. See Chapter 3 of this volume, above.
2. See Chapter 2 of this volume, above.
3. R. Page Arnot, *The Miners: a history of the Miners' Federation of Great Britain*, vol. 2, *Years of Struggle* (1953), vol. 3, *In Crisis and War* (1961).
4. See W. Thompson, *The Good Old Cause: British communism 1920-1991* (1992), ch. 1.
5. Ablett's position towards Lenin and the Communist International was similar to Kautsky's. (Interview with Dai Dan Evans, 7 August 1973, by H. Francis and D. Smith, transcript in South Wales Miners'

Library.) For Arthur Cook, see P. Davies, *A.J. Cook* (Manchester, 1987), pp. 42-4.

6. In Derbyshire, the Hicken brothers, Henry and Phil, were supporters of the reform movement. Phil joined the Communist Party. Henry remained staunchly leftwing and became a prominent supporter of the Miners' Minority Movement. The Kane family emigrated from the west of Ireland to Scotland before 1914. The father, Michael, became a miner in West Lothian; three children, Martin, Mick and Annie were foundation party members. Their elder brother Tam was involved in gun running for the IRA. Their younger brother Jock, born in 1907, became a party member when he was old enough.

7. L.J. Macfarlane, *The British Communist Party: its origin and development until 1929* (1966), p. 129.

8. Ibid., p. 131. Macfarlane observes that the question of the Fed affiliating to RILU 'was hotly debated ... with the CI [Comintern] representative Borodin, when he visited branches in South Wales but it was finally rejected because of the grave danger that the South Wales Miners' Federation would be expelled from the MFGB'.

9. J. Klugmann, *History of the Communist Party of Great Britain*, vol. 1, 1919-1924 (1968), pp. 278-9 and Macfarlane, *British Communist Party*, p. 131. The MMM's inaugural meeting had representatives from South Wales, Scotland, Durham, Yorkshire and Lancashire and Cheshire. Nat Watkins disappeared from party and MMM work without explanation in 1929. Some details about him are given in R. Martin, *Communism and the British Trade Unions, 1924-1933: a study of the National Minority Movement* (Oxford, 1969), p. 48.

10. 'Despite the distance and expense involved the Miners always sent a substantial delegation to [National] MM conferences' (Martin, *Communism*, p. 57).

11. A. Horner, *Incorrigible Rebel* (1960), pp. 43-4 and Davies, *A.J. Cook*, pp. 55-8 and pp. 65-8. In 1924, the South Wales Reform Committee, (the South Wales MMM), convened a conference of 200 delegates to endorse a candidate for MFGB secretary. Horner used his casting vote as chairman in favour of A.J. Cook rather than W.H. Mainwaring who was a party member. Cook eventually defeated Joseph Jones of Yorkshire.

12. Macfarlane, *British Communist Party*, pp. 158-9. Horner made a fortnight's tour of the Durham coalfield in 1925. As a result nine MMM groups were formed with a combined membership of 250. (Ibid., fn. 97, p. 159.)

13. Quoted in Horner, *Incorrigible Rebel*, pp. 73-4. See also Martin, *Communism*, p. 68. In June 1923 Horner had joined the party

politbureau, or cabinet, as a part-time member. During the imprison-
ment of the full-time leadership in anticipation of the General Strike,
Horner temporarily ran the party's industrial department. (Macfarlane,
British Communist Party, p. 83 and p. 138.)

14. Martin, *Communism*, pp. 71-4.
15. Macfarlane, *British Communist Party*, p. 166-9, p. 175; Trotsky's
    speech to the Soviet Communist Party politburo on 3 June 1926 is
    reprinted in Appendix F.
16. Ibid., p. 173. and N. Fishman, *The British Communist Party and the
    Trade Unions 1933-45* (Aldershot, 1994), Appendix One.
17. Arnot, *Years of Struggle*, pp. 470-1 and Macfarlane, *British
    Communist Party*, pp. 170-2.
18. Macfarlane, *British Communist Party*, pp. 173-4.
19. Horner, *Incorrigible Rebel*, p. 92. For Johnny Campbell, see
    Fishman, *The British CP*, pp. 4-10 and ch. 2.
20. H.A. Clegg, *A History of British Trade Unions Since 1889*, vol. 2,
    1911-1933 (Oxford, 1985), pp. 419-20.
21. Fishman, *The British CP*, pp. 31-4 and pp. 54-6. Assessments differ
    about the extent of Pollitt's complicity (willing or otherwise) with
    'class against class' and also when he turned away from the extreme
    left position he had adopted after 1926. For a discussion of Pollitt's
    position, see K. Morgan, *Harry Pollitt* (Manchester, 1993), chs 2 and
    3.
22. Ibid., pp. 33-6.
23. H. Francis and D. Smith, *The Fed: a history of the South Wales
    Miners in the twentieth century* (1980), pp. 153-4 and N. Branson,
    History of the Communist Party of Great Britain, 1927-1941 (1985),
    pp. 38-51.
24. Francis and Smith, *The Fed*, pp. 175-80 and Horner, *Incorrigible
    Rebel*, pp. 110-12.
25. Fishman, *The British CP*, pp. 40-1.
26. From the available evidence, Durham was the other coalfield with
    more than a token rank and file movement. See *Daily Worker*, 9
    April, 26 and 31 May, 8 December 1934. For the South Wales
    Miners' Rank and File Movement, see Fishman, *The British CP*, pp.
    71-3 and Francis and Smith, *The Fed*, pp. 245-7. By 1938, 360
    members of the SWMF were enrolled in the party and five members
    of the CP sat on the SWMF Executive (CPGB Archive, Politbureau
    Meeting, 22 June 1938, 'South Wales District Report').
27. Fishman, *The British CP*, pp. 73-80 and Branson, *History of the CP*,
    pp. 124-8.
28. Francis and Smith, *The Fed*, p. 201.

29. Ibid., p. 204 and fn. 109, p. 210.
30. *Daily Worker*, 15 September 1934.
31. N. Fishman, 'The British Communist Party and the Trade Unions, 1933-45: the dilemmas of revolutionary pragmatism', unpublished PhD thesis, University of London, 1991, pp. 295-6. The Taff Merthyr strike is discussed on pp. 295-300.
32. Horner, *Incorrigible Rebel*, pp. 125-6.
33. See Fishman (thesis), pp. 297-309.
34. *Daily Worker*, 21 May 1936.
35. Ibid., 14 April 1937. See also ibid., 26 April 1937. For relations between the Fed and the coalowners, see W.J. Anthony-Jones, 'Labour Relations in the South Wales Coal Industry', unpublished PhD thesis, University of Wales, 1959.
36. MFGB Conference Report 1937, pp. 296-7.
37. *Daily Worker*, 23 July 1937. The Fed motion proposed that delegates should be entitled to represent their union in all Labour Party institutions, from local ward to party conference, whatever their political allegiance. It was rejected by 413,000 to 130,000.
38. Fishman, *The British CP*, pp. 233-5.
39. N. Fishman, unpublished manuscript, 'Coalmining and communism, 1933-45', 1981, pp. 40-7.
40. *Daily Worker*, 17 October 1935.
41. Ibid., 21 and 22 November 1935.
42. Ibid., 15 January 1936.
43. Arnot, *Years of Struggle*, p. 178. Delegates from South Wales, Northumberland, and Cumberland voted against the settlement, with Scottish delegates remaining neutral.
44. *Daily Worker*, 25 January 1936.
45. Quoted in A.R. Griffin, *The Miners of Nottinghamshire 1914-44* (1962), p. 257. MFGB officers and party leaders had both spoken at meetings in the coalfield during the national wages dispute. They tried without success to rally miners around the national demands and back into the NMA. During the dispute, the Nottinghamshire owners made it known that they would produce and sell coal during a national strike.
46. For the Communist Party's involvement in Harworth and an analysis of the dispute on which the following account is based, see Fishman, *British CP*, ch. 7.
47. See Chapter 7 of this volume, below.
48. See Fishman, *British CP*, ch. 10.
49. The last annual conference of the National Union of Scottish Mineworkers passed an anti-war resolution, (*Daily Worker*, 4 May 1940).

50. Fishman, *The British CP*, pp. 267-9. The anti-war campaign in the Fed is analysed in S.R. Broomfield, 'South Wales in the Second World War: the coal industry and its community', unpublished PhD thesis, University of Wales, 1979, pp. 573-81. A similar conflict erupted over the People's Vigilance Movement, a counterpart to the People's Convention in South Wales. Neither Horner nor Labour activists on the Fed executive had any qualms about these 'popular movements' and the executive officially supported them in the face of the MPs' determined opposition. (Broomfield, pp. 580-92)

51. Labour relations in coalmining during World War II are dealt with in the official wartime history, W.J.B. Court, *Coal*, 1951.

PART TWO
Regional Studies

CHAPTER FIVE

'The hope of the British proletariat': the South Wales miners, 1910-1947

Chris Williams

Introduction

Given their remarkable history, it is not surprising that the South Wales miners have been well served by successive generations of historians, each with its own political and intellectual agenda. The coalfield's turbulent past has given rise to a highly politicised and deeply committed historiography. Some writers have operated with a manifest personal commitment to the industry and its working class. Thus Ness Edwards, author of *The History of the South Wales Miners* (1926) and *The History of the South Wales Miners' Federation* (1938), was variously agent for the SWMF and Labour MP for Caerphilly. Robin Page Arnot, responsible for the first two volumes of the 'official' history (*South Wales Miners*, 1967 and 1975), was a veteran and leading member of the Communist Party. Only a generation removed from the struggles themselves, and writing very much in the aftermath of the victorious miners' strikes of 1972 and 1974, Hywel Francis and David Smith, in their third volume of the 'official' history *The Fed: a history of the South Wales miners in the twentieth century* (1980), played a self-conscious role in re-establishing the centrality of the union's history and that of its members to the understanding of modern South Wales. Whilst Edwards and Page Arnot provided traditional, institutional labour histories, Francis and Smith were able to break the shackles of that mould (in part through pioneering usage of oral evidence) whilst retaining its virtues in a captivating account of a trade union 'in its society'. The establishment in the 1970s of the Welsh Labour History Society, Llafur, was, along with the opening of the South

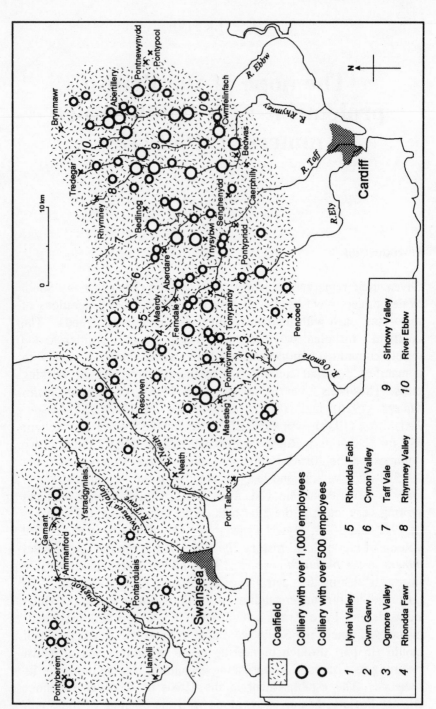

Map 2 The South Wales coalfield at nationalisation in 1947.

Coalfield

◯ Colliery with over 1,000 employees

○ Colliery with over 500 employees

1	Llynei Valley	5	Rhondda Fach	9	Sirhowy Valley
2	Cwm Garw	6	Cynon Valley	10	River Ebbw
3	Ogmore Valley	7	Taff Vale		
4	Rhondda Fawr	8	Rhymney Valley		

Wales Miners' Library and the collection of the South Wales Coalfield Archive, not just a reflection of academic awakening in labour history, but equally a statement of the significance of the area's history to its then current affairs. The severance of that umbilical link was signalled by the defeat of the miners' strike of 1984-5, and with the subsequent near-extinction of the deep-mined coal industry, it was inevitable that historical perspectives should be refocussed. Whatever their many qualities, the existing union histories, with their emphasis upon the union and political activists, particularly those with distinctive syndicalist, communist or internationalist credentials to display, cannot provide the last word. With all the old certainties of labour history in distant retreat, it would not be surprising if the ideological commitment of much of the existing historical record proves unfashionable to latter-day scholars. Recent years have witnessed the beginnings of a 'revisionist' historiography, which has questioned the meaning and nature of industrial and political 'militancy', and which has emphasised the prevalence of prosaic concerns and parochial horizons amongst the coalfield's working class. Such a reassessment of the history of South Wales will be welcomed by those prepared to marginalise its challenging experiences within accounts of both Welsh national and British political history. Whatever the fate of 'South Wales' as historical object and contemporary society, it is to be hoped that in their haste to shed rhetorical excesses and assert new narratives, the 'revisionists' do not fail to learn from the sensitivity of their predecessors to the complexity and integrity of their historical subjects.

Chronological overview

> A great gulf is fixed between the psalm-singing colliers who during the strike of 1898 begged their bread in the streets of English towns and the colliers who, 12 years later, looted Tonypandy, tried to drown the horses at Clydach, and did their ferocious best to destroy the surface works and the winding plant of the Glamorgan Colliery at Llwynypia. They do not seem the same breed of men.[1]

Despite its inaccuracy, this evaluation in the *Western Mail*, the Tory daily paper regarded as the organ of the coalowners, contained

more than a grain of truth.[2] For the events of the year 1910
probably have greater significance in the history of the South Wales
coalfield than of any other in Britain. The Rhondda-based Cambrian
Combine dispute, partnered by a shorter if no less bitter strike in the
neighbouring Cynon valley, heralded the emergence of South Wales
as a 'storm centre' of industrial unrest. The Combine dispute was
remarkable for four characteristics: it encompassed approximately
eleven thousand workmen spread across four separate collieries but
all under the control of one coalowner; it lasted longer than any
major strike in living memory; it involved large-scale and persistent
violence not only during the Tonypandy riots of November 1910
(which occasioned the notorious importation of the military) but for
months thereafter; and it inspired a critique of both the existing
personnel and traditions of the South Wales Miners' Federation
(SWMF or 'Fed') leadership which drew upon syndicalist and
industrial unionist theory, and which was embodied in the Unofficial
Reform Committee's 1912 publication, *The Miners' Next Step.*

Of course the 'class of 1910' was not a breed wholly apart from
that of 1898 (the strike that had acted as an essential prelude to both
the establishment of the SWMF and the replacement of the old
sliding scale method of wage negotiations with the Conciliation
Board), as many of the developments that became fully evident in
and after 1910 had deep roots in the preceding decade. Miners'
leaders had never been immune to criticism, and the influence and
status of SWMF president, the class-conciliatory William Abraham
('Mabon') had been under challenge since the bitter strikes of 1893
and 1898. By the late 1900s the style of compromise he personified
had to face the criticisms not only of advocates of a more resolute
industrial and political policy such as James Winstone, but also the
scorn of the flamboyant 'young man in a hurry' Charlie Stanton,
miners' agent for Aberdare, who attacked 'the faint-hearted, over-
cautious, creeping, crawling, cowardly set who pose as leaders but
do not lead (and) are responsible for the rotten condition of things
today'.[3] Industrial relations had been deteriorating in the coalfield
prior to the conflagration of 1910, with the conciliation and
arbitration procedures resulting in lengthy delays before arriving at
settlements, if settlements arrived at all. The economic background
to such deterioration included falling productivity, placing downward
pressure on both wages and profits. Such problems were exacerbated

(for both owners and miners) by the 1908 Eight Hours Act, and (for miners alone) by the judicial decision in 1908 that compensatory allowances for colliers working in difficult and less productive conditions ('abnormal places') were a matter of custom (and therefore revocable) rather than of law. Finally, the early years of the new century had witnessed the development of a radical critique not only of mining union leadership but also of capitalism, particularly amongst the devotees of the workers' education movement. Welsh miners were in the van of the Plebs League (advocating independent working class education), the Ruskin College strike of 1909, and the newly formed Central Labour College.

Nevertheless such developments were markedly accentuated by the Combine dispute, which simultaneously exposed the stark opposition of labour and capital in a manner that drastically undermined the viability of Lib-Lab notions of industrial cooperation and wider social harmony. In this conflict between the archetypal authoritarian (if also progressive and far-sighted) coalowner D.A. Thomas and a body of miners organised through a combine committee to meet the challenge of capitalist combination and led on the ground by a new generation who were, if not all syndicalists, at least cognisant of the 'advanced' views now in circulation, the language of industrial relations shifted from assertions of the identity of interest of the two sides of the industrial equation to proclamations of their incompatibility. If 'Mabon''s ostensible motto had been 'half a loaf is better than none', Ruskin College-product, Cambrian Combine Committee vice chairman and *Miners' Next Step* co-author Noah Rees could pithily respond that '[we] are demanding the bakehouse'.[4] Of even greater significance was the realisation that the object of industrial struggle was henceforth not simply an improved relationship between wages and profits but the determination of both the leadership and the future trajectory of South Walian society.

Exhausted by an ultimately unsuccessful conclusion to the Combine dispute, South Wales miners had nevertheless played a major role in radicalising British miners generally over the issues of 'abnormal places' and the minimum wage, realised in regional form after the first national strike of the MFGB in 1912. They had also acquired a reputation for militancy, divesting themselves of the timid image acquired during the late nineteenth century. Naturally there were limits to such militancy and to the advancement of new and radical ideas within the coalfield. Most representative positions in the union continued to be held by those with attachments to the Mabonite era. William Brace, as president of the SWMF from 1912, represented continuity not novelty. Syndicalist-inspired schemes for the central-isation of the SWMF were clearly defeated in 1912 and 1913, and politically the tenor of the SWMF remained constitutional, not revolutionary, in sympathy.

A brief period of industrial quiescence after 1912 (which allowed the coalfield to reach peak production figures of 57 million tons in 1913) was terminated by the pressures of the Great War. The coal-field strike of July 1915 needs to be understood as resulting neither from an 'excess of patriotism' nor from any appreciable 'anti-war feeling', but from the material interests and grievances of the miners, incensed that the coalowners who were themselves making fortunes should be so resistant to passing any of the surplus thus generated on to their employees.[5]

The 1915 dispute impelled the imposition of government control upon the coal industry, an act that offered political confirmation of the economic and strategic strength of the miners. In 1916 the SWMF secured an agreement from the coalowners that all colliery workmen should be members of one of the recognised trade unions: assisting the extinguishing of non-unionism whilst also strengthening the central position of the SWMF itself, the appropriate home for all in the mining industry excepting a few thousand enginemen, craftsmen, and colliery officials. Of more immediate importance were the improvements secured in pay that saw average money earnings more than double between summer 1914 and summer 1918, and the gathering of support for the realisation of the MFGB's objective of the permanent nationalisation of the mines, based upon a belief that the miners had a right to a higher standard of living and to special treatment by the state and by the nation it represented. The war years, although not introducing novel vistas of miners' ambitions, at least helped to generalise, popularise and confirm the combativeness that had been so marked in 1910-12.

In the aftermath of the war South Wales miners continued to benefit from the circumstances offered by the continuation of government control and the upsurge of the postwar boom. Employment in the coalfield rose to an all-time high of 271,516 in 1920, whilst average earnings were more than treble those of 1914. Such prosperity was both temporary and fragile, however, given the decline by a quarter of labour productivity during the same period, and given that the collapse of the export price of coal at the end of 1920 (vital to a coalfield where half of total output was exported) resulted in South Wales coal being produced at a loss of six shillings per ton by the beginning of 1921.[6] With Lloyd George's government declining the opportunity to nationalise afforded by the Sankey Commission, the return of the coalfield to private control in April 1921 led to the halving of average earnings in the course of that year.

The miners' fight for a reasonable standard of living was not completely lost until the defeat of 1926, a trauma that marked the point at which the ambitious projects of the coalfield's revolutionaries had at last to be shelved, as they began to come to terms with living in an undeniably non-revolutionary situation. But although ultimately beaten, the miners' struggles of the 1920s explicitly and unambiguously completed the process of societary redefinition in which South Wales had been engaged since 1910. The Lib-Lab *gwerin* had now taken the form of a proletariat, and the defiant resilience exuded in these years moulded the consciousness of successive generations in ways that were to redound down to the equally vital struggles of the 1980s.

However despite the fact that in historical retrospect and popular legend the defeats of 1921 and 1926 acquired an epic status, at the time they resulted in a substantial shift of power away from the miners and towards the coalowners. Union and political activists were subjected to widespread victimisation, wages were cut, hours extended, and conditions worsened. Employment in the coal industry fell steadily every year from 1926 to 1937, and by 1932 male unemployment across Wales as a whole was averaging 39.1 per cent. The SWMF, reacting slowly to the changed circumstances under which it had to operate, found itself regarded by some miners as powerless to defend their interests, and blamed by others for the disasters that had befallen them and their society. Non-unionism, encouraged by some employers and a constant nuisance at the best of times, became rife, with at worst (between 1929 and 1933) less than half of the coal industry's employees being members of the SWMF.[7] Some workers were attracted by other unions, such as the AEU, NUGW, and D.B. Jones's craftsmen and surfacemen's union, all of which could at least be regarded as 'legitimate' if unwelcome. Not so the South Wales Miners' Industrial Union (SWMIU), an explicitly 'non-political' organisation founded in 1926, and one that was to plague the Fed for more than a decade before its extinction in 1938.[8]

The SWMIU was a shadowy organisation, with an uncertain membership (probably of two to six thousand) sharing a complex set of motivations and principles. It was fostered by coalowners such as the Ocean Coal Company and Instone's, and drew upon sympathies present within the Conservative Party, yet the clearest affinities of some of its most prominent members were either with the Liberal Party, or with liberalism's legacy of the vision of coal trade unity. Identifiable motivations amongst its adherents ranged from avowed anti-communism, through a naive faith in the benefits obtaining to 'non-political' trade unionism, to a more fundamental desire simply to work and earn money at a time when both were goods in short supply. Whilst there is no denying that the SWMIU has to be understood as part of coalfield society rather than as an alien import, it is also the case that the struggle waged between the SWMF and the MIU was much more one determined by the former's resolution not to have its centrality displaced and its representativeness questioned by the coalowners, than it was characterised by any equal competition between the two unions for the allegiances of South Wales miners. Even at its moment of greatest weakness, the SWMF was between ten and thirty times larger than the SWMIU.

In explaining the Fed's ultimate victory, one may identify organisational, tactical and strategic elements. In 1933 the decision was taken to reorganise the SWMF along more centralised lines (presaged by the Unofficial Reform Committee some twenty years previously), including the creation of an executive council dominated by 'rank and file' miners. The eight 'areas' thus created were larger, stronger and more efficient sub-units than the pre-existent nineteen districts, many of which had been devastated by unemployment, short-time working and non-unionism. In the 'stay-down' strikes of 1935 the SWMF found an imaginative tactical weapon that met with no effective response from either the SWMIU or the employers, whilst in those colliery settlements proximate to SWMIU-infected pits, the range of collective action and social ostracism practised carried echoes of the 'Scotch Cattle' of the nineteenth century coalfield. All of this was spearheaded by intelligent and resourceful leaders such as James Griffiths, S.O. Davies, and, in particular,

Arthur Horner, the latter belying his received image as a firebrand communist (itself no handicap in commanding the loyalty of a membership congenitally suspicious of betrayal) with an acute sensitivity to the art of the possible.

The rebuilding of the SWMF was one facet of a many-sided politicisation of the coalfield in the late 1920s and 1930s. The spectre of unemployment and its attendant poverty, malnutrition and disease occasioned national hunger marches, localised campaigns (often spearheaded by the NUWM), and vast, spectacular and successful demonstrations against the Means Test in 1935. This society in crisis still had time to look elsewhere than simply at itself as the mobilisation in support of Republican Spain testifies. In what was only the most tangible expression of a widespread anti-fascist commitment, South Wales supplied 134 volunteers to the International Brigade, 33 of whom died in the conflict.[9]

By the late 1930s the SWMF was back in control of its members, actual and potential, and if not on wholly secure ground in its dealings with employers (in what was still an uncertain economic climate), at least it could look to the future and concentrate on improving wages and conditions rather than on simple survival. The 1937 wages agreement was evidence of the new, disciplined style of industrial relations being established by Horner, whatever the reservations of others on the left.[10]

During the Second World War the mood of the 1930s remained highly influential. Insofar as rearmament and the exigencies of the war economy resulted in an increased demand for coal and its workers, then unemployment eased and wages rose. But the deep embitterment of industrial relations could not be so easily reversed, and a high level of unofficial strikes was the result. The conviction grew that private ownership of the coal industry was damaging not just the coalfield societies but also the efficiency and flexibility of the practice of mining itself. From mid-way through the war, reconstruction became a prominent theme in the leadership circles of the Welsh labour movement, and nationalisation of coal was centrally embedded in any proposals resulting from such discussions. When Labour's sweeping election victory of 1945 was followed a year later by the Coal Industry Nationalisation Bill, those many mining trade unionists who had sacrificed time, effort, earnings and even liberty to fight for their organisation and their class could indeed believe that this was a major step on the road to a new Britain. Looking back at this era from the post-industrial, economic desert that is the South Wales valleys in the 1990s, it is easy to be drawn to the views of those historians who stress the continuities in managerial personnel and attitudes across the nationalisation watershed, and who describe the sometimes prosaic approach to state control taken by non-activist miners.[11] Yet, in its context as part of Labour's grand enterprise of building the welfare state and moving towards a mixed economy, the nationalisation of coal could be seen as a vindication of the struggles of the South Wales miners across the preceding four decades.

The economic and geographical context

> A fundamental fact as to this industry [coal] in South Wales, is that the life of the workers engaged in it is conditioned at every point, and in every form of activity, by the physical and geographical conditions of the district itself. The physical configuration of the coalfield is markedly different from that of any other coal area in Great Britain, and is a factor that profoundly affects and largely conditions the social life of the inhabitants.[12]

The South Wales coalfield is 70 miles in length and up to 18 miles in width. It is divided into a score of valleys of varying sizes, around whose floors mines have been sunk and residential areas grown. Communications have most naturally followed the rivers, and have thus tended to run north-south rather than east-west, hampering contact between adjacent valley communities. Certainly this landscape has conditioned aspects of the emergence of mining trade unionism and traditions of loyalty and solidarity, as observed by the Commissioners of Enquiry into Industrial Unrest in 1917, perhaps the *locus classicus* of this case. Nineteenth century mining unions tended to be valley-based, and the SWMF, from 1898 through to reorganisation in 1933, was organised around districts also predominantly identified with these geographical confines. Local identifications have been seen as of prime importance in understanding the dynamics of collective action up to 1926, and there is evidence that they remained of considerable significance throughout the interwar years at least.[13] A common factor in explaining the presence of the SWMIU in collieries such as Raglan, Taff-Merthyr and Bedwas may have been the relative geographical isolation or uniqueness of these pits. Thus Raglan drew upon the semi-rural communities of Pencoed and Heolycyw to the north east of Bridgend, Taff-Merthyr was opened during the 1926 dispute midway between Bedlinog and Trelewis in the Taff-Bargoed valley, and Bedwas, on the very edge of the coalfield in the lower Rhymney valley, and serviced by the twin and young colliery villages of Trethomas and Bedwas, was regarded as 'an oasis in a desert'.[14]

Colliery companies were not unaware of the advantages that could flow from breaking the hold of a particular mining settlement over the labour supply for their pit, and the Powell Duffryn company was by the 1930s deliberately recruiting its workforce from as far afield as possible as a deterrent to union solidarity.[15] Of course there was no necessary link between isolation and company unionism, as the very different history of Mardy, 'Little Moscow', at the top end of the Rhondda Fach indicates.[16] Nor did such settlements have to be anything other than rather ordinary, as seems to have been the case for both Senghenydd, at the top of the Aber valley, and Ynysybwl, an offshoot of the Taff north of Pontypridd.[17] Rather these self-contained colliery areas were able to sustain traditions of industrial and political behaviour, sometimes against the prevailing current, calling upon social and communitarian resources in the process.

Nevertheless one must not overstate the relevance of the geographical parameters of colliery settlement. Labour turnover and in-migration within the coalfield were sufficiently common to ensure that many miners would have experience of working in a number of pits, and perhaps in a number of different areas throughout the coalfield. The prevalence of miners travelling to work by train, also severs any simple connection between settlement and specific 'occupational community'. Thus miners resident in the 'north crop' areas of Monmouthshire would increasingly travel down the valley to the newer and more profitable collieries opened there. Miners' trains ran to the coalfield from the seaside town of Porthcawl, whilst during the 1921 dispute miners resident in Cardiff asked to form their own lodge so as to manage the relief of distress during the crisis.[18] Overall, collieries cannot be understood simply as reflections of their proximate colliery settlements, although that is not to say that such settlements did not exert a considerable influence over traditions of activism and leadership.

Sensitivity to the wide variation in sizes and ages of mines, their markets and their ownership patterns is also required if the 'stereotyped images' from which the South Wales coalfield has long suffered are to be reassessed. Across the 37 year span, the tendency was towards medium sized mines (See Table 5.1). At the lower end of the scale many small mines closed during the mid-to-late 1920s, whilst large pits slashed their workforces in an attempt to reduce costs during unprofitable times. Thus in the Garw valley, six of the smaller mines closed between 1924 and 1927 with a total loss of over nine hundred jobs, and the workforce at the Ffaldau colliery, Pontycymmer, still numbering 1100 in 1927, was halved by the mid-1930s. Older mines, particularly those along the north crop of the coalfield, were highly vulnerable, and by 1934 not one pit in the northern half of the borough of Merthyr Tydfil was working.[19]

The unemployment which bit into the South Wales coalfield in these years did so unevenly. Forty-eight per cent unemployment in the Merthyr area in 1935 was paralleled by 31 per cent in the Rhymney-Tredegar area.[20] Even within these districts there was enormous variation, so that unemployment in Abertillery in 1937 was less than half that of Brynmawr, 5 miles to the north.[21]

An even greater contrast was to be found with the position in the anthracite coalfield, to the west of the Vale of Neath.[22] The economic development of this area had proceeded after the most rapid expansion of the central steam coalfield, and the peak of production came not in 1913 but in 1934. Anthracite coal was not subjected to the same slump in demand that afflicted steam coal in the 1920s, and as a result continued to maintain relatively buoyant employment levels throughout the interwar years. Production was characterised by a higher number of smaller mines than elsewhere, and unemployment stood at around 20 per cent in the anthracite area in 1935. Wyndham Portal in his 1934 report considered it appropriate to concentrate on the 'Eastern Section' of the coalfield as 'the outlook in the Western Section is definitely brighter'.[23] The anthracite coalfield had a reputation for a more homogeneous ethnic composition than the rest of the coalfield, which was considered to explain its pre-1920s industrial and political moderation.[24]

Settlement patterns in the anthracite were also markedly different from those in the central coalfield. Larger houses with substantial gardens, many of which were owner-occupied, provided a stark contrast to the ribbon terraces of the Rhondda, a higher proportion of which were rented. A minority of miners in the anthracite lived in cottages in the countryside, perhaps combining a small holding with colliery employment. Elsewhere, in the Swansea valley and Llanelli districts, alternative futures could be countenanced in the tinplate and copper industries. Even outside the anthracite there were qualifications to the common image of mono-industrial mining communities. In Ebbw Vale, Tredegar, Merthyr and Pontypool, iron and steelworkers rubbed shoulders with miners, whilst Pontypridd had its chainmakers, and everywhere its railwaymen. The traditions of industrial cooperation and peace in these industries may account for their lack of prominence relative to the miners in the labour history of South Wales, but community studies exploring the relations between these different occupational groups are urgently needed.

The South Wales coalfield was thus an area of such economic, social and geographical variation as to force one to question any assumption that a particular settlement can be seen as 'representative', 'typical' or 'universal'. However there were developments making for a greater uniformity and commonality of experience, and thus it remains possible to describe South Wales miners, be they from Pontnewynydd (in the east) or Pontyberem (in the west), as increasingly coming to share in a common industrial and political culture.

Most obviously, pre-1914 traditions of employer paternalism, even then being overshadowed by the growth of organisations such as the Cambrian Combine, were made redundant in the interwar years by the concentration of coal ownership in the hands of a small number of companies. The physical withdrawal of first coalowners and then colliery managers from the coalfield, the eradication of customs and concessions at individual collieries as companies attempted to impose standard arrangements across their growing number of concerns, and the progressive integration of coal production, horizontally with that of iron and steel, tinplate and copper, and vertically with marketing, transport and banking interests, all led to an atmosphere of facelessness and austerity in industrial relations, and an apparent lack of concern on the part of the distant owners for the fortunes of the communities whose economic destinies they controlled. By 1938 over two-thirds of coalfield output was in the hands of five companies, with Powell Duffryn Ltd responsible for one-third in its own right.[25] Allen Hutt did not exaggerate when he wrote that to

Table 5.1 Size distribution of coal mines according to employment, South Wales coalfield, 1910-1947

Wage-earners	1910			1929			1947		
	No. of mines	Wage-earners employed	% of total	No. of mines	Wage-earners employed	% of total	No. of mines	Wage-earners employed	% of total
Under 20	126	1,053	0.49	132	887	0.48	32	235	0.22
20-49	75	2,409	1.13	45	1,426	0.77	5	167	0.16
50-99	65	4,868	2.28	30	2,272	1.22	13	1,058	0.99
100-249	103	15,716	7.37	57	9,557	5.14	33	5,702	5.32
250-499	61	20,938	9.82	71	26,391	14.19	44	15,585	14.55
500-749	42	25,810	12.10	33	20,276	10.90	43	26,656	24.89
750-999	21	17,889	8.39	28	24,319	13.08	25	21,637	20.20
1000-1499	28	32,721	15.34	25	31,131	16.74	19	22,118	20.65
1500-1999	21	37,127	17.41	19	32,902	17.69	8	13,939	13.02

contd

2000-2499	8	17,568	8.24	8	17,466	9.39	-	-
2500-2999	6	16,505	7.74	6	16,320	8.78	-	-
3000 and over	6	20,686	9.70	1	3,001	1.61	-	-
Total	562	213,290	100	455	185,948	100	222	107,097	100

Source: Lists of Mines (HMSO).

Note: Only those mines taken into production by the NCB are listed for 1947.

'journey in South Wales is not to journey from one county or one valley to the next, but to travel from territory to territory of one or other of these combines.'[26]

The SWMF response to such developments was to attempt to match the enemy pit for pit by organising its own combine committees, composed of representatives of all concerns held by a single employer, and important statements of the ability to overcome latent geographical parochialism through the formation of united fronts. By the late 1920s there were combine committees in the anthracite, and for the Powell Duffryn, Cory's, Ocean and Cambrian workers.

Finally, technical changes within coal mining such as the introduction of coal cutting and conveying machinery had a prolonged and widespread impact upon industrial relations and the experience of work, whatever the relative lack of coal cutting in South Wales more generally. Whilst formulating a response to the challenges posed by mechanisation never became central to the strategy of the SWMF, the introduction of machinery proved to be a common experience that disrupted traditional patterns and assumptions concerning the organisation and remuneration of labour underground. It involved the recasting of control and authority, the redefinition of skills and the displacement of others. As such it was regularly the occasion for a labour dispute on a pit by pit basis, as miners reacted to what they felt was the 'speed up' of work, with its attendant pressures and dangers. After 1926 colliery companies capitalised upon their position of strength over labour by breaking up existing work practices at the same time as they eliminated union activists, although they did not always require the pretext of mechanisation to do either. For some miners the loss of pride in their work was keenly felt, whilst others were unable to retrain to use the new equipment and were downgraded or made redundant. Mechanisation furthered a commonality of experience of exploitation and powerlessness throughout the coalfield that exacerbated industrial relations hostility.

The clearest example of how these developments had the capacity to transform every part of the coalfield is afforded by the experience of the anthracite after the Great War. Here rapid postwar combination saw the Amalgamated Anthracite and United Anthracite combines emerge as dominant, their rise accompanied by an assault on customs and practices underground. This sparked the violent disturbances of the 1925 strike, as the anthracite miners cast off their reputation for moderation and proceeded to display support for the full range of socialist political and cultural icons in the interwar period, culminating in the election in 1933 by Gwendraeth valley miners of Arthur Horner as agent. At a time when the traditionally more militant miners of the central steam coalfield were being devastated by unemployment, victimisation and company unionism, it was the anthracite miners who provided the SWMF with one of its strongest and most consistent reservoirs of support.

The South Wales Miners' Federation: a social, industrial, political and male institution

> There is probably no organisation in the world which has such a close relationship to the community it serves as the South Wales Miners' Federation has to the people of the mining areas of South Wales. For the last twenty or thirty years it has become so much a part of the life of the people of this Coalfield that every man and women living in this area turn instinctively to it for advice and protection in almost every kind of difficulty or trouble they meet from time to time.[27]

The social centrality of the SWMF within mining communities has become a commonplace of modern historiography, albeit one that still needs further exploration in order to locate its origins and the way in which it intermeshed with Welsh nonconformity in providing a range of reference points, services and interpretations for its people.[28] The SWMF lodge was an educational and recreational focus as well as an advice bureau, although it was this latter role that secured its placement at the core of mining communities. With the retreat of capital from the coalfield, the absence of a strong, educated and professional middle class, and the decline of the public role of nonconformity, there were few obstacles to the redefinition of mining communities as working class entities, appropriately led by representatives of the most prominent working class institution of the age.

Such leadership could only be secured through effective industrial strategies, and in this respect it is necessary to contextualise the ideological differences exhibited by different generations of miners' leaders. The world view of an Ablett or a Horner was far removed from that of a Hartshorn or a 'Mabon', and an education in Marxism or a commitment to the Communist Party offered budding miners' leaders intellectual guidance and resources. But in terms of the handling of practical matters such as disputes, negotiations for new price lists, and the running of non-unionist campaigns, what was critical was a pragmatic clear-sightedness and an ability to cooperate, conciliate and choose very carefully the grounds on which to fight. Paynter saw himself as 'a miner and trade unionist first and a communist second', and applied this label also to Arthur Horner.[29]

The SWMF also played a vitally important political role in coalfield communities. By 1922 sixteen parliamentary constituencies with high percentages of miners amongst the electorate, from Gower in the west to Pontypool in the east, were all returning Labour MPs, and continued to do so throughout the following decades. At the general election of 1931, when the Labour Party went into massive retreat across Britain, the South Wales coalfield made a major contribution to its avoidance of parliamentary extinction with this contingent of supporters. Not every Labour MP in these constituencies was identified with the SWMF and there were occasional clashes with other interests within the Labour Party, but even if the Fed did not return the MP for the constituency, it invariably dominated the local government arena where its agents, lodge secretaries and checkweighers were regularly returned as councillors and guardians. Parties to the right of Labour were marginalised: the Liberals unable to recover from the combination of the Great Unrest and the Great War, the Conservatives and Welsh Nationalists irrelevant to the needs of coalfield society. Even the most obvious manifestations of an alternative political tradition, the large and popular Conservative clubs, concealed quite different allegiances. In the Sirhowy valley in the 1930s the Cwmfelinfach club was dominated by miners loyal to the SWMF intent on ousting the SWMIU from the nearby Nine Mile Point colliery, whilst in the Rhondda Fach the Ferndale Conservative club was actually populated by members of the CPGB.[30]

Finally, much of the gender history of the coalfield has yet to be written, an absence in part explained by economic history. Throughout South Wales there was little available paid work for women, and the census recorded an average of less than a fifth of women in Glamorgan and Monmouthshire as being economically active across the period 1911-1931, whilst the comparable figure for men was well over four-fifths. The vast majority of working women were young and single, with activity rates among married women being lower than 5 per cent in many valleys. The 'separate spheres' of the economy were reproduced in much associational and political activity in the coalfield, with trade unions, trades councils and political parties being male-dominated preserves. Women played a regular part in collective action against non- and company-unionists, but their participation in the more routine channels of the labour movement was generally limited to the articulation of 'welfarist' issues (such as the campaigns for pithead baths and maternity and child welfare clinics) through the Cooperative Women's Guild and the Women's Sections of both the Labour and Communist parties. Even Mrs James Griffiths, writing about 'Co-operative housekeeping' in the official SWMF publication *The Colliery Workers' Magazine*, saw social improvements as helping to make 'joyous, healthy and happy women - true comrades to their menfolk, and willing mothers of happy children!'[31]

Radicalism, militancy and culture in the South Wales coalfield

> During the last ten or fifteen years the South Wales miners have come to be regarded by critics, both friendly and hostile, as being in the very fore-front of the revolutionary movement in this country and their lodges, economic classes and conferences as the natural and, almost, the original home of advanced opinion as to the ultimate objective of the workers and the correct means of getting there. They have been bracketed with the engineers of the Clydeside as the twin hopes of the British proletariat.[32]

South Wales miners have, in the course of the twentieth century, established a powerful reputation for industrial militancy, with an unsurpassed degree of 'strike-proneness'. Recently, however, revisionist scholarship has argued for a dual qualification of this reputation. First it has been suggested that industrial militancy should not be seen as necessarily expressive of either an 'archetypal proletarian' identity or a set of 'proletarian internationalist' beliefs held by those engaged in strike activity. Strike activity should instead be seen as stemming from immediate material grievances rooted in the profitability or otherwise of individual collieries, rather than from either the political culture of the surrounding community, or from a more generalised ideological predisposition. Second any necessary connection between industrial militancy and political militancy (defined as 'membership of or support for political organizations to the left of the Labour Party, primarily the CPGB') is denied, and the overwhelming support for the Labour Party exhibited throughout the interwar period is instead seen as indicative not of militancy but of conformity and an acceptance of 'the established order'.[33]

Such work is undoubtedly valuable for forcing historians to consider carefully the nature of the links between occupational and political consciousness, and for providing a corrective to any easy assumptions of the inevitability of solidarity amongst coal miners. However there are significant weaknesses in the 'revisionist' case. It is highly doubtful whether any historian of the South Wales miners would subscribe to the 'archetypal proletarian' caricature as deployed by the critics. More substantially the stress on any given pit's lack of profitability as the key explanatory variable for industrial relations may be feasible for the mid-1930s onwards but cannot apply with such regularity to the earlier period.[34] It was precisely when colliery companies were making unsurpassed profits from their concerns (1914-1920) that industrial unrest was at its peak in the coalfield. Friction between employers and employees may be determined primarily by lack of profitability, but only in conditions under which issues of strategic control and power have been 'depoliticised', either by the assertion of managerial-capitalist authority (as after 1926) or by nationalisation.

As for the revised assessment of political radicalism, it is sorely deficient in understanding the nature of coalfield politics. The definition of political militancy is unduly restricted and of an ahistorical character: if militancy is to have any meaning then it must acknowledge that South Wales provided the Labour Party with one of its regional heartlands, and that support for the Labour Party was not seen as support for the established order, particularly during the first half of the twentieth century. The development of 'revolution-ary' strategies such as syndicalism and communism took place within the context of a more generalised and hegemonic labourism. Both syndicalism and communism took root only to a limited degree, and in quite geographically circumscribed areas. Their growth was dependent, in part, upon the success of the Labour Party in routing

Liberal and other opposition, and in providing a secure environment for the contemplation of more extravagant alternatives to parliamentary socialism. Leftwing organisations inhabited a common cultural terrain suffused with a popular socialism, albeit one tied closely to occupational and trade union identifications.[35]

This understanding of the political consciousness of the South Wales miners stands between the revisionist account of miners' history and the characterisation proffered by Francis and Smith of an 'alternative culture', defined as including a 'hostility to capitalism' and the increasing rejection of 'social, political and cultural norms', which created 'a new behavioural pattern' most evident in the 1925 and 1926 disputes.[36] This culture ('founded on class discipline, resourceful quasi-political illegality, direct action resulting often in guerrilla and open warfare, collectivist action of various forms, perverse humour and escapism') has been seen as producing 'a society within a society'.[37] Whilst it is important to stress both the internationalist and the independent working class education traditions within the history of the South Wales miners, as well as to recognise the titanic scale of the clashes between coalfield communities and the state in the 1920s and 1930s, the label of an 'alternative culture' may prove misleading. Miners had resilient links to the traditional coalfield culture, enjoyed patterns of leadership and behaviour that exhibited continuity over many decades, and, largely, supported a Labour Party that generally aimed to secure gradualist changes within the boundaries of the law.

South Wales miners shared in a common trade union and political culture that, if not 'alternative', was certainly distinctive in a British context. This culture could be exported (not without modification and realignment) to the new industrial centres of the Midlands and the South of England through the processes of out-migration: in Oxford ex-miners dominated the local Transport and General Workers' Union (TGWU) and provided an important stimulus to the growth of the local Labour Party.[38] Above all, it was a culture that could also be dispersed as both ideological inspiration and historical memory, contributing to the self-realisation of 1945 and 1947 and to the struggles of the British working class in the 1970s and 1980s.

Notes

Place of publication is London unless otherwise stated.

1. *Western Mail*, 27 February 1912; cited in D.K. Davies, 'The Influence of Syndicalism and Industrial Unionism on the South Wales Coalfield 1898-1921: a study in ideology and practice', unpublished PhD thesis, University of Wales (Cardiff), 1991, p. 147.
2. D. Smith, 'Tonypandy 1910: definitions of community', *Past and Present*, no. 87, 1980, pp. 158-184.
3. D. Evans, *Labour Strife in the South Wales Coalfield, 1910-1911* (Cardiff, 1911), p. 35.
4. Cited by Davies (thesis), p. 41.
5. A. Mor O'Brien, 'Patriotism on trial: the strike of the South Wales miners, July 1915', *Welsh History Review*, vol. 12, no. 1, 1984, pp. 76-104; H. Francis and D. Smith, *The Fed: a history of the South Wales miners in the twentieth century* (1980).
6. B. Supple, *The History of the British Coal Industry*, volume 4, 1913-1946 (Oxford, 1987), pp. 154-155. In 1913 65 per cent of coal was exported, but this had fallen to 45 per cent by 1920.
7. Francis and Smith, *The Fed*, p. 117.
8. Ibid., especially pp. 113-144.
9. H. Francis, *Miners Against Fascism: Wales and the Spanish civil war* (1984), pp. 179, 248.
10. N. Fishman, *The British Communist Party and the Trade Unions, 1933-45* (Aldershot, 1995), pp. 242-3.
11. K. Howells, 'A View From Below: tradition, experience and nationalisation in the South Wales coalfield, 1937-1957', unpublished PhD thesis, University of Warwick, 1979; I.M. Zweiniger-Bargielowska, 'Industrial Relationships and Nationalisation in the South Wales Coalmining Industry', unpublished PhD thesis, University of Cambridge, 1989.
12. *Industrial Unrest, Commission of Enquiry, (Reports) No.7 Division*, 1917-18 (Cd.8668).
13. D. Gilbert, *Class, Community, and Collective Action: social change in two British coalfields, 1850-1926* (Oxford, 1992) p. 54.
14. H. Francis, 'Society and trades unions in Glamorgan 1800-1987', in P. Morgan (ed.) *Glamorgan County History Vol.VI: Glamorgan Society 1780-1980* (Cardiff, 1988), pp. 89-107, p. 101; A. Morgan, 'Bedlinog: glimpses of a pre-war society', in R. Denning (ed.) *Glamorgan Historian* vol. 11, (Cowbridge, 1975), pp. 137-148; and Dai Dan Evans cited in Francis and Smith, *The Fed*, p. 314.

15. Francis and Smith, *The Fed*, p. 391.
16. S. Macintyre, *Little Moscows* (1980).
17. Gilbert, *Class*; M. Lieven, *Senghennydd: the universal pit village, 1890-1930* (Llandysul, 1994).
18. P.N. Jones, 'Workmen's trains in the South Wales coalfield 1870-1926', *Transport History*, vol. 3, 1970, pp. 21-35 and *Colliery Settlement in the South Wales Coalfield 1850-1926* (Hull, 1969), p. 30; SWMF EC Minutes, 30 April, 9 May 1921.
19. J.W. England, 'The Merthyr of the twentieth century: a postscript', in G. Williams (ed.) *Merthyr Politics: the making of a working-class tradition* (Cardiff, 1966), pp. 82-101.
20. National Industrial Development Council of Wales and Monmouthshire, *The Second Industrial Survey of South Wales Volume Three: Part Three: Development*, Appendix III.
21. The Labour Party, *South Wales: Report of the Labour Party's Commission of Enquiry into the Distressed Areas* (London, 1937), pp. 4-5.
22. My thanks to Ioan Matthews for allowing me to consult the proofs of his doctoral thesis upon the anthracite miners.
23. W. Portal, *Reports of Investigations into the Industrial Conditions in Certain Depressed Areas: III, South Wales and Monmouthshire* (Cmd. 1934), p. 129.
24. Ministry of Health, *Report of the South Wales Regional Survey Committee* (1921), p. 11.
25. Ministry of Fuel and Power, *South Wales Coalfield Regional Survey Report* (1946), p. 144.
26. A. Hutt, *The Condition of the Working Class in Britain* (1933), p. 4.
27. SWMF, *An Outline of the Work Accomplished on Behalf of the South Wales Colliery Workers* (Cardiff, 1927), p. 3.
28. W. Paynter, *My Generation* (1972), p. 10; Francis and Smith, *The Fed*, p. 34; C. Williams, 'The South Wales Miners' Federation', *Llafur*, vol. 5, no. 3, 1990, pp. 45-56; Gilbert, *Class*, pp. 88-93.
29. Paynter, *My Generation*, p. 109.
30. A. Burge, 'In search of Harry Blount: scabbing between the wars in one South Wales community', *Llafur*, vol. 6, no. 3, 1994, pp. 58-69; O. Stutchbury, *Too Much Government: a political Aeneid?* (Ipswich, 1977), pp. 11-12.
31. *Colliery Workers' Magazine*, vol. 3, no. 11, November 1925.
32. J.T. Walton Newbold, *The Doom of a Coalfield: 'Big Business' in South Wales* (1922), p. 2.
33. Zweiniger-Bargielowska, (thesis), pp. 102-113.
34. I.M. Zweiniger-Bargielowska, 'Miners' militancy: a study of four

South Wales collieries during the middle of the twentieth century', *Welsh History Review*, vol. 16, no. 3, 1993, pp. 356-383.
35. C. Williams, 'Democratic Rhondda: politics and society, 1885-1951', unpublished PhD thesis, University of Wales (Cardiff), 1991.
36. Francis and Smith, *The Fed*, pp. 54-56.
37. Ibid., p. 66.
38. A.J. Chandler, 'The Re-making of a Working Class: migration from the South Wales coalfield to the new industry areas of the Midlands c.1920-1940', unpublished PhD thesis, University of Wales (Cardiff), 1988.

CHAPTER SIX

The social history of political conflict in the Scots coalfields, 1910-1939

Alan Campbell

Introduction

The Scottish coalfields witnessed the sharpest clashes between the Labour and Communist Parties in British trade union politics during the interwar period. It was in Scotland that the major attempt was made to establish a communist-led 'red union' in Britain, the United Mineworkers of Scotland (UMS), and two out of the three communist MPs elected in the interwar period represented seats in the Scots coalfields. By the Second World War, Communist Party members held leading positions in the Scottish miners' unions; yet electoral politics in the Scots coalfields were dominated (though not totally) by the Labour Party.

This chapter examines the complex relations between these trade union traditions and the influences which nurtured or retarded their development. It does so by reference to three ideal types of mining trade unionism: the independent collier, the bureaucratic reformist and the militant miner.[1] Their defining characteristics are summarised schematically in Table 6.1 and their empirical expression is discussed more fully in the central section of this essay. Here we need only introduce our argument that trade unions simultaneously pursue a number of methods to achieve what Flanders described as internal and external job regulation. The former includes unilateral workgroup regulation, such as restriction of output and apprentice-ship controls, and bilateral, often informal, negotiations within the workplace enforced through unofficial sanctions. The latter category includes regulation by unions and employers' associations of their respective members, formal collective bargaining between unions and

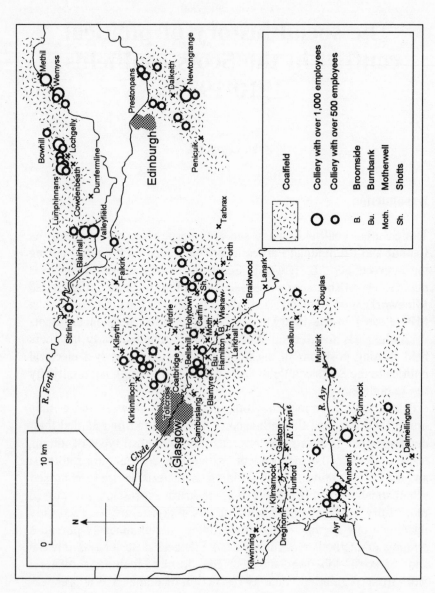

Map 3   The Scottish coalfields at nationalisation in 1947.

employers or their associations, and state regulation through legislation.[2] Our ideal types suggest an alignment between processes of internal regulation and the independent collier and the militant miner, and between external regulation and bureaucratic reformism. Such a framework provides linkages between the mining labour process, trade unionism and mineworkers' political behaviour: the industrial policies of the Communist Party were more congruent with the pit activities of the militant miner while the Labour Party's promise of state regulation appealed to supporters of the trade union bureaucracy.

However it should be emphasised that such relationships were not simple nor reductionist. As we note below, the impact of mechanisation prior to the First World War evoked a reaffirmation of the 'exclusive' policies associated with the independent collier. Therefore although our ideal types display a chronological sequence in their emergence, it is not suggested that they were historically discrete: all three can be seen as coexisting and competing during the early decades of the century, although by the 1920s the primary conflict was between bureaucratic reformism and militancy. However it is suggested that struggles for control of the labour process and the contours of industrial concentration conditioned the plausability of the differing industrial and political strategies associated with our ideal types. But such factors in themselves cannot fully explain political behaviour. Those elements influencing the adoption or rejection of these strategies which were rooted in the highly variegated communities of the Scots coalfields must also be considered. We begin therefore by examining the contexts of the industry and its communities.

The regions of the Scots coalfields

The Scottish coal measures have been split by geological disturbances into four separate fields: Ayrshire; the large West-Central field centred on Lanarkshire but extending into Dunbartonshire, Stirlingshire and West Lothian; Fife and Clackmannan; and Mid and East Lothian. The differing structural, social and institutional characteristics defining these four regions must be examined before we can fully understand the political conflicts which developed within them.[3]

Table 6.1 Ideal types of orientation to trade unionism in the Scottish coalfields

Ideal type	Independent collier	Bureaucratic reformist	Militant miner
Historical period	18th Century———	———1880s———	———>1930s
			c.1912——————>
Union recruitment	Exclusive	Open	Open (including miners' womenfolks)
Union organisation	Federations of local and district unions	Federations of county unions	One industrial miners' union
Industrial relations methods	Unilateral regulation of recruitment and output (and hence wages) by hewers	Collective bargaining within context of State regulation of hours and minimum wage	Militant waging of all disputes as expression of class struggle

contd

Politico-industrial goal	Cooperative production	Nationalisation of the mines	Socialist Revolution involving socialisation of the mines
Political affiliation	Liberal	Independent Labour	Communist
Typified by	Alexander Macdonald (1821-1881); General Secretary, Scottish Coal and Ironstone Miners' Assoc. 1885-1881; Elected Liberal MP for Stafford 1874	Robert Smillie (1857-1940); President NUSMW 1894-1912, 1922-1928; President MFGB 1912-1921	Willie Allan (1900-1970); President LMCU, General Secretary elect, NUSMW 1927; General Secretary, UMS 1929-1931
'Corresponding' stage of labour process and mine ownership structure	Hand mining / Small mining enterprises, local markets	Hand and machine mining / Larger mining companies, national market	Machine mining / Monopoly combines, international markets

The productive base

The modern exploitation of the Scots coalfields was both chronologically and geographically uneven. In the west, each decade after 1830 witnessed new areas being opened up. The eastern coalfields experienced intensive development only after 1890. By the early years of the twentieth century the West-Central field was increasingly dependent on thin seams and during the 1920s and 30s this structural decline was overlain by the cyclical depression in domestic markets. As Table 6.2 indicates, the numbers employed in the West-Central field more than halved between 1919 and 1932.

Contingent upon the geology of the coalfields was the size and spatial distribution of the productive units. In 1927 the average number of employees per mine was 169 in Ayrshire, 193 in Lanarkshire, 364 in Fife and 437 in Mid and East Lothian.[4] Yet these county averages could conceal wide variations. In Lanarkshire, there was a significant number of large mines concentrated in the central Clyde valley but these were surrounded by many small ones. In Ayrshire, a pattern of scattered mining developed along river valleys. The few large mines were geographically separate and mining settlements were dispersed throughout a largely rural environment. Fife's large pits were densely concentrated in central and east Fife, with small mines extending west of Dunfermline and into Clackmannanshire. In the Lothians, generally larger collieries were located in a ten mile radius in the countryside south and east of Edinburgh.

The ownership of capital

The structure of the Scots coal industry displayed considerable regional differentiation. One company, William Baird, dominated Ayrshire, employing 47 per cent of all mineworkers in the county in 1927. In the West-Central region, piecemeal development had created a more fragmented structure. Although by 1939 there were five major companies, almost two-thirds of the region's output was produced by small employers owning one or two mines. Fife and Clackmannan were largely controlled by four companies while in the Lothians, there was a larger number of medium sized firms.[5] Even the largest enterprises tended to exhibit a strong regional bias in the

Table 6.2 Numbers employed in the Scottish coalfields, 1913-1935

	1913	1919	1921	1925	1927	1932	1935
West-Central	79,128	80,422	75,850	66,986	57,651	38,585	38,167
Fife and Clackmannan	30,776	29,577	27,942	28,597	23,634	19,928	21,725
Ayrshire and Dumfries	15,576	16,500	15,453	15,169	14,189	11,362	11,261
Mid and East Lothian	13,944	14,692	14,529	15,222	13,534	12,483	12,305
Total: Scotland	139,424	141,191	133,774	125,974	109,008	82,358	83,458

Source: *Twentieth Abstract of Labour Statistics of the United Kingdom* (1931), pp. 26-27; *Twenty Second Abstract of Labour Statistics of the United Kingdom* (1937), p. 38.

location of their colliery operations, despite some interlocking directorships. In the face of economic depression, Scots mining companies survived by rationalisation and increased mechanisation, and, unusually, most of the large firms made profits in almost every year of the interwar period.[6] That they did so by constant pressure on wages and hours directs our attention now to the control of the labour process.

The labour process

At the end of the 19th century, the job control of the skilled, 'independent collier' remained remarkably intact. Although there was a gradual, though incomplete, shift to longwall working, the hewer retained the functions of an all-round tradesman; faceworkers in Scotland comprised over two-thirds of the underground workforce compared with a British average of 57.8 per cent in 1905.[7] Furthermore, piecerate payments continued to allow considerable freedom from managerial control. A director of the largest mining company in Scotland stated in 1909 that 'the Scotch collier is of a very free and independent nature and is not very subservient to discipline ... [he is] a free man and very much his own master'.[8] It was such freedom from managerial control which continued to underpin traditional working practices: in particular collective restriction of both daily output (or 'darg') and working hours in order to manipulate favourably the demand for coal, and hence the level of wages.[9]

The frontier of this job control was strongly contested, its shifting contours shaped by the trade cycle, labour markets and union organisation in the pit, as employers waged recurring but only partially successful attempts to erode it through the use of subcontractors and unskilled labour. For their part, colliers sought to defend piece rates and conditions by frequent resort to strikes. Analyses of offical strike data confirm that Scotland was the most strike-prone mining region in Britain after 1921 (being second only to South Wales prior to that date). As Church and his colleagues note: 'by the outbreak of the Second World War, Scotland was more than 10 times as strike-prone as Lancashire, more than 15 times as strike-prone as the North East, and about 20 times as strike-prone as the Midlands'. Within Scotland, the incidence of disputes was consistently highest in the large West-Central field.[10]

It is against this background that we must view the impact of mechanisation, which was introduced more rapidly in Scotland than elsewhere in Britain: in 1927 55 per cent of Scotland's coal output was cut mechanically compared with a British total of 23 per cent; by 1935, the figures were 79 and 61 per cent respectively.[11] Coal cutting machinery replaced the most skilled work of undercutting the face and degraded the large majority of hewers to fillers. Both regularity of working and the completion of the allocated work each shift was essential if the benefits of the capital invested in the machinery were to be fully realised and managers frequently forced men to work longer hours.[12] However, it is important to note that geological conditions prevented the simultaneous and uniform introduction of machinery within individual collieries and across the coalfields. It was a gradual and uneven process until the 1920s: in 1927 machinery was used in 43 per cent of Ayrshire pits, 65 per cent West-Central, 76 per cent Mid and East Lothian and 84 per cent Fife.[13] By then, in the contexts of the increased use of mechanical conveyors underground and the aftermath of the 1926 lockout, a more systematic approach to mechanisation was adopted by mine managers. By 1927 a mining consultant was spelling out the implications of such an integrated strategy in greater detail:

> Discipline is an essential feature of the machine mining face ... but owing to the concentration of output such closer supervision can be effected at a reduced cost per ton. Time studies of the operations conducted on machine faces are of great use in furthering the efficiency of the system ... [By telephone] the under-manager is able to keep a check on the performances of the machines at any hour in the loading shift.[14]

The Mines Inspector for the Scottish division, who had noted in 1923 that discipline in mines under his charge was 'the despair of inspectors and managers', observed in 1927 the 'striking change' in underground operations. Interconnected mechanised face conveyors allowed the geographical concentration of miners and other workers at the face and hence their easier supervision.[15] One outcome of this concentration of different grades of workers in closely supervised, mechanised units was that common grievances were generated within the workgroup. Not only was there an increase in the incidence of local and sectional strikes from the 1920s, particularly in West-

Central and Fife, it is significant that there was a marked increase in the percentage of strikes over discipline and dismissal after 1926.[16]

Social relations in mining communities

We should first note the range of settlements and authority relations within them which existed in the Scots coalfields. Gilbert has suggested a fourfold categorisation of mining communities, and examples of each type were in evidence to varying degrees.[17] The first, villages dominated by miners and characterised by social homogeneity, was the most typical and was widely found throughout Scotland. The second was similar but under the authority of the mining company. Scottish examples include the family-owned Wemyss Coal Company in east Fife which followed a policy of welfare paternalism in its villages built on the 'garden city' model, and the Lothian Coal Company in Mid-Lothian whose general manager ruled like a king over the company-owned village of Newtongrange through a network of contractors, informers and the company policeman.[18] The third group consisted of occupationally heterogeneous towns and these were found in the urban archipeligo of settlements based on heavy industry in the central Clyde valley; in 1921, for example, Motherwell's 3000 mineworkers were merely the largest occupational group among the town's 14,000 male workers. Finally, there was the homogeneous mining town of more than ten thousand people, relatively rare in Scotland but typified by Cowdenbeath and Lochgelly in Fife.

Although there was some movement out of the industry and some mobility from the West-Central field to Fife, the mining communities were relatively stable. Interviews conducted by the Social Survey with over 1700 Scottish miners before the end of the Second World war indicated that 85 per cent were the sons of miners (and 70 per cent of the 'housewives' were miners' daughters); 69 per cent of miners in the West-Central region lived within five miles of their birthplace; in Fife the figure was 58 per cent.[19] Nevertheless, pit closures, particularly in the west but in all other regions also, meant that the link between a pit and its community was often broken as miners travelled long distances to work: for example, of the 610 miners employed in the Kingshill no.2 colliery near Forth, Lanarkshire in the early 1940s, 157 travelled distances of between six and fifteen miles from thirteen different villages.[20]

Within these communities, one significant but regionally differentiated fissure was that based on ethnic and religious identity. Religious sectarianism had been a feature of the western coalfields since the waves of Irish immigration in the 19th century, and was given fresh impetus with the rise of Sinn Fein and rebellion in Ireland. Lanarkshire miners and steelworkers were involved in a number of incidents relating to the theft of explosives for the IRA.[21] During the 1921 lockout, catholic miners built a shrine at Carfin near Motherwell which attracted tens of thousands of pilgrims. The Orange Order could mobilise even larger numbers on its processions on the 12th of July. Some pits and villages were popularly identified as orange or catholic, and these divisions were symbolised by the formation of an ephemeral protestant miners' union in 1921.[22] Even in 1926 the solidarity of the Lanarkshire miners was balanced precariously upon the potential of sectarian division, as A.J. Cook recognised when he urged a mass meeting in Hamilton not to 'allow religious differences to divide them where their bread and cheese were concerned'. In Fife, catholics remained a smaller minority than in the west and Abe Moffat recalled that 'You never had the problems with catholics and protestants as you had in Lanarkshire. They were all in one place. Valleyfield and Blairhall'.[23]

A second regional variable was the willingness of the miners to engage in violent social disorder. In the turbulent and densely populated mining communities of Lanarkshire, major industrial disputes witnessed sabotage and civil disorder; there were mass pickets, riots and attacks on pitheads during strikes in 1912 and 1921. The 1926 lockout highlighted a division between the more peaceable regions of Ayrshire and the Lothians, and the West-Central and Fife coalfields. In Ayrshire, the Chief Constables of Ayr and Kilmarnock reported in early November that not one case of intimidation or assault had arisen in the county during the dispute. In Fife and Lanarkshire, the miners were ferocious in their prosecution of quasi-guerilla warfare involving arson and the use of explosives to sabotage colliery machinery and railway lines.[24]

One social relation common to all regions was a rigid gender division. Although most young women worked prior to marriage, the onerous domestic labour of maintaining a mining household was almost invariably a full-time task. Kelogg Durland, who worked in the Fife mines in 1901, noted the 'servitude' of women in the home: 'their slavery to the men was almost universal in the district'.[25] While oral testimony suggests such patriarchal subjection was ameliorated in later years, the gendered division of public and private spheres persisted. Whereas one-third of the miners surveyed during the Second World War participated in union and political meetings, only 3 per cent of housewives attended any.[26] When the UMS attempted to involve miners' wives in UMS Women's Guilds, it met with only limited success. This was an innovation about which the Fife UMS organiser complained that 'every committee without exception are very timid and chary about facing up to' because of 'the old antiquated idea still prevalent amongst the workers that a woman's place is at the fireside'.[27] But if women remained outside formal political institutions, this should not obscure their public mobilisation during strikes in mass pickets and soup kitchens.

Trade union structure

Union organisation was based on a fragmented pattern of seven county unions covering Ayrshire, Lanarkshire, Stirlingshire, West Lothian, Fife and Clackmannan, Mid and East Lothian, and until 1927, Dunbartonshire. In the West-Central field, there were thus four separate unions (until 1927) while in contrast, the large employers in the region were organised by the Lanarkshire Coal Masters' Association. The autonomous county unions were loosely linked in the Scottish Miners' Federation (SMF) until 1914, thereafter equally loosely in the federal National Union of Scottish Mine Workers (NUSMW). Within this already fragmented official structure, there persisted further schisms based on parochialism, religion and politics. In Ayrshire, three branches seceded from the county union in 1921 and operated as district unions for a number of years, 'only combining when attacked by the county union'.[28] In Fife, leftwing militants formed the Mineworkers' Reform Union (MRU) in 1923 which amalgamated with the county union in 1927. There were also attempts to set up 'non-political' unions in Fife and Stirlingshire but these failed, perhaps because employers preferred to utilise the county unions to counteract the communist-led United Mineworkers of Scotland formed in 1929. For example, when the UMS began recruiting in 1933 in Hamilton Palace Colliery, which had been unorganised since 1926, the manager invited the Lanarkshire county union to represent the miners there.[29] The fissiparous nature of Scottish mining unionism is part of the reason why trade union density fluctuated considerably over time and varied significantly between regions. After 1926, density was lowest in Lanarkshire (where it fell below 25 per cent in 1932) and West Lothian; highest in Ayrshire and Mid and East Lothian.[30]

The foregoing analysis is intended to demonstrate the regional specificities of the four coalfields. The particular configurations of their social relations and economic structures gave each its own identity and influenced the willingness of their miners to support differing trade union and political traditions. It is to a more detailed consideration of these that we now turn.

A typology of trade union cultures in the Scots coalfields, 1910-1926

The independent collier

The writer and others have analysed the policies of miners' unions in Scotland during the 19th century by reference to the work culture of the independent collier and we need only briefly comment further here on its persistence into the twentieth century, sustained in part by the continuing underground autonomy of the hewer. A five day working policy to restrict output was pursued, albeit raggedly, in Lanarkshire until 1925, although the NUSMW unsurprisingly failed to persuade their English and Welsh colleagues of the efficacy of such an archaic strategy during the crisis of 1921.[31] The spread of mechanisation also evoked traditional attempts to defend the hewers' skill. For example, a resolution was passed unanimously at the 1910 SMF conference 'with a view to protect the trade' which sought to revive the traditional training system whereby boys entering the mines were permitted to put out only a fixed proportion of a man's 'darg'. The following year, the conference agreed to impose a heavy entrance fee on all unskilled workers entering the mines.[32] But the manifest difficulties in implementing such aspirations rendered them nugatory.

The political aspirations of the independent collier were most easily accommodated within popular Liberalism. Alexander MacDonald, the leader of the Scottish miners who most clearly embodied the values of the independent collier, was returned to parliament as one of the first two Lib-Lab MPs in 1874. Yet his election as MP for Stafford rather than a Scottish constituency, and the fact that no other Scots miners' official was elected until December 1910, underlined the weakness of the 'Lib-Lab' tradition in the poorly unionised Scots coalfields.

Bureaucratic reformism

From the 1880s onwards, renewed attempts to organise the Scottish miners' unions were led by socialists who adopted a policy of legislative reform including a state-enforced restriction of output through the legal eight hour day, state arbitration of wage disputes and nationalisation of the mines. In the face of Liberal opposition, such a policy could only be achieved through independent labour representation, which in turn required the extension of trade union organisation committed to this end.

By 1913, 80 per cent of Scots miners were unionised. The leadership cadre which painstakingly built up trade union organisation had had to wrench recognition from employers, at least in the west. Initially they were forced to defend wages and conditions vigorously - for example, the Lanarkshire Mineworkers' Union spent a total of £60,000 on sectional disputes between 1901 and 1907.[33] Once recognition was secured, the leadership was anxious to maintain formal bargaining relationships with employers and to settle disputes by negotiation wherever possible to protect the carefully accumulated union funds. James Brown, secretary of both the Mid and East Lothian union and the NUSMW was reported to 'have always tried to avoid fighting with the employers on questions of wages; he often tried to restrain the demands of the more excitable and less responsible members'.[34] The minutes of the Lanarkshire union executive committee indicate the routine pressures on this evolving bureaucracy: meetings were often held several times per week to discuss sectional disputes, receive reports from the law, medical and political subcommittees and the NUSMW executive, and consider resolutions from the delegate council. Such routinism placed a premium on internal union discipline. Faced with widespread unofficial strikes in 1919, the executive committee of the Lanarkshire union made every effort to get their members to return to work until negotiations between the MFGB and the Coal Controller were completed. In the aftermath, Robert Smillie proclaimed to the NUSMW conference that,

> he was exceedingly anxious to prevent these local outbreaks. He wanted to maintain the power of lightning strikes if necessary, but he wanted to have an organisation which by negotiation would make the local strike impossible.[35]

Such views led to accusations of collaboration with employers which were not always misplaced. We should note the tone and implicit assumptions in the following extract from a private letter from Charles Carlow, managing director of the Fife Coal Company, to William Adamson, general secretary of the Fife county union. It was prompted by press reports that surface workers at Bowhill had rejected a national agreement on the working week at the end of 1918. 'It is necessary that you should put yourself in communication with the Bowhill men and see that there is no trouble over the adoption of this agreement ...', commanded Carlow. He noted that a national meeting would consider a further reduction of one hour:

> No promise was given that the concession would be made. This information, however, may help you to keep down any trouble arising under the agreement ... I hope you will be able between this and Monday to get the men to resume their work on Monday morning without fail.[36]

The formal union organisation which was built up in Scotland was constructed on interconnecting layers of lay delegates and full-time agents within an increasingly oligarchic, federal structure. Full-time county agents, who were usually also officials of the county unions, were elected by ballot of a county's miners but formally employed by the NUSMW, enjoyed tenure at that body's discretion, and could be drafted by it to handle official disputes in other counties whose miners therefore had no control over them. The executive committee of the NUSMW was made up of representatives from each county union, in only very approximate proportion to the affiliated membership so that the smaller county unions were over-represented. The mechanisms by which the county representatives were appointed to it varied from election by ballot in Lanarkshire and Fife to self-selection by officals in the smaller county unions. Thus, some of the 'national' agents (of whom there was a total of 19 by the the 1920s) appointed themselves to sit on the Scottish executive which also employed them. 'At present autocracy rules in the Scottish Miners' Union', wrote James C. Welsh, a Lanarkshire checkweighman in 1918, although ironically he became one of its leading defenders following his election as an agent and vice-president of the Lanarkshire union the following year.[37]

Holders of positions at each level of this complex structure received financial perquisites which increased as one ascended it. Branch officers and committee members normally received 'salaries' and commission was paid to dues collectors. Council delegates in Lanarkshire were paid six shillings expenses plus the county average daily wage to attend meetings. In Ayrshire, full-time 'local agents' were employed 'in almost every branch', paid a weekly wage of £3 5s and represented the branch at delegate meetings of the county union. The cost of a national agent's salary and expenses amounted to an average of £240 per annum by 1929 and agents in different county unions were involved in unseemly public rivalry over their salaries on occasion. Officials who were elected as miners' MPs received an annual salary of £650 from the MFGB, first class rail travel and a retaining fee of £50 from the NUSMW plus expenses.[38] There were thus substantial material as well as ideological interests at stake in the conflicts which developed within the Scots miners' unions.

Bureaucratic trade union practice was coupled with a commitment to parliamentary reformism: before 1914, ten Scots miners' agents stood for parliament; between 1918 and 1935 the figure was fourteen. Although many were nominal members of the ILP, their political views ranged from the pacifism and socialism of Lanarkshire's Robert Smillie to the pro-war labourism of Robert Brown and William Adamson. Whatever their position in the spectrum of Labour politics, their repeated electoral attempts as Labour candidates before the First World War were unsuccessful except for Adamson in West Fife. Reasons for this failure included the absence of any pact with the Liberals as in England, the radicalism of Scottish Liberals and their continuing working class support, particularly from the significant element of Irish extraction in the mining workforce, the operation of the registration process for lodgers and the weakness of local electoral organisation.[39] In 1908, Joseph Duncan, the Scottish ILP organiser lamented the poor state of the party in the mining districts, complaining that 'the Lanarkshire miner is the most disagreeable animal I ever met with'.[40] As union organisation improved, the local miners' branches constituted the effective unit of Labour's electoral campaigning. The NUSMW acted as 'a party within a party', employing five 'political agents' as full-time organisers by 1921. Mining constituencies were jealously regarded as the union's electoral fiefdoms. For example in 1926, when the Bothwell constituency selected an ILP candidate in preference to the miners' union nominee, both the NUSMW and the MFGB forced his withdrawal after the Labour Party national executive accepted that Bothwell was a 'miners' seat'.[41] No doubt for similar reasons, Jennie Lee, the prominent ILPer elected MP for North Lanarkshire in 1929, recalled that, despite coming from a Fife mining family, she met considerable hostility from the Scots miners' MPs whose 'faces curdled up like a bowl of sour milk' whenever they met her in Westminster.[42] We shall consider the electoral performance of miners' MPs in the interwar period in the concluding section; but first we must consider our third ideal type which emerged partly in response to the failure of electoralism as a strategy before 1922 and which embodied an alternative conception of trade unionism in opposition to the bureaucratic practice of the miners' officials.

The militant miner

During the first nationwide miners' strike in 1912 demanding a national minimum wage, Scottish miners displayed a new mood of militancy. In Lanarkshire, a large crowd at Tarbrax attempted 'in a most systematic manner to try and destroy the pithead'; in Fife, crowds up to eight thousand strong besieged pits and in one instance smashed a thousand windows in the pithead buildings. When a miners' agent, despatched to the scene to restore order described the perpetrators as hooligans, 'great disorder' ensued and he required police protection from the crowd. The Chief Constable of Fife learned from an informant 'in close touch with the militant strikers' that the destruction of the pumping apparatus at all the pits in the district was contemplated which, he suggested, 'clearly shows the malicious and depraved spirit of a large section of the miners'.[43]

The calling off of the strike by the MFGB and a settlement based on district minima fuelled dissatisfaction with the union leadership. A demonstration in Hamilton, organised by a 'Miners' Indignation and Reform Committee' was addressed by a number of speakers including W.F. Hay of South Wales, an author of *The Miners' Next Step*. One claimed that there was 'not a more autocratic organis- ation' than the Lanarkshire union and motions were passed calling for its reconstruction.[44] Nothing more was heard of this committee but the motivation behind it re-emerged in 1917 when a hundred or so miners met again in Hamilton to form the Lanarkshire Miners' Reform Committee. Its manifesto, 50,000 of which were circulated, noted the growing competition between large combines, the 'continual struggle to reduce the time taken to produce the coal' and increased mechanisation. Its aims included a repudiation of nationalisation and the demand for direct control of the mines by the miners; 'the methods of the union to be based on the principle of class struggle'; the annual election of agents and officials who would sit on the executive committee in a consultative capacity only; the establishment of pit committees to handle local disputes; and the organisation of all workers in the coal industry in one industrial union. Approximately a fifth of the Lanarkshire union's branches affiliated to the committee and similar bodies were established in Fife and the Lothians. In Lanarkshire Reform Committee activists led unofficial strikes against food prices, fought against conscription of miners and led a successful campaign leading to the removal from office of the pro-war secretary of the county union. A vital element in imbuing these grievances with a political content was the agitational intervention of the revolutionary socialist John Maclean and his 'first lieutenant' James MacDougall, both of whom conducted Marxist education classes in Lanarkshire and Fife before and during the war.[45] In 1919 Scottish military intelligence sources lamented that 'for some considerable time now the working class interest in sociological, economic and historical subjects has been entirely directed by the extremists and "un-offical" party'.[46]

The height of the reform committees' influence took place in early 1919 against the background of a general strike of engineering and shipbuilding workers in western Scotland for a forty hour week and the MFGB's demands for nationalisation of the mines and a thirty hour week. An unofficial strike in Fife over surface workers' hours was broadened by the Fife committee into a demand for the MFGB's claim. The Lanarkshire committee initiated a wave of unofficial strikes in sympathy, supported by flying columns of mass pickets. At the head of thousands of demonstrating supporters, the Reform Committee seized control of the Lanarkshire union offices, allegedly at gunpoint, and forced the union leadership to declare the strike official. This call was swiftly retracted by the union executive from the safety of an office in Edinburgh, and after the Fife miners narrowly voted to return to work, the strike movement collapsed.[47]

The aftermath of the 1921 lockout saw union membership in steep decline. That year was an unpropitious one for the fledgling Communist Party to begin its attempt to group the former reform committee militants under its banner. John Maclean's antagonism to the CP delayed their entry further, but by 1924 the majority of militants supported the CP-controlled Scottish Miners' Minority movement. In Fife, despite opposition from the CP leadership, communists had joined with other leftwing union members to form the Mineworkers' Reform Union with a membership of over 7,000. The MRU was an important proving ground for the communist cadre in Fife and helped build a significant following for the party there. In Lanarkshire, communists remained active within the formally more democratic county union and by 1925, William Allan, a young Blantyre communist and a graduate of Maclean's Scottish Labour College, secured over 42 per cent of the vote when he stood for the post of general secretary.[48]

We can discern a number of influences on the emergence of the militant miner. Support for the Lanarkshire Reform Committee was strongest in the large, mechanised pits around Hamilton, Blantyre and Burnbank in the central Clyde valley and in the recently exploited seams around outlying Douglas and Coalburn. It was significant too that Marxist education classes had been conducted at Burnbank since 1908 and at Coalburn since 1912. Of the seventeen branches where Allan received 60 per cent or more of the votes, sixteen were within a circle six miles in diameter in the central Clyde valley; the seventeenth was at Douglas. In Fife, the Reform Committee was strongest at Bowhill, the largest pit in Fife where Maclean had taught a class since 1910 and for which a hundred miners enrolled in

1918.[49] A further factor was the strong advocacy of Irish republican-
ism (an important theme in Maclean's propaganda) by the reform
committee militants which attracted support from sections of the
catholic population. A final important influence was generational.
The militants were active in a particularly youthful workforce due to
the expansion of the coal industry up to 1921: in that year over a
third of Scottish miners were under 25 years of age while almost 60
per cent were under 35. A central influence on this new generation
was the experience of the war and its aftermath, either in the pits or
in the trenches. The new communist cadre self-consciously claimed
to represent the aspirations of 'the young miners'. It is also
significant that donations from Soviet miners during the 1926 lockout
were distributed largely to young single men who were excluded
from parish relief.[50] In 1927, Allan, then only 27 years of age, won
the posts of secretary of both the Lanarkshire and Scottish unions; his
fellow communist, the 31 year old John Bird from Bowhill, defeated
the 70 year old Smillie for the Scottish presidency. The stage had
been set for a political contest unprecedented in British trade union
politics.

The struggle for control, 1926-39

The Communist Party's militants played a major role during the 1926
lockout, organising pickets, poor relief demonstrations and soup
kitchens. In Lochgelly, the Council of Action was 'practically the
Miners' Reform Union'; the Chief Constable of Fife reported that the
county union refused to collaborate with it' and they are always
willing to tell the police anything they know of the workings of the
council'.[51] Miners and their families flocked to join the CP and its
Scottish membership doubled to a peak of 1,560 in September 1926:
in Fife there were over 600 members in 1927 and the large Shotts
and Blantyre branches in Lanarkshire had 58 and 40 members
respectively.[52] The election victories of Allan and Bird in 1927 were
reinforced by further gains in the Lanarkshire and Fife unions.
However the defeated NUSMW officials and executive members
defied the mandates of their county unions and repeatedly postponed
the annual conference at which their communist opponents would
have taken office.

In 1928 the Scottish unions were plunged into increasing chaos as both left and right secured injunctions restraining the manoeuvres of the opposing faction; police were called on two occasions to eject Allan from the NUSMW executive; and William Adamson, under threat of suspension by the Fife executive, formed a breakaway union of his own. The Communist Party came under increasing pressure from the Comintern to implement the 'new line' of forming revolutionary unions, a strategy supported by many local militants with little respect for the organisational skullduggery of 'the old gang' of defeated officials.[53] Faced with a haemorrhaging union membership since the end of the lockout, communists in Lanarkshire at the end of 1928 felt that 'there is no union to save, that we should immediately set about the formation of a new union'.[54] With the recognition of Adamson's breakaway by the MFGB and the NUSMW, and faced with the prospect of the now communist-controlled Fife county union being disaffiliated from the NUSMW because of arrears of dues accumulated during Adamson's term of office, the CP leadership authorised the formation of a new union, the United Mineworkers of Scotland in 1929.

At the UMS inaugural conference, the county affiliations of the 132 delegates conformed to the uneven parameters of communist support in the Scots coalfields: Lanarkshire accounted for 64, Fife 47, Ayrshire 8, West Lothian 6, Stirlingshire 4, Mid and East Lothian 3. The new union was launched with some optimism, Allan, its first general secretary, claiming that it represented 'the only line of salvation ... away from the self-wrecked and discredited rump' of the county unions.[55] Unfortunately, the desire for one union for the Scots miners was not to be met so easily. There were three unions in Fife alone in 1929. In Lanarkshire, communist activists who had been criticised by the party leadership for their 'trade union legalism' now swung to a desperate ultra-leftism, calling tactically ill-judged strikes and making virulent attacks on the 'social fascists' remaining in the county union. Faced with the collapse of mining employment in the west, the threat of victimisation and the unremitting hostility of employers, paid up membership of the UMS also declined from a peak of less than 4000 in 1929 to around 2000 in 1932, by which time over 65 per cent of the membership was in the large mines of central and east Fife.[56] Allan was relieved of his post by the CP politbureau in December 1930, temporarily 'banished' to Moscow and replaced by David Proudfoot who in turn was succeeded by Abe Moffat in 1931.[57] Under Moffat's leadership, and in step with the CP's shift towards 'revolutionary pragmatism', the emphasis within UMS activities focussed more on militant trade unionism rather than revolutionary struggle. To combat the intensification of labour associated with mechanisation, the union supported a number of strikes to secure the 'pool' or cooperative tonnage system whereby men were paid according to the total output of a unit team rather than individual shift or yardage payments which removed the legal entitlement to checkweighmen. A vigorous campaign was waged to secure the election of statutory workmens' inspectors to monitor safety in the mines: of 29 inspections carried out in Fife in 1932, all but three were conducted by UMS members.[58]

The concentration of its membership in Fife's large pits allowed the UMS to exert strike leverage and secure a limited and grudging recognition from employers there. By 1930 the CP had decided that in other regions the UMS should recruit only unorganised workers and by 1932, the CP leadership openly advocated the need for work in the reformist county unions.[59] In Lanarkshire, a communist cadre began re-entering the county union to the consternation of the union leadership.[60] For example, James McKendrick, a former president of the Lanarkshire Miners' Minority Movement and a CP member rejoined the county union in the early thirties and was the secretary for Blantyre's militant Priory branch by 1935; its mine, Bothwell Castle Nos 3/4, was one of the most strike prone in Britain, experiencing thirty three disputes between 1936 and 1940.[61] William Pearson, a UMS executive member in 1933, was president of the county union Broomside branch by 1936.

If the UMS had not fulfilled its hopes of growth, the county unions also struggled to survive in the first half of the decade. In the Lanarkshire county union it was reported that, despite recruitment efforts, 'collieries and sections of collieries were being closed more rapidly than members were coming in'.[62] This loss of membership meant that most of the money which the unions received in dues went to pay the officials' salaries and expenses. Despite a reduction in the number of agents, 67 per cent of the dues income of the NUSMW in 1931 was spent on agents' salaries and executive expenses.[63] Age was inevitably catching up with this older generation: 1935 saw the deaths of Robert Smith, Secretary of the NUSMW, Joseph Sullivan, former MP and NUSMW executive member, and James Tonner, a 78 year old agent of the Lanarkshire union (since 1904) and long standing county councillor who had been appointed Deputy Lieutenant of Lanarkshire two years earlier. William Adamson died the following year.

In the face of increasing sectional and 'lightning' strikes, the county union officials condemned such actions as communist-inspired and unofficial. At the 1934 NUSMW conference, the president complained of 'a spirit of anarchy' in some districts: 'none of us seek to curb the natural desire of our members to resist ... tyranny but we cannot ignore the [negotiating] machinery set up ... '.[64] Communists did indeed seek to seize the leadership of such strikes, although they can scarcely be credited with the conditions which gave rise to them. After the dissolution of the UMS in 1936, communists increasingly won union positions. John Sutherland, a communist workman's inspector from Bowhill was elected as a Fife agent in 1936; James McKendrick, who had organised a stay-down strike in Blantyre in 1936, secured the Lanarkshire union secretaryship in 1937 with over two-thirds of the vote; William Pearson became Lanarkshire president in 1940; in 1942, Abe Moffat was elected president and Pearson treasurer of the NUSMW.[65]

The communists' successes with the UMS in Fife and in the Lanarkshire county union were not translated into a significant CP membership in the coalfields, despite repeated exhortations by the leadership of the party and Comintern. In 1931, only 55 Scottish CP members were actually employed in the mining industry.[66] The paradox of the simultaneous growth of party influence in the pits with declining party membership was a constant refrain in the discussions of the politbureau and central committee in the 1930s. For example, in 1931 Page Arnot complained that 'in strike after strike, as soon as a strike begins, the Party ends and only resumes again when the strike is finished ... '; whereas the UMS leaders in Fife 'had real contact with the masses in several villages, this was more as individuals and not as members of the Party ... [during strikes] the Party disintegrates and becomes a series of active strikers ... '.[67] The growing disjuncture between pit and community may have been one element in explaining the CP's success in leading strikes but failing to build a mass membership in mining communities. But such leadership is perfectly conceivable as being despite, rather than because of, their Communist Party membership. Although the sectarian milieu of the party and the dream of the workers' state may have sustained the small party cadre, there is little evidence of communism's wider political appeal.[68]

Communist successes in trade union politics were generally not matched in the electoral sphere. The CP's abrupt shifts in policy towards the Labour Party precluded effective campaigning, except in West Fife. Here William Gallacher polled sufficiently well to allow a Conservative to unseat Adamson in 1931 and for Gallacher to defeat Adamson in 1935. This victory was due to a combination of Gallacher's long term nurturing of the seat, the abstention of both catholic priest and local orange lodges from directing voters, and the role of the UMS in a strike over a dirt scale at Valleyfield in the constituency during the election campaign.[69] Refused assistance by Adamson's county union, the strikers' public assistance claims were handled by Abe Moffat who was subsequently elected a workman's inspector for the pit.[70] Communists were more consistently active in parish and county councils in Fife and Lanarkshire where they achieved some limited electoral success in mining wards. But once elected, communist councillors functioned as militant and occasionally critical supporters of the Labour Party.[71]

The Labour Party dominated the mining parliamentary constituencies but it too failed to build a mass membership and its electoral presence was not hegemonic. Between 1918 and 1935, of the 77 general election results in the eleven Scottish constituencies where miners comprised more than 30 per cent of the electorate, the Labour Party was victorious in only 47.[72] In part this was because there was only one constituency - West Fife - in which miners were a majority of voters. Moreover, the Conservative victories at Lanark in five out of these seven general elections and at Rutherglen in two suggest the continuing political influence of orangeism.[73] A further conclusion which might be drawn is that many miners in Lanarkshire and Fife voted unenthusiastically for Labour's distant promise of nationalisation and welfarism but also sought aggressively to defend wages and conditions in the mines through industrial militancy. The tragedy of the Scots coalfields in the interwar period is that while the potential for a more militant reformism may well have existed, it was denied political space between the sterility of Stalinism and the bankruptcy of an ageing and corrupt labour bureaucracy.

Notes

Place of publication is London unless otherwise stated.

1. For the tradition of the independent collier, see A. Campbell and F. Reid, 'The independent collier in Scotland', in R. Harrison (ed.), *Independent Collier: the coal miner as archetypal proletarian reconsidered* (Hassocks, 1978) and A.B. Campbell, *The Lanarkshire Miners: a social history of their trade unions, 1775-1874* (Edinburgh, 1979), especially ch. 2; for the new tradition of the militant miner, see S. Macintyre, *Little Moscows: communism and working-class militancy in interwar Britain* (1980), p. 169.
2. For a useful discussion of Flanders' categories, see D. Lyddon, 'Industrial relations theory and labour history', *International Labor and Working-Class History*, no. 46, Fall 1994, pp. 122-141.
3. This approach to the study of regions draws on the work of Philip Cooke; see his 'Class practices as regional markers: a contribution to labour geography', in D. Gregory and J. Urry (eds), *Social Relations and Spatial Structures* (1985).
4. P. Long, 'The Economic and Social History of the Scottish Coal Industry 1925-39, with particular reference to industrial relations', unpublished PhD thesis, University of Strathclyde, 1978, Table 11.
5. *List of Mines, 1927*; Long (thesis), pp. 84, 88.
6. Long (thesis), p. 111; B. Supple, *The History of the British Coal Industry, vol. 4, 1913-1946* (Oxford, 1987), p. 393.
7. R. Church, *The History of the British Coal Industry, vol. 3, 1830-1913* (Oxford, 1986), p. 213.
8. *Royal Commission on Mines*, First Report, Minutes of Evidence, vol. iv, *Parliamentary Papers* (PP) 1909, XXXIV, 200-1.
9. *Royal Commission on Trade Disputes and Trade Combinations*, Minutes of Evidence, PP 1906, LVI, 265.
10. R. Church et al., 'British coalmining strikes 1893-1940: dimensions, distribution and persistence', *British Journal of Industrial Relations*, vol. 28, no. 3, 1990, p. 333; PRO LAB 34/2-51, Board of Trade Record Books of Strikes and Lockouts, 1902-1936.
11. Supple, *History*, p. 380.
12. A. Campbell, 'Colliery mechanisation in Lanarkshire', *Bulletin of the Society for the Study of Labour History*, no. 49, Autumn 1984, pp. 37-45; Macintyre, *Little Moscows*, pp. 63, 114.
13. *List of Mines, 1927*.
14. L.J. Barraclough, 'Some general considerations on machine mining practice', *Transactions of the Institute of Mining Engineers*, vol. 74,

1927-28, pp. 194-5.

15. *Report of HM Inspector of Mines, Scottish Division, 1923* (1924), p. 40; *Report of HM Inspector of Mines, Scottish Division, 1927* (1928), p. 4.

16. PRO LAB 34/2-51, Board of Trade Record Books of Strikes and Lockouts, 1902-36.

17. D. Gilbert, *Class, Community, and Collective Action: social change in two British coalfields, 1850-1926* (Oxford, 1992), pp. 44-6.

18. J. Frew and D. Adishead, 'Model colliery housing in Fife: Denbeath Garden Village, 1904-1908', *Scottish Industrial History*, vol. 10, nos 1 and 2, 1987, pp. 45-59; I. MacDougall, 'Mungo MacKay and the green table', in B. Kay (ed.), *Odyssey: the second collection* (Edinburgh, 1982).

19. PRO RG 23/72, Scottish mining communities, pp. 21, 10.

20. *Report of the Scottish Coalfields Committee*, PP 1944, IV, 604.

21. *Motherwell Times*, 6 and 13 May, 30 December 1921; I. MacDougall, *Militant Miners* (Edinburgh, 1981), pp. 35-6.

22. G.Walker, 'The Orange Order in Scotland between the Wars', *International Review of Social History*, vol. 37, 1992, pp. 176-205; *Motherwell Times*, 15 July and 12 August 1921.

23. *Motherwell Times*, 19 February 1926; P.Long, 'Abe Moffat, the Fife miners and the United Mineworkers of Scotland: transcript of a 1974 interview', *Scottish Labour History Society Journal*, no. 17, 1982, p. 17.

24. Scottish Record Office (SRO) HH56/22, Letters from Chief Constables of Ayr and Kilmarnock to Scottish Office, 2 November 1926; *Glasgow Herald*, 6 July, 13 October, 15 November 1926.

25. K. Durland, *Among the Fife Miners* (1904), pp. 116-19.

26. PRO RG 23/72, Scottish mining communities, p. 108.

27. Buckhaven and Methil Public Library (BMPL), Proudfoot Collection, Letter from D. Proudfoot to G.A. Hutt, 2 September 1929.

28. *Miner*, 27 September 1924; *Workers' Life*, 28 October 1927.

29. Interview with D. Meek, 25 July 1984; *Daily Worker*, 10 February 1933; National Library of Scotland (NLS), Deposit 227/45A, Lanarkshire Mine Workers' Union (LMWU) Records, Minutes of Council, 8 March 1933.

30. Long, (thesis), Tables 27, 28 and 31.

31. NLS Deposit 227/37A, LMWU Minutes of Council, 26 February 1921.

32. NLS, Scottish Miners' Federation, Proceedings of the Seventeenth Annual Conference, 1910; *Glasgow Herald*, 18 August 1911.

33. *Colliery Guardian*, 26 June 1907.

34. *Dalkeith Advertiser*, 27 December 1917.
35. NLS Deposit 227/99, NUSMW, Proceedings of Annual Conference, 1919.
36. NLS Accession 4311/250, Fife, Clackmannan and Kinross Miners' Union Miscellaneous Papers, Letter from C. Carlow to W. Adamson, 21 December 1918.
37. J.C. Welsh, 'The Scottish miners and their union', *Socialist Review*, vol. 15, 1918, p. 78.
38. *Miner*, 18 August 1923, 27 September 1924; NLS Deposit 258/1, Ayrshire Miners' Union, Minutes of Delegate Meeting, 5 July 1930; NLS Deposit 227/88, NUSMW Minutes of Special Sub-Committee on Finance and Organisation, 5 August 1929; J. Doonan et al., *A Trade Union Tragedy in Scotland: some dark deeds which should be known to all trade unionists and trade union officials* (1902), pp. 72-4; *Forward*, 7 October 1922.
39. I.G.C. Hutchison, *A Political History of Scotland, 1832-1924* (Edinburgh, 1986), pp. 257-65.
40. Quoted ibid., p. 246.
41. G. Brown, 'The Labour Party and Political Change in Scotland, 1918-1929: the politics of five elections', unpublished PhD thesis, University of Edinburgh, 1981, pp. 393-95.
42. J. Lee, *This Great Journey* (1963), p. 99.
43. SRO HH 55/388, Letter from Chief Constable, Hamilton, to Sheriff of Lanarkshire, 8 March 1912; SRO HH55/341, Memorandum from Chief Constable of Fife to Standing Joint Committee, 15 May 1912; *Scotsman*, 6 April 1912.
44. *Hamilton Advertiser*, 3 August 1912.
45. *Plebs*, vol. 9, no. 9, October 1917, pp. 208-9; J.D. MacDougall, 'The Scottish coalminer', *Nineteenth Century*, December 1927, pp. 767-73; NLS 7.57, *Manifesto of the Lanarkshire Miners' Reform Committee*; NLS 6.1484 (11), *Manifesto of the Fife Miners' Reform Committee*; BMPL, Proudfoot Collection, K033, *Manifesto of the Lothian Miners' Reform Committee*.
46. PRO AIR 1/554, GHQ Intelligence Summaries, Scottish Command, 18-24 May 1919.
47. *Dunfermline Press*, 25 January 1919; *Glasgow Herald*, 27 January-5 February 1919; *Hamilton Advertiser*, 1, 8 February and 3 May, 1919.
48. NLS Deposit 227/41, LMWU Minutes of Council, Annual Elections of Officials, 1 July 1925.
49. N. Milton, *John Maclean* (1973), pp. 43, 68, 71; NLS Accession 4251, Box 2, File 9, John Maclean Papers, 'Recollections written down from the dictation of J.D. MacDougall'; *Call*, 11 October 1918.

50. *Workers' Weekly*, 25 June 1926.
51. SRO HH 56/26, Police Report, Miners' Strike, 11 June 1926.
52. *Workers' Life*, 4 and 25 March 1927; National Museum of Labour History (NMLH), CPGB Archive Notes made by the late James Klugmann at the Central Party Archive, Moscow, Folder 4.
53. R. Martin, *Communism and the British Trade Unions, 1924-1933* (Oxford, 1969), pp. 91-2, 127-8; Long (thesis), ch. 12.
54. BMPL Proudfoot Collection, D. Proudfoot to G.A. Hutt, 25 December 1928.
55. W. Allan, 'The position of the Scottish miners', *Labour Monthly*, vol. 11, 1929, p. 284.
56. M. Sime, 'The United Mineworkers of Scotland', unpublished paper.
57. NMLH, CPGB Archive, Minutes of the Political Bureau, 23 December 1930.
58. A. Moffat, *My Life with the Miners* (1965), pp. 50-1.
59. NMLH, CPGB Archive, Minutes of the Central Committee, 13 September 1930; *Daily Worker*, 12 October and 10 December 1932.
60. NLS Deposit 227/45A, LMWU Minutes of Council, 5 September 1934; NLS Deposit 227/90, NUSMW Minutes of Executive Committee, 29 May 1935.
61. R. Church *et al.*, 'British coalmining strikes 1893-1940: dimensions and distribution', University of Leeds School of Business and Economic Studies, *Discussion Paper*, 1989, p. 24.
62. NLS Deposit 227/45A, LMWU Minutes of Council, 4 May 1932.
63. Calculated from NLS Deposit 227/89, NUSMW Statement of Accounts for year ended 31 July 1931.
64. NLS Deposit 227/90, NUSMW Annual Conference Proceedings, 1934.
65. *Daily Worker*, 7, 17 August 1936; NLS Deposit 227/45A and 46LMWU, Annual Elections of Officials, 1937 and 1940; R. Page Arnot, *A History of the Scottish Miners* (1955), pp. 250-1.
66. NMLH, CPGB Archive, Scottish District Party Committee Organisation Report, Minutes of the Political Bureau, 9 April 1931.
67. NMLH, CPGB Archive, Minutes of the Central Committee, 19-20 September 1931.
68. For further evaluation of the CP, see A. Campbell, 'The Communist Party in the Scots coalfields in the interwar period' in G. Andrews, N. Fishman and K. Morgan (eds), *Opening the Books: the social and cultural history of British communism* (1995).
69. NMLH, CPGB Archive, Minutes of the Political Bureau, 21 November 1935.
70. *Daily Worker*, 28 October 1935, 12 March 1935.
71. For example, see the reminiscences of former CP councillors John

McArthur in MacDougall, *Militant Miners*, pp. 151-63 and Abe Moffat, *Life*, pp. 31-6.

72. Calculated from M. Kinnear, *The British Voter: an atlas and survey since 1985* (2nd edn, 1981), p. 116, and F.W.S. Craig (ed.) *British Parliamentary Election Results 1918-1949* (Glasgow, 1969).

73. Walker, 'Orange order', p. 188.

CHAPTER SEVEN

The landscape of Spencerism: mining politics in the Nottinghamshire coalfield, 1910-1947

David Gilbert

Introduction

Any history of mining politics in the twentieth century Nottinghamshire coalfield is necessarily dominated by two events: the decisive return to work during the 1926 lockout; and the refusal of the majority of Nottinghamshire miners to join the national strike in 1984-5. In both strikes breakaway unions were formed, and during the 1984-5 dispute the earlier history of the Nottinghamshire coalfield assumed great significance. In the heat of the conflict of 1984-5, understanding of the position of the Nottinghamshire miners and their past politics hardly progressed beyond knee-jerk demonologies or eulogies. In this account of mining politics in Nottinghamshire between 1910 and 1947, a central place is given to events of the 1926 lockout. The role of the Nottinghamshire miners in 1926 cannot be explained by simple one-dimensional accounts of their exceptionalism. Rather the drift back to work, and the subsequent formation and relative success of the Nottinghamshire Miners' Industrial Union (NMIU or the 'Spencer Union') needs to be understood in the context of the character of the coalfield. The first section of the chapter examines the context and background to that dispute in Nottinghamshire. Mining politics were shaped by the nature of the regional society, by traditions of political identification and action, by the working order within the collieries, and even, indirectly, by the geology of the coal seams. In particular the politics of the Nottinghamshire Miners' Association (NMA), affiliated

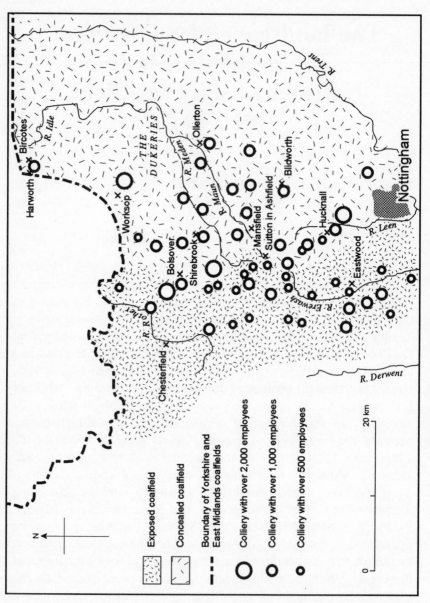

Map 4 The East Midlands coalfield at nationalisation in 1947.

to the MFGB, cannot be understood without reference to this context.

The central part of this chapter looks in detail at the 1926 lockout in Nottinghamshire. The drift back to work was not consistent across the county, and the timing of different returns to work says much about the political micro-geography of the coalfield. Five months into the dispute, with around three-quarters of Nottinghamshire miners back at work, the Labour MP and NMA leader George Spencer made his (in)famous intervention which established the NMIU. The new union rapidly became known as the 'Spencer Union', and 'Spencerism' entered the lexicon of the labour movement as a term of abuse to describe the organisation of rightwing, anti-strike unions. Yet Spencer was no *deus ex machina*, and the breakaway resulted from much more than the actions of a single man. The NMIU built upon long-established traditions of accommodation and conciliation in Nottinghamshire labour relations, and was able to use a pre-existing network of rightwing and anti-socialist labour activists in the coalfield.

The politics of the Nottinghamshire coalfield after 1926 were dominated by the division between the NMIU and the rump NMA. A series of tactics were used against the NMIU during the late 1920s and early 1930s, but its membership remained stubbornly high. The end of the split came only after the bitter dispute at Harworth in 1936-7. Harworth is sometimes celebrated as a great victory against non-political unionism, but the amalgamation terms which created the new Federated Union in Nottinghamshire were highly favourable to the old Spencer Union. Spencer himself remained president of the new union until nationalisation.

The Nottinghamshire coalfield and the Nottinghamshire Miners' Association

The experience of Spencerism in Nottinghamshire sets the political history of the coalfield apart during the interwar years. However in many other ways Nottinghamshire can be regarded as representative of a different kind of coalfield from those most prominent in the historiography of British mining. Mining in Nottinghamshire and in other parts of the English Midlands took place in a very different context from the conditions found in the North East, South Wales and parts of Yorkshire and Scotland. The Nottinghamshire coalfield was a place where traditional stereotypes of the isolated, self-contained mining community were of limited relevance. In Nottinghamshire, as in other parts of the Midlands, miners lived in a variety of social settings. Some Nottinghamshire miners lived in single industry, single class communities, but many lived in more industrially and socially diverse situations.

In many ways the most distinctive and isolated mining communities were associated with the new pits of the Dukeries sunk and opened during the interwar period.[1] The Dukeries pits were larger and deeper than the existing Nottinghamshire pits, and situated some way to the east of Mansfield in an area dominated by large aristocratic estates. In the new pit villages like Ollerton and Clipstone, the colliery companies adopted a policy of social control through the design of the physical and social environment. The 'new feudalism' in these model colliery villages was marked by close company control of both the workforce and of local associational culture.[2] In the surrounding countryside there were strong traditions of deference to the local elites and of Conservative voting. It was unsurprising that these pits were marked by low rates of support for the NMA, and experienced some of the earliest breaks in the strike in 1926.

The Dukeries pits were working within traditions of company involvement in local affairs which had developed in other parts of the county. However these earlier traditions had somewhat different political consequences. In particular, close relations between colliery owners and the early leadership of the NMA in the Leen Valley area during the late nineteenth century had helped to establish a moderate, Lib-Lab style of conciliatory industrial politics. The Liberal MP and owner of the Hucknall collieries, John Ellis, may even have had a hand in drafting the NMA's constitution in the 1880s. However straightforward social and industrial paternalism was limited by the complexity of local society. Even in towns like Mansfield, Sutton-in-Ashfield and Hucknall where the mines were the largest employers of male labour, other industries were important influences on local politics. The trade unions of the traditional industries of the East Midlands, especially the lace and hosiery industries, had long favoured conciliation and close involvement with employers. The leaders of the NMA, even after the First World War, drew upon these developed regional traditions of industrial relations, which went back at least as far as the ideas of Mundella and the Liberal conciliators of the mid-Victorian period.[3]

One particularly important influence on the Nottinghamshire coalfield was the size and scope of the female labour market. Significant numbers of women were employed in the traditional lace and hosiery industries, and in newer pharmaceuticals and consumer goods factories. In this respect the Nottinghamshire coalfield was both more socially diverse and less patriarchal than other coalfields. It is hard to judge the direct effects on mining politics. While female wages could provide a secondary source of income during strikes, some have suggested that reliance on women's income helped to shame proudly masculine miners back to work, and that many women actively urged their men to return.[4]

The nature of the female labour market in Nottinghamshire certainly helped to weaken the link between pit and local community, which was fundamental to rank and file mining politics in many other coalfields. Many women were employed in factories, offices and shops outside of their immediate localities. The city of Nottingham itself was an important focus for this labour market. Statistics from the 1921 census show that even in mining towns like Mansfield, Sutton-in-Ashfield and Hucknall, nearly half the women were in paid work, and that a significant proportion commuted to work outside of their immediate areas.[5] The coal industry itself was more open and flexible than in most other coalfields. Many miners did not live in the town or village containing their pit. A dense network of railways, tramways and bus routes made the commuting miner a familiar figure in the coalfield. The miners were increasingly concentrated in urban areas, including the northern suburbs of Nottingham, with many miners travelling to pits away from significant settlements. By the interwar period the coalfield towns of Nottinghamshire had commuting rates nearly as high as the suburbs of London.[6] Many mining people were drawn outside of their localities for leisure and culture. The attractions of Nottingham had a significance in the lives of mining people that was quite unmatched in cities like Cardiff, Swansea or Newcastle, which served coalfields where local associational culture remained unchallenged by more metropolitan temptations.[7]

The relative weakness of the relationship between pit and community had its expression in the political structure of the NMA.

Because local union branches were not the key local social institutions that they were in other parts of the country, they did not provide the same basis for rank and file organisation as in, say, South Wales or the North East. In many of the other mining unions there was a difficult and contested relationship between strong local lodges and the regional union bureaucracy. The NMA had a settled and centralised structure from 1885 onwards, and the local lodges were relatively weak.[8] The political history of the NMA was more often a story of continuities and disputes within a small oligarchic leading group than one of tensions between the leadership and the grassroots. One significant effect of this was that organised leftwing politics were often marginalised.

Another factor which was an important influence on mining politics in Nottinghamshire was the nature of the working order. In common with hosiery and the lace industries, East Midlands mining had a strong tradition of subcontracting. In the nineteenth century subcontractors or 'butties' had overseen the sinking of pits and their day to day management. The development of professional mining managers and engineers downgraded the role of the butty, but even in the interwar period the butty played a central part in the organisation of the labour process. The butty was responsible for the recruitment of his gang of men, and paid them out of the contract negotiated with the colliery management.[9] This so-called 'little butty system' maintained a clear income differential between the butties and other miners. The system had a number of effects beyond the pit. The butties formed a distinctive stratum in local society, which had the effect of fragmenting the mining population. Butties tended to live in larger houses, often in separate streets or areas, and were members of different chapels or churches from the rest of the mining people.[10] The butties formed a kind of middle class among the miners, and their traditions of material aspiration and independence were often expressed in anti-collectivist and rightwing politics.

Butties were to form the organisational backbone of the Spencer Union, but prior to 1926 were already active in rightwing politics. One of the main issues for the organised right in the coalfield was the defence of the butty system from attempts to abolish it. The butty William Holland, vice-president of the NMA in 1919, led the anti-socialist British Workers' League (BWL) in the East Midlands.[11] Under Holland's leadership, Nottinghamshire became one of the

League's strongest areas of support. The organisational centre of the BWL was in Mansfield, but the real strongholds of the movement were in more isolated pits where the colliery companies had significant control over local society. The BWL flourished in the pits of the Barber-Walker Company and the Bolsover Company. Joseph Birkin, a butty at the Barber-Walker Moor Green pit had already reduced the local NMA branch to 'a virtual company union', even before the 1926 breakaway.[12] After the formation of the NMIU, Birkin became its Eastwood area agent, taking many of the local men with him.[13]

The political culture of the Nottinghamshire miners was also conditioned by the geology and economics of their coalfield. Although in the west of the county there were many small and relatively uneconomic pits, in general Nottinghamshire pits were more efficient and profitable than those in most other coalfields. The oldest pits in the county were in the west in the exposed coalfield which extended into Derbyshire. There the pits tended to be relatively small, working into seams which outcropped on the surface. Development of the coalfield in the late nineteenth and early twentieth centuries moved from west to east, requiring deeper and larger pits to mine the seams which dipped down from the surface. Developments in the Leen Valley and the Mansfield area preceded the sinking of the Dukeries pits in the 1920s.

During the interwar period the only pits which faced closure were smaller pits in the exposed coalfield. The first pit to close in the Leen Valley was at Bulwell in 1945, and production from the Mansfield area and Dukeries pits continued to rise after the Second World War. Although some Nottinghamshire coal was exported, most was used for domestic consumption and increasingly for electricity generation, and the effects of the depression were not as disastrous as in the main export coalfields. Nottinghamshire's share of British coal production rose from under 5 per cent before the First World War to over 8 per cent on the eve of nationalisation. Productivity in Nottinghamshire was consistently higher than the national average. In 1913 production per miner in Nottinghamshire was 21 per cent higher than in Durham, and 25 per cent higher than South Wales. By 1939 Nottinghamshire's productivity advantage over both had increased to more than 33 per cent.[14]

The political consequences of Nottinghamshire's relatively strong economic position were complicated. In a different context the economic position of the coalfield could have strengthened the position of the union movement. However in Nottinghamshire job security and relatively high wages tended to increase political apathy and weaken the Nottinghamshire miners' commitment to the MFGB. In 1921 and 1926 the organised right were very hostile towards national settlements and to pooling arrangements, and these views seemed to have been shared by a sizeable proportion of the workforce.[15] In the June 1921 MFGB ballot on a national wages pool, a small majority of NMA members voted for the pool, but less than a third of the membership bothered to vote, and less than 15 per cent of the workforce voted for industrial action.[16] The central issue in George Spencer's career can be seen as not industrial unionism as such, but rather independent district agreements. As early as 1915 Spencer had been involved in a campaign to disaffiliate the NMA politically from the MFGB, and during the early 1920s the leadership of the union was generally sceptical about pooling proposals. Many years later, after the fusion of the NMA and NMIU, Spencer continued to argue for district agreements inside the Federation.

The three most important figures in the NMA between 1910 and 1926 were Spencer, Frank Varley and J.G. Hancock, all of whom were also MPs for mining constituencies in the East Midlands. Hancock had been one of the permanent officials of the NMA since the early 1890s, and was Liberal MP for Mid-Derbyshire (later Belper) from 1909 to 1923. Among the paid officials of the union, Hancock provided a direct link between the nineteenth century Liberal conciliators and a later generation of leaders. On his retirement from union politics in 1927, one local paper celebrated Hancock as a 'staunch Liberal in politics ... he stands for sane and moderate trades unionism'.[17] Hancock was a consistent critic of any form of socialism, who lost the Labour whip in 1914 and stood against the Labour Party in 1922 and 1923. He opposed nationalisation bitterly, and for a time flirted with the BWL.[18] It is indicative of the weakness of the organised left in the NMA that there were several futile attempts to remove Hancock from office during the 1920s. Hancock's continuing employment by the NMA also gives some clues as to the nature of the Labour supporters in the leadership.

George Spencer and Frank Varley represented a different generation of miners' leaders in Nottinghamshire. Spencer was elected president of the NMA in 1912, and was elected Labour MP for Broxtowe in 1918. Varley first came to prominence when he was elected vice-president of the union in 1913. He was Labour MP for Mansfield from 1923 until his death in 1929. Spencer and Varley were rivals for power in the union, and their bitter enmity after 1926 built on earlier tensions. However they shared many political characteristics. If anything Varley was to the right of Spencer until the early 1920s, but both 'reflected the temper of the men as the chameleon reflects the colour of its surroundings'.[19] In the early postwar period both men seemed to be moving to the left. However as it became clear that the influence of groups like Herbert Booth's ILP branch in Hucknall or Jack Lavin's Socialist Labour Party (SLP) branch in Mansfield was rather limited, both men returned to the Nottinghamshire leadership's traditions of 'ultra-moderation'.[20]

The Nottinghamshire coalfield in the great lockouts

The 1921 dispute was relatively uneventful in the Nottinghamshire coalfield. The strike certainly held firm and there were few direct indications of the weakness of the NMA which was to be so apparent five years later.[21] However beneath a superficial impression of solidarity, there were tensions which prefigured the breakaway of 1926. The strike remained solid and peaceful at most pits in the Mansfield area and the Leen Valley, but weak links were already being identified in June 1921. Towards the end of the strike, mass picketing took place at Gedling, where the butties' organisation was notoriously powerful, and there were confrontations near Eastwood between Birkin, who was organising outcropping, and militant pickets from the Leen Valley.[22]

At the end of the dispute the NMA was weakened severely by strike payments of over £150,000, and many mining people faced severe debts.[23] This situation was of course repeated in other coalfields, but in Nottinghamshire the economic situation made it difficult for the union to justify the hardship. Whereas miners in some other coalfields had stood to lose a significant proportion of their wages, the reductions proposed for Nottinghamshire were minimal. Some Nottinghamshire miners would even have gained from the proposals.[24] Dissatisfaction with the cause, conduct and result of the 1921 strike led to defections from the NMA from the left, the right, the hard-up, and the apathetic. Membership dropped rapidly from 45,684 in August 1921 to 39,084, and significantly the proportion of fully paid-up members dropped from 96 per cent to 61 per cent.[25]

The 1921 lockout strengthened opposition to wage pooling arrangements in Nottinghamshire and the leadership moved further to the right. For many miners their inclusion in the new Eastern District, along with the other Midlands coalfields and Yorkshire, represented an unacceptable subsidy to less profitable areas. In 1923 Varley and Spencer opposed MFGB moves to end the 1921 agreement on the grounds that the Nottinghamshire miners would gain little and were still too weak after the lockout. By mid-1925, when the Mining Association's new terms were presented to the MFGB, the possibility of a Nottinghamshire breakaway and independent agreement (as had happened after the 1893 lockout) was recognised as a real danger by Herbert Smith and Arthur Cook. Although radicals in the coalfield, particularly the unofficial Mansfield District Committee, had close relations with Cook and were pushing for confrontation in 1926, the leadership of the NMA was extremely unsympathetic and provided the chief dissenting voices at MFGB conferences leading up to the General Strike.

In many British coalfields the General Strike passed off with very little incident because of the local strength of the mining unions. There was more conflict in Nottinghamshire, where mining took place in more socially and industrially mixed locations, and where branches of the NMA had been unable to establish themselves as key social institutions. The response to the strike call was very good but there was also a significant mobilisation of the counter-strike organisation, especially in Nottingham with its large middle class and student population. Up to 5,000 people volunteered for the OMS and over 1,000 new special constables were recruited.[26] Volunteer-run transport was attacked and there were several violent confrontations in the Old Market Square in the centre of the city. Other clashes took place elsewhere in the coalfield. Lorries and buses were attacked in Mansfield and Sutton and a tram on the line between the two towns was derailed. A number of communists were arrested and charged under the Emergency Regulations, and for a time the BBC relay station at Nottingham broadcast unofficial news items including the Mansfield District Committee's provocative intent to 'keep the Fascisti out of the town by all and any means'.[27] However none of the Nottinghamshire strike committees styled themselves 'councils of action', a title which usually indicated the coordinating influence of the Minority Movement or other organised leftwing groups.

Nottinghamshire remained relatively solid during the early months of the miners' lockout. Unsurprisingly the first returns to work were in the new pits of the Dukeries where the NMA had great difficulty in organising. Ollerton and Blidworth (a newly sunk pit south east of Mansfield) reopened in early June, and Harworth colliery started work later in the month. The Bolsover Company opened its pits at Rufford and Clipstone in July. The company used its position as landlord and provider of local amenities to bring pressure on strikers. At one point its villages were even 'roped and wired off to prevent speakers and pickets approaching'.[28] However during the early summer it was the Warwickshire pits which were seen as the 'cockpit of the entire struggle', and the place where the strike seemed most likely to break.[29] It was not until August that the situation started to change dramatically in Nottinghamshire. There were significant returns to work in early August in the Mansfield and Eastwood pits and, when new terms were posted by the Nottinghamshire owners on 20 August, 12,740 men signed on for work.[30]

The Mansfield area had become the key to the whole dispute. During the weekend of 21 and 22 August, Arthur Cook spoke at twenty-five meetings in Nottinghamshire. This work met with some success as only 4,500 men turned up for work on the Monday, and less than 4,000 worked the following day. However this intensive and highly charismatic campaigning could produce only short term results, and as the police became more successful at managing mass picketing the numbers at work increased steadily. The owners and government estimated that one in five Nottinghamshire miners were working at the start of September, one in four by 15 September, and one in two by the end of the month. The NMA disputed the figures but not the trend. At the start of October, only the pits at Manton, Cotes Park and Shireoaks remained closed, all in the north of the county, and all with significant numbers of YMA members.

There were a number of dimensions to the return to work. The collieries of a number of companies led the way, notably the Bolsover, Barber-Walker, and Butterley companies. Company support for the butty system was important. The political role of many butties has been mentioned, but their entrepreneurial opportunism also helped to break the strike. Where union lodges were powerful institutions capable of disciplining the local population, as in South Wales or the North East, outcropping was sanctioned to provide coal for homes or collective kitchens. In the East Midlands, outcropping was organised by the butties on a commercial basis. Thousands of men crossed into Derbyshire to work the exposed seams there.

It has been suggested that hardship and starvation were primary causes of the return to work in Nottinghamshire.[31] The NMA had only just cleared its debts from the 1921 dispute, and provided only nominal financial support for strikers. In Nottinghamshire the miners faced unsympathetic Poor Law Boards outside of the control or influence of the labour movement. Labour members were in a minority even on the Mansfield Board. As the return increased in pace, the Boards in the county threatened to remove support on the grounds that the pits were open and work was available. Many miners chose not to apply for relief. There were about 32,600 miners in the Mansfield Poor Law Union, but the number applying for relief never exceeded 10,000. There seemed to be a distinctive moral economy of debt and pauperage in Nottinghamshire and most mining families privatised their responses to hardship by drawing upon their savings, or by relying on a second wage (often of a wife or daughter). Hardship in Nottinghamshire was also a consequence of the failure to mobilise the resources of the wider population. Donations to relief funds were small when compared with those in other coalfields. During the lockout the Mansfield relief funds collected donations of about £2,500 from a town of 40,000, many of whom were in work. By contrast, £2,200 was gathered in the South Wales mining village of Ynysybwl, which had one-tenth the population and no other industries.[32] The hardships faced by the Nottinghamshire miners were a contributory factor in the return, which requires understanding in terms of differences in regional political culture. The miners were not simply starved back to work.

Another contributory factor was the equivocal position of the NMA leadership. While attempting to maintain the discipline of the strike, both Varley and Spencer were publicly critical of Arthur Cook and consistently supported moves towards a compromise settlement. On

28 August, with thousands of miners already back at work, the NMA formally applied to the MFGB for permission to begin district negotiations.[33] This approach was of course rejected. The NMA leaders were also increasingly worried that the men who had returned were starting to organise and negotiate with the owners independently. The pressures increased when the remaining solid area in the county, the Leen Valley, began to crack from early October onwards. Cook mounted one last great campaign of meetings in Nottinghamshire but again the effects were short-lived. *The Miner* optimistically trumpeted that the campaign had fired the enthusiasm of the 'thousands of men who drifted back on account of the defeatist tactics of Mr George Spencer and others'.[34] But by this time all the leaders of the Nottinghamshire miners acknowledged that the strike had collapsed. The conflict was now about the future nature of mining unionism in the county.

The Spencer Union and the NMA

On 5 October 1926 Spencer attended a meeting of men from the Digby and New London pits where the strike had collapsed. Faced with a situation where the management was excluding strike-loyalists from returning to their old jobs, Spencer negotiated a return to work for practically all the men who had previously worked in the pits. Spencer was then approached by men from seven other pits and negotiated similar arrangements. At this point it is unclear whether or not Spencer was clearly committed to a breakaway organisation. These initial negotiations were not incompatible with a final pragmatic attempt to save the NMA's authority and credibility with the majority of the workforce. What is clear is that positions hardened over the next few days, aided greatly by the pre-existing personal antagonisms between Spencer and Varley, and Spencer and Cook. Spencer was called before the conference of the MFGB on 8 October and denounced by Cook as 'a blackleg of the worst order. A conscious blackleg'.[35] The NMA was more equivocal, only suspending Spencer on 16 October, and continuing to make overtures in an attempt to heal the split. However by this time the die was cast and Spencer was already actively negotiating a district settlement with the Nottinghamshire owners. Spencer was not formally expelled from the NMA until after the formation of the NMIU on 22 November.

In a speech at Welbeck in December 1926, Spencer claimed that he was not the 'originator of the new movement', and that the inspiration had come from 'the rank and file, who were disgusted with the way in which the dispute was conducted by the Miners' Federation'.[36]   Butties like Birkin and Holland were already organising outside the NMA before Spencer's intervention, but he gave the new organisation coherence and increased its respectability in the eyes of the Nottinghamshire owners.   In December 1926 the new union was recognised by the Nottinghamshire Coal Owners' Association (NCOA) as the official union for all future negotiations.

Company support for the NMIU went well beyond official recognition.   The Bolsover Company was one of a number which made financial donations to the new union and the NCOA agreed to allow contributions to be deducted from wages.   Many companies excluded NMA activists from employment.   Others operated a NMIU closed shop policy, as at the New Hucknall and Annesley collieries.[37] A combination of company policy and the association between butties and the NMIU also produced discrimination underground where those loyal to the NMA were given the worst places and the dirtiest jobs. The NCOA set up a joint pension scheme with the NMIU, which was a powerful incentive to join as the NMA's own pension fund had collapsed.[38]   Support for the new union was strongest where the company was a significant force in the community and where pressures could be brought to bear on those in company housing.   By the end of 1927, the *New Statesman* was reporting that the NMA 'has disappeared from the Dukeries.   The men who fought are still hanging round the streets of Mansfield and the neighbouring villages, collecting for the Union, opening back-street shops to live, looking for jobs of any kind'.[39]

The split had drastic effects on the NMA which had already lost thousands of members in the lockout.   Membership dropped from around 34,000 before the strike to less than 9,000 paid-up members at the end of 1926.   There was some subsequent recovery but the NMA could never again claim to represent more than a small section of the labour force.   In 1928 a TUC organised ballot of the Nottinghamshire workforce voted 32,277 to 2,533 in favour of representation by the NMA rather than the NMIU, but no further action was taken and there was no great rush to join the NMA. The split had the effect of both marginalising and radicalising the NMA. Frank Varley, who had come in for every bit as much criticism from the left as Spencer, found himself leading the campaign against the rogue union. Until his death in 1929, Varley conducted an aggressive campaign fuelled partly by intense personal animosity towards Spencer. The Minority Movement greatly increased its influence in the NMA after 1926, although prominent activists were blacklisted by the coal owners. The NMA switched from its reactionary position to become one of the most leftwing unions in the MFGB, bitterly opposed to 'Mondism'.

Within the NMA and the MFGB there were strong differences of opinion about the proper strategy required to combat the Spencer Union. Some officials of the NMA, like Herbert Booth, took the line that negotiations could reunite the two unions; others, like William Bayliss and William Carter, argued that no compromise could be made.[40] Various tactics were used, but if anything the NMIU increased its strength during the early 1930s and there were no real challenges to its position before the strike at Harworth in 1936-7. The MFGB subsidised the NMA, but had little practical involvement in the coalfield until the mid-1930s.

Despite the advantages it had in the coalfield, the NMIU also failed to attract a majority of Nottinghamshire miners. During the late 1920s and early 1930s the main struggle for the Spencer Union was not with the NMA loyalists and the organised left, but with the indifference and confusions of the Nottinghamshire miners. For much of the period between the end of the lockout and the fusion of the unions in 1937, over half the workforce were non-unionised, and the proportion of miners not belonging to the NMA or NMIU never fell below 38 per cent. Indeed because some members of the NMA also paid dues to the Spencer Union to avoid victimisation, the actual rate of non-unionism was even higher than this. Although the NMIU was more than a mere owners' tool, and did enter into meaningful negotiations over issues of pay, conditions and welfare (albeit without the sanction of industrial action), for many ordinary miners it was a rather pointless organisation.[41] Without a long tradition of participation in the organisation, the NMIU was almost designed to encourage 'free riding'. Many miners were quite happy to take the benefits of separate district pay settlements, but were less willing to join the Industrial Union except when coercion was used.

The impact of the Spencer Union on local electoral politics was rather muted. If anything the split strengthened the Labour Party. There were reports that the Conservative Party had recruited extra members during the closing months of the lockout, but in the first local elections after the split Labour loyalists captured council seats in Eastwood (one of the strongest areas of NMIU organisation) from Conservative-backed 'Independents'.[42] In general the Spencer Union seems to have been something of liability for the Conservatives, and while not approaching the dominance found in most other coalfields, Labour did relatively well in Nottinghamshire when compared with other Midlands mining areas. In 1931 all but one of the Derbyshire mining seats were won by National candidates, while Labour held both Broxtowe and Mansfield. Spencer himself sat on the Liberal benches as an Independent from 1927, and did not resign from the Broxtowe seat until just before the election of 1929, despite various campaigns in the local Labour Party to force him to go earlier.[43]

At the end of the lockout there were fears in the MFGB and the wider trade union movement that the NMIU would provide a model for 'company' unions in other coalfields and industries. Havelock Wilson's National Union of Seamen (NUS) supported Spencer both politically and financially from the time of the split, and the two organisations formed the 'Non-Political Trade Union Movement'. However this organisation received relatively little backing except from small marginal groups of the political right like the Economic League, and was effectively defunct after Wilson's death in 1929. There were moves to establish similar non-political unions in other coalfields, but only in the case of the South Wales Miners' Industrial Union (SWMIU) was there any success. The spread of such unions was limited by the general balance of power in industrial relations after 1926. Most employers were happier to work with the weakened official trade union movement rather than risk the confrontations often associated with breakaway unions.

Harworth and after

Harworth has been described as 'one of the classic battles in the history of Trade Unionism' and contemporary reports in the leftwing press made comparisons with Tolpuddle.[44] Yet the Harworth dispute was a complicated event and can be read in a number of different ways. At one level it was the culmination of various campaigns by the NMA, MFGB, and the Communist Party against the Spencer Union.[45] This had become more urgent for the MFGB after the 1935-6 national wages dispute, when Spencer's promise to maintain coal supplies from the Nottinghamshire coalfield had seriously weakened the federation's position. It seems likely that the Communist Party had targeted Harworth as a site for confrontation with the Spencer Union long before events came to a head.[46] The communist Mick Kane, who had been laid off from Harworth in 1931, returned at the end of 1935 and set about reinvigorating the NMA branch. Between January and August 1936, NMA membership increased from 157 to 640 and Kane was elected branch president in June. By the autumn, conflict on the representation issue seemed inevitable. A series of disputes over harassment, 'snap time', dirt allowances and the subsequent victimisation of NMA activists developed into the anticipated confrontation over recognition.

However the Harworth dispute cannot be understood in terms of political developments alone. While Kane's intervention was crucial in organising the men at the colliery and the growing involvement of the MFGB gave Harworth national significance, the dispute was also about the nature of the local social order. At Harworth, like the other new interwar pits in Nottinghamshire, the Barber-Walker Company had attempted to control closely the lives of their workforce. Although the strike was primarily about the issue of company unionism, it was equally a rejection of a certain form of community by a considerable proportion of the local population. Barber-Walker had built nearly 1,000 houses in a new development called Bircotes, an extension of the existing village of Harworth. The company used its position as landlord to influence behaviour and used the threat of eviction as a sanction against trouble-makers at the pit. The company also owned and controlled most of the social facilities in the village, including the institute building.

The mining people of Harworth were significantly less acquiescent in this social order than those in the other Dukeries pits. This was in part due to a combination of political culture and geography. Harworth is in the north of the county and the closest pits were Maltby and Dinnington in South Yorkshire. Almost half the miners

192 MINERS, UNIONS AND POLITICS, 1910-47

who came to the village between 1925 and 1931 came from
Yorkshire, bringing with them quite different experiences of union
affiliation, community organisation and collective action in the
lockouts of 1921 and 1926.[47] For much of the interwar period
Harworth was also the first pit with work available for North East
miners travelling south on the Great North Road. Miners from the
North East including Kane himself played a leading role in the re-
emergence of the NMA at Harworth.

From an early stage the dispute was marked by violent
confrontations. While about 1,000 miners supported the strike, on
most days during the dispute between 600 and 1,100 were at work.
A sizeable proportion of these were outsiders, bussed into the village.
Twice a day the police processed the 'chain gang' of working miners
through the village to the colliery gates past protesting strikers and
their supporters. The dispute was marked by highly visible and
aggressive policing. Parts of the village were shut off to known
activists, and the police made considerable use of the new Public
Order Act of 1936. Many of those arrested at Harworth were
charged with vague and potentially far-reaching public order offences
such as the use of 'insulting language' or 'threatening behaviour'.[48]

There were also outbreaks of serious rioting during the strike. On
16 December 1936, working miners and police were stoned outside
the colliery gates, a police car was wrecked, and a baton charge was
used to restore order. These events received little attention outside
of Nottinghamshire, but further violence on the nights of 23 April
and 24 April 1937 made the front pages of the Fleet Street papers.
The events in Harworth were receiving national attention because the
MFGB had given the NMA greater support and a national ballot had
voted by an overwhelming majority in favour of a strike on the issue.
The tensions had been increased by Captain Muschamp, one of the
Nottinghamshire owners, who had publicly called for 'German'
methods to be used against the strikers.[49] On 5 May, just before
strike notices were due to be handed in, Prime Minister Baldwin
pleaded in the House of Commons for a compromise solution to the
dispute. The MFGB leadership was very uneasy about the prospects
for a national dispute and their negotiators seized the opportunity to
push for a fusion of the unions. The subsequent agreement was
approved by a delegate conference of the MFGB on 28 May, and the
new Nottinghamshire and District Miners' Federated Union (NMFU)

came into being on 1 September 1937.

The Harworth dispute had achieved the end of the NMIU, but the terms and circumstances of the settlement were decidedly ambiguous. Almost all sides in the dispute could (and did) represent the final outcome as a victory. For Mick Kane and the Communist Party it was a vindication both of the role of activism and of the strategies used.[50] Kane and eleven other activists were given jail sentences after the April disturbances, but this contributed to a sense of martyrdom for the cause. As president of the MFGB, Joseph Jones was able to represent the outcome as a victory for pragmatism and for concerted action, even though the threatened national strike would have placed great strain on the federation. Both Attlee and Baldwin were able to claim credit for their political interventions and the outcome strengthened the developing industrial relations system.

Whoever were the winners in the dispute, it was clear that neither George Spencer nor the Barber-Walker company were losers. (The real losers were the NMA rank and file at Harworth, for despite pledges made by the company in the settlement, many were victimised and never returned to work at Harworth.) Spencer became president of the Federated Union, and the NMIU supplied three of the five officials of the new organisation. Significantly Herbert Booth, who had resigned from the presidency of the NMA in January 1937 and defected to the NMIU, became one of the new miners' agents, despite strong objections from the NMA. The new executive also contained many of the NMIU activists who were most detested by the NMA, particularly Joseph Birkin. There was initial reluctance to join a new 'Spencer' union on the part of many ex-NMA members, but membership of the NMFU climbed to 28,000 by the end of 1937, greater than the combined membership of the NMA and MMIU before Harworth.[51] While non-unionism and apathy remained significant problems for the new union, membership continued to rise in the years before the formation of the NUM.

The Federated Union was admitted to the MFGB, and under Spencer Nottinghamshire returned to its traditional reactionary position. Spencer consistently opposed both national wage negotiations and moves towards the establishment of one big union. Spencer criticised the imposition of national bargaining arrangements during the war, and was the dissenting voice on the Joint National Negotiating Committee formed in 1943. Rank and file attitudes in

Nottinghamshire were more contradictory. Most miners were content with the line Spencer was taking on district agreements but also favoured the formation of a single miners' union. Spencer found himself increasingly marginalised on the centralisation issue, and an overwhelming majority of miners (88 per cent of those voting) chose to take Nottinghamshire into the NUM.

In many ways this marked the end of an era in Nottinghamshire mining politics. Spencer himself was forced into retirement, along with a number of other significant figures from the struggles of the interwar years. The Nottinghamshire Area of the NUM gave full support to nationalisation and by the 1960s and 1970s it had some reputation for militancy. Nonetheless lukewarm support for the strikes of the early 1970s and enthusiasm for local productivity agreements indicated that Nottinghamshire remained a distinctive environment for mining politics. It would be an over-simplification to make direct parallels between the 1920s and the events of 1984-5, but it is clear that the main dimensions of Nottinghamshire's exceptionalism were similar and were reinforced by awareness of the coalfield's past industrial politics. Nottinghamshire never provided fertile ground for the kind of all-embracing, community-based unionism so commonly associated with British mining people. Instead the Nottinghamshire unions had to work within a more diverse and fragmented political culture where the collective loyalty of miners could not be guaranteed, and where the ordinary miner was likely to give paramount concern to his own interests and those of his immediate family.

Notes

Place of publication is London unless otherwise stated.

1. The history of the Dukeries coalfield is discussed in detail in R.J. Waller, *The Dukeries Transformed: the social and political development of a twentieth century coalfield* (Oxford, 1983).
2. The term 'new feudalism' is taken form an article on the Dukeries pits in the *New Statesman*, 24 December 1927.
3. P. Wyncoll, *The Nottinghamshire Labour Movement* (1985), pp. 24-5.
4. A.R. Griffin, *Mining in the East Midlands, 1550-1947* (1971), pp. 248-9.

5. Source: 1921 Census. Women comprised almost exactly 25 per cent of the workforce in each of the three towns mentioned. Of these, 30 per cent commuted to work from Hucknall, 25 per cent from Sutton, and 9 per cent from Mansfield.

6. In 1921 the aggregate daily movement in and out of Mansfield was 25 per cent of the night population. In Sutton-in-Ashfield, 29 per cent of the population moved in or out of the area during census day. The comparable figures for Barnes, Mitcham and Wimbledon were 31, 33 and 29 per cent respectively.

7. A much fuller discussion of the miners' place in a developing regional society can be found in D.M. Gilbert, *Class, Community and Collective Action: social change in two British coalfields, 1850-1926* (Oxford, 1992), pp. 162-70.

8. A.R. Griffin, *The Miners of Nottinghamshire: a history of the Nottinghamshire Miners' Association, vol. 1, 1881-1914* (Nottingham, 1956), p. 39. There is a marked contrast with Durham and Northumberland where established central bureaucracies were counterbalanced by strong lodges.

9. R. Mottram and C. Coote, *Through Five Generations: the history of the Butterley Company* (1950), p. 139.

10. See Jessie Chambers' recollections of the Congregational Chapel or 'Butty's Lump' in Eastwood, quoted in J.D. Chambers, *D.H. Lawrence: a personal record* (1965), pp. 16-17.

11. *Empire Citizen*, October 1926. The *Empire Citizen* was published by the BWL, a supposedly rank and file organisation which had been set up during the First World War as the Socialist National Defence Committee to oppose pacifism in the labour movement. By the 1920s the primary aims of the BWL were patriotic propaganda and non-political trade unionism.

12. P.W. Shorter, 'Electoral Politics and Political Change in the East Midlands of England, 1918-35', unpublished PhD thesis, University of Cambridge, 1975.

13. See C.P. Griffin (ed.), *The Nottinghamshire Miners' Industrial Union ('Spencer Union'): Rufford Branch Minutes 1926-36, District Minutes 1926-7* (Thoroton Society Record Series XXXVIII, Nottingham, 1990).

14. Waller, *Dukeries*, pp. 2-3.

15. See for example William Holland's attack on 'the fantastic futility' of pooling during the 1921 dispute. (*Mansfield Chronicle*, 23 June 1921.)

16. MFGB Minute Book, 1921, p. 391. The ballot in Nottinghamshire is discussed in A.R. Griffin, *The Miners of Nottinghamshire: a history of the Nottinghamshire Miners' Association, vol. 2, 1914-44* (1962), pp. 91-2.

17. *Mansfield and Kirkby Chronicle*, 26 May 1927.
18. See discussion of Hancock's politics in Wyncoll, *Nottinghamshire Labour Movement*, pp. 148-53.
19. Griffin, *Miners of Nottinghamshire, vol. 2*, p. 62.
20. D. Howell, *British Workers and the Independent Labour Party* (Manchester, 1983), p. 50.
21. At the end of the national strike less than 600 miners were reported working in Yorkshire, Nottinghamshire, Derbyshire and Leicestershire combined. (PRO CAB 27 80/81, Cabinet Papers 1921.)
22. PRO CAB 27 80/81, 20 June 1921; G.C.H. Whitelock, *250 Years in Coal: the history of the Barber Walker Company Limited, 1680-1946* (Derby, 1955), p. 57.
23. NMA Minutes, 1921.
24. Griffin, *East Midlands*, pp. 222-4.
25. Griffin, *Miners of Nottinghamshire, vol.2*, p. 109.
26. Wyncoll, *Nottinghamshire Labour Movement*, p. 198.
27. Ibid., p. 204.
28. *Miner*, 4 September 1926.
29. Ibid., 30 July 1926.
30. PRO CAB 333.
31. Griffin, *East Midlands*, pp. 248-9.
32. Gilbert, *Class, Community*, p. 190.
33. Griffin, *Miners of Nottinghamshire, vol. 2*, p. 172.
34. *Miner*, 23 October 1926.
35. Quoted in R. Page Arnot, *The Miners: years of struggle* (1953), p. 495.
36. *Mansfield and Kirkby Chronicle*, 16 December 1926.
37. C.P. Griffin, *NMIU*, p. 18.
38. C.P. Griffin, 'Nottinghamshire miners between the wars: the Spencer Union revisited', *University of Nottingham Occasional Papers in Local History*, 4, 1984, p. 4.
39. *New Statesman*, 24 December 1927.
40. C.P. Griffin, *NMIU*, p. 22.
41. Ibid., p. 12.
42. *Eastwood and Kimberley Advertiser*, 3 December 1926.
43. Wyncoll, *Nottinghamshire Labour Movement*, p. 214.
44. Ibid., p. 218; *Daily Herald*, 30 April 1937. There are detailed accounts of the Harworth dispute in N. Fishman, *The British Communist Party and the Trade Unions* (1995), pp. 164-99; R. Page Arnot, *The Miners in Crisis and War* (1961), pp. 199-243; Griffin, *The Miners of Nottinghamshire, vol. 2*, pp. 255-89.
45. See N. Fishman, Chapter 4 of this volume.

46. Fishman, *British Communist Party*, pp. 173-5.
47. Waller, *Dukeries*, p. 35.
48. The Public Order Act was also a mainstay of the policing strategies used in divided mining communities in 1984-5.
49. Quoted in Arnot, *Miners in Crisis*, p. 219.
50. See N. Fishman, Chapter 4 of this volume.
51. Griffin, *Miners of Nottinghamshire, vol. 2*, p. 278.

CHAPTER EIGHT

Work, class and community: social identities and political change in the Lancashire coalfield, 1910-1939

Trevor Griffiths

Of the coalfields under review in this volume, the one which departed most profoundly from 'traditional' community patterns was Lancashire. Across much of the county, mining was pursued not in geographically remote settlements dominated by a single mode of work, but in large urban areas in which occupational diversity was the norm and where colliers were integrated into a wider industrial workforce. In 1911, 67 per cent of Lancashire miners resided in areas where the pit accounted for fewer than 30 per cent of all jobs; the equivalent figures for South Wales and North East England, the two largest fields by output at that time, were 19 and 16 per cent, respectively. The contrast carried over into individual neighbourhoods: Bill Naughton recalled street corners in Bolton during the 1920s populated by colliers, mill hands, and foundry workers.[1] More significantly, the span of a 'typical' Lancastrian mining career encompassed more than pit work. Many of those raised in districts where coal and cotton coincided gained their first work experience in local textile mills; entry into the pit was delayed until their later teenage years. For some, the mill provided a more permanent source of employment. A survey of continuation classes across the county in 1912, revealed that almost one-third of children with fathers in mining were employed in the textile trade. Over time, the tendency to explore alternative job avenues increased, so that, during the 1920s, miners were observed to be seeking work for their sons in mills or in 'sheltered' public sector work.[2]

From this it is clear that familiar typologies are of little use in

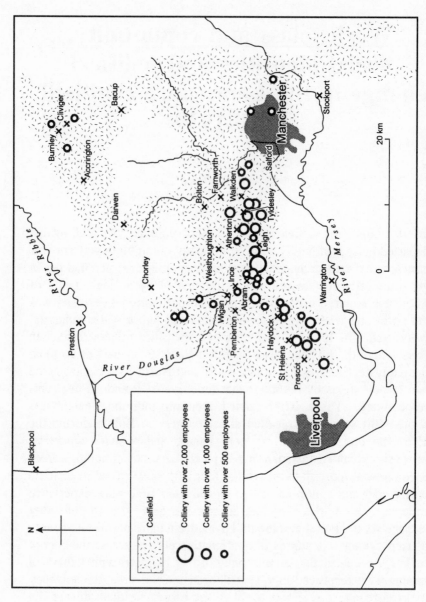

Map 5 The Lancashire coalfield at nationalisation in 1947.

seeking to comprehend the inner workings of Lancastrian mining society. In no sense did the county's colliers constitute an 'isolated mass', nor were their lives encompassed by the ties of an 'occupational community'.[3] Other facets of local society exemplify this observation. The presence of a large textile sector encouraged high rates of participation in paid employment among women. On average, over 40 per cent of females aged 10 and over were wage earners. National and religious differences were also crucial to Lancashire's social and political development. Irish catholics made up between a quarter and one-third of the populations of late-Victorian Leigh, St Helens, and Wigan, three towns central to mining activity in Lancashire.[4] The need to confront issues such as gender and ethnicity indicates that this was not a society susceptible to analysis through the work process and the internal dynamics of trade union organisation alone. Lancashire's social complexities demand that a more rounded approach be adopted, relating the world of the pit to that of home, family and neighbourhood. The contribution of the work experience to social and political trends across the region can then be placed in its proper perspective. Lancashire's significance extends beyond its social peculiarities. The Lancashire and Cheshire Miners' Federation (LCMF) was the first miners' organisation to affiliate to the Labour Representation Committee (LRC) in 1903, some five years in advance of the national Federation. The reasons for that decision, and its subsequent impact on political allegiances have much to tell us about the values and associations around which colliery society in Lancashire was structured. In addition to pointing up regional variations in social and political development, the experience of the county's miners, as workers tied in to the complex rhythms of urban society, throws more general light on the nature of class identities in early twentieth century Britain.

At one level of analysis, political change merely reflected underlying industrial realities. As a declining coalfield marked by poor working conditions, low wages, and an employer elite seemingly indifferent to the needs of its workforce, Lancashire appeared a natural setting for fundamental social division. Reviewing the county's mining history to 1912, the Liberal *Daily News* noted a succession of disputes, the cumulative effect of which was 'an estrangement between masters and men such as exists nowhere else except in South Wales'.[5] If the evidence calls into question the accuracy both of this observation and broader accounts of class alienation, the facts of decline at least are incontestable. The fourth largest field in terms of output in 1850, Lancashire ceded precedence to faster growing areas over subsequent decades. From 1907, however, decline was no longer merely comparative. Over the following quarter century, the annual level of output was halved, from 26.2 million to 13.2 million tons. Employment figures plotted a similar course from 115,475 in 1920 to 66,264 in 1932. Marketing agreements arrested the pace of such losses after 1930.[6] By then, however, Lancashire was reconciled to a diminished economic role.

Yet decline, rather than acting as a catalyst for social conflict, provided the context for lasting industrial accord. Throughout the period, both sides of industry were acutely sensitive to Lancashire's growing competitive problems. Although 80 per cent of coal raised was marketed locally, the county's pits were unable to satisfy demand. In meeting the needs of domestic and industrial consumers, fuel was imported from more productive fields to the east. Awareness of comparative disadvantage, heightened by the actions of one local cooperative society which invited its members to 'Try our Selected Yorkshire Best, it will certainly please you', hampered the development of conciliation arrangements within the county.[7] Owners were reluctant to conclude agreements which would further weaken their hold on the regional market. National bargaining machinery became a necessary precondition for the introduction of joint negotiating procedures in Lancashire. Bodies such as the Federated Districts Board, which from 1888 regulated wage movements across Lancashire, Yorkshire, and the Midland counties, provided some security against competitive undercutting. Union officials were equally convinced of the need for interdistrict cooperation. Experience in the 1880s indicated that strike action would only be effective if coordinated nationally, eliminating alternative sources of supply. Lancashire's representatives thus became convinced advocates of the 'nationalisation' of industrial politics through the MFGB and the Federated Districts' Board.[8]

The virtues of national regulation were confirmed by the experience of war from 1914. Consistent full-time working and the pooling of 'surplus' profits offered some insulation against the effects of long term decline and provided the essential context for an accommodation of interests within the county. In October 1915 it was agreed that differences left unresolved by joint negotiation should be subject to independent, binding arbitration. This unprecedented surrender of the strike weapon had little practical effect. No recourse was had to third party arbitration in the years that followed. Nevertheless the agreement exemplified the absence of conflict across the coalfield from 1914. Stephen Walsh was guilty of only slight exaggeration in claiming that 'the only body of miners that had worked without a break during the war was Lancashire and Cheshire'.[9] In retrospect, the war came to be regarded as a period of 'Augustan Peace' down Lancashire's mines, marked by a 'complete smoothness and freedom from disputes'. The contrast with South Wales, where evidence of political radicalisation occasioned acute government concern, was obvious.[10]

The unity of purpose so evident in wartime survived the armistice. Although the county's joint committee, representing owners and miners, registered an 'emphatic protest' against decontrol, the objections of a declining inland field carried little weight in the formulation of national policy. The reversion to district settlements inaugurated a period of limited profitability and declining wages across Lancashire. Nevertheless cooperation endured. At the end of 1921, the joint committee voted to apply money from the Sankey Welfare Fund, raised by a penny per ton impost on coal sales, to augment the wages of low paid workers. The Central Welfare Committee vetoed the proposal, adjudicating that it constituted an improper use of the fund. In its place, the county introduced a system of minimum shift payments for all miners on day wages.[11] Yet if agreement reigned within the county, Lancashire acquired a reputation for industrial radicalism at the national level. Few matched the county's representatives in the determination with which they opposed trends in mining politics during the 1920s. Alone among the major fields, Lancashire opposed a return to work on the conditions agreed in June 1921. Five years later, the county's only ally in rejecting compromise at the end of the seven month dispute was South Wales. Nevertheless a radical stance in national politics, driven by concern over the county's increasingly precarious economic position, failed accurately to reflect feeling within the coalfield where the tone remained more one of compromise than of conflict. Throughout the 1920s, monthly joint committee meetings provided an effective forum for the resolution of points of dispute. As a measure of the discipline secured within the trade, the refusal of one firm to observe joint agreements on meal breaks for surface workers in 1927 was considered as being without precedent.[12] Few pit stoppages occurred, so that, contrary to the claims of the *Daily News'* correspondent, the Lancashire miner emerges from the institutional record an industrial moderate whose propensity to strike was no greater than that of colliers in the prosperous East Midlands.[13]

Of course this conveys only a partial truth. Conditions underground provided a potential source of friction throughout, with the issue of control a persistent cause for concern. Managerial spokesmen regularly testified to the problems encountered in ensuring discipline within the pit. Conditions at the coal face were particularly troublesome. Hewers, responsible both for undercutting the coal and for the maintenance and safety of their section of face, appeared free to determine the pace and hours of work. For much of the period, owners relied on the wage mechanism as the most effective guarantee of consistency of effort. Piece rate payments sought to reconcile the interests of owners, anxious to guard against 'ca' canny' tactics, and miners, endeavouring to secure an adequate income without undue expenditure of effort. Difficult working conditions, frequently encountered given Lancashire's variable geology, often rendered such differences irreconcilable. In such circumstances, the colliers' most likely sanction was not strike action but mobility. The social context facilitated this response. As the Wigan colliery director, George Caldwell, observed, whereas miners in remote settlements were dependent on their local pit for work, 'in West Lancashire, where there are plenty of houses ..., they ship about from one house to another and from one colliery to another, there being so many collieries in the same neighbourhood, they change about as often as two or three times sometimes in a week'.[14] It remains impossible precisely to quantify the extent of voluntary mobility, particularly as over time the numbers involved were swollen by the enforced movement of men thrown out of work through pit closures. Nevertheless its significance is suggested by repeated managerial protests at the tendency for miners to move between pits, seeking the most 'comfortable' places. The capacity of employers to control colliery development was often compromised. Problems were encountered in staffing difficult workplaces, while attempts to inaugurate a second cutting shift after 1921 were frustrated.[15]

This point had important implications for trade union development also. If mobility constituted the most characteristic form of labour protest across the Lancashire coalfield, it proceeded for the most part outside union control. Although the LCMF operated a system of 'clearances', enabling miners to move between branches without affecting their right to membership, it was an arrangement utilised by only a small minority. A recruitment campaign at pits across Leigh and St Helens in the mid-1920s, revealed over 600 colliers who had previously worked elsewhere; fewer than one-third had made use of clearances.[16] The roots of this less than wholehearted commitment to the Federation can be traced to wider social conditions. High rates of labour turnover loosened the tie between home and work, the basis of that close sense of community detected in many other coalfields. Many Lancashire collieries drew manpower from well beyond their immediate area. The 344 miners killed in the explosion at the Hulton Colliery Co., Ltd's No.3 Bank (or Pretoria) Pit, near Westhoughton in December 1910, resided in 14 separate towns and townships.

The effects of this dispersal carried over into the home. It was not unusual for recruitment to extend beyond the family tie, as employment patterns reconstructed from compensation returns relating to each Pretoria victim indicate. Of 76 unmarried miners for whom full information was available, only 23 had fathers working at the same pit. Examples of cross-company employment were numerous. The father of James Edward Hogan, a haulage hand at the Pretoria, was employed at Ramsden's Collieries in Tyldesley, while an elder brother worked at the Fletcher, Burrows complex of pits in Atherton. The kinship tie was no more evident underground. Several work teams at the Pretoria (comprising two or three hewers to one drawer) included members from different townships.[17] Work was only one of several factors shaping social and political developments across the coalfield.

The task of union organisers, engendering unity based on a shared commitment to agreed industrial and political goals, was rendered far from straightforward. Reflecting the coalfield's social complexities, miners were originally organised in district associations, in which branch membership was determined by ties of residence rather than of employment. Meetings brought together colliers working at different pits under separate ownerships. In this way, the union sought to integrate the worlds of work, family and neighbourhood. The emergence of a permanent county organisation from 1881 presaged a fundamental re-ordering of union structures whereby district associations would be dissolved, executive authority would be centred at county level, and the pit would become the basic unit of branch administration. If such changes could be justified on grounds of efficiency, by eliminating intermediate levels of authority and by removing the confusion caused when a colliery located in one district drew much of its labour from another, their implications for the Federation's industrial and political influence were less obviously favourable.[18] For many, union organisation appeared increasingly out of step with wider social realities. Opponents of reform argued that pit-lodge meetings would be inaccessible to miners who lived some distance from their place of work. Furthermore, with members of the same household dispersed across several branches, the lodge would be denied the important socialising influence of the family. Interdistrict comparisons indicate the problems which flowed from this. While commissioners inquiring into the causes of industrial unrest in 1917, found lodges of the South Wales Miners' Federation to be 'centres of social and political activity more potent perhaps than any other ... in the community', the LCMF struggled throughout against non-membership and rank and file indifference.[19]

Levels of allegiance, as measured by the proportion of the county workforce paying to the Federation, fluctuated markedly over the period. Pre-war membership levels peaked in 1908, at 76 per cent of eligible miners. Within two years, poor trading conditions had reduced that figure by a quarter. Full-time working and cooperation from owners under the agreement of October 1915 virtually eliminated non-membership in the months immediately before and after the armistice. However decontrol from April 1921 heralded renewed losses. Although aggregate workforce levels remained substantially unaltered over the following two years, Federation membership fell by 40 per cent. From that point, at least a quarter of all miners remained outside the LCMF.[20] In 1923, national union officials contrasted Lancashire's aggressive stand against existing wage agreements with the failure to secure wholehearted rank and file support. In response, the LCMF president, Thomas Greenall, pointed to the absence of effective community sanctions within the county: 'in Northumberland and Durham, the men live in villages, purely mining villages, and if a man does not pay, every man, woman, and child knows about it, and he does not get any peace. In Lancashire, a man may live miles away from the place where he works'.[21]

The problem went beyond non-membership, however. Low levels of participation suggest that the commitment of union members as a whole was slight. In November 1924, the delegate from Worsley Mesnes, near Wigan, warned the Federation's monthly conference that branch meetings were attended by 'not five per cent' of members. It was not an unreasonable estimate. Pit-head meetings, called to press for a uniform wage list at all collieries owned by the Wigan Coal and Iron Co., Ltd, in 1903, attracted an attendance of 200 out of a workforce of 10,000.[22] Such indifference reflected, in part, the absence of a clear supportive role for the Federation. Whereas union officials in areas such as County Durham administered various friendly benefits, support from county funds in Lancashire was limited to strike and victimisation cases. Few branches possessed the means to elaborate on this basic provision; most opted to divide their funds at the end of each year. Alternative sources of relief were utilised. In cases of accident or death, families sought assistance from funds administered jointly by miners' and owners' representatives. Union members dismissed attempts to transform the Federation into 'a kind of Savings Club'. The LCMF's own accident benefit scheme, launched in 1898, failed to secure the support of more than a small and diminishing proportion of the county workforce.[23] The financial, organisational, and structural weaknesses of trade unionism suggest the need to look beyond the institutional record in seeking to reconstruct the values and associations which shaped Lancastrian pit society.

Consideration of the role of industrial elites assists in clarifying such points. Lancastrian owners constituted a regionally different-iated elite. Of the 339 colliery directors active in the mid-1920s for whom place of residence could be established, over three-quarters lived within the region. Reflecting this local identification, many applied their wealth to the benefit of surrounding communities, donating land for church and school building. Such endowments, not directly connected with work, gave expression to a broad moral sensibility and were informed more by religious ideas of stewardship than by cruder calculations of 'social control'. Local circumstances placed decisive limits on the extent of proprietorial initiatives. For example, abundant manpower reserves in neighbouring towns discouraged investment in company housing. In the few cases where accommodation was provided, tenancies were rarely restricted to company employees. In the 1920s, dwellings owned by the Sutton Manor Colliery Co., Ltd, near St Helens, were occupied by miners employed elsewhere. The only recorded instance of evictions from company property occurred in the exceptional circumstances of manpower shortage in wartime.[24] The ready supply of hands also discouraged experiments in welfare capitalism. Investment in workplace amenities (such as canteens and recreation grounds) remained, for the most part, small scale and piecemeal. Financial difficulties, although considerable, were not a crucial constraint on policy, given that money was made available from the Sankey Welfare Fund. However the tendency for miners to reside in towns at some distance from their place of work discouraged expenditure on facilities designed to centre social functions arounds the pit. As a result, the first instalment of the Sankey Fund was applied to other purposes: the construction of a County Convalescent Home on Blackpool's North Shore.[25]

A more important area of proprietorial activity was the administration of accident relief benefits. The everyday dangers of pit work reiterated the need for some provision against loss of earnings through death or disablement. In the Edwardian period, reportable, non-fatal accidents, involving an absence from work in excess of seven days, affected one in five of the underground workforce each year. Assistance in these cases was provided by a variety of agencies. Across southern and western areas of the coalfield, benefits were administered by the Lancashire and Cheshire Miners' Permanent Relief Society. Elsewhere, companies operated independent schemes. All had certain features in common. Employers were involved in relief administration at all levels. Business was transacted through colliery offices, contributions being deducted from wage packets. Owners also exercised executive authority, alongside elected workmen's representatives.[26] Initially, membership of benefit schemes was compulsory. Miners were obliged to contract out of the Employers' Liability Act of 1881, in return for which proprietorial donations to society funds were fixed at between 10 and 25 per cent of total contributions. This arrangement obtained until the passage of workmen's compensation legislation in 1897. Yet although contracting out ceased from that date, relief structures endured. Society benefits now supplemented compensation awards, being paid in the first two weeks of disablement, a period not covered by the act, and thereafter at a level sufficient to guarantee claimants a weekly income of 10 shillings. More importantly, coalowners retained their executive roles even though aggregate donations, which had averaged £12,000 a year before 1897, fell to a mere £63 by 1905.[27]

Federation officials criticised such arrangements, arguing that a system of relief based on deductions from wages constituted a powerful instrument of proprietorial influence. However there is little evidence that the societies' survival owed much, if anything, to compulsion. Miners had endorsed the principle of joint administration of benefits in a series of ballots in 1897-8. What is more, loyalty to the Lancashire and Cheshire Society held firm despite the emergence of a separate agency under union control. Membership losses immediately following the ending of contracting out were reversed in the decade to 1914. Thereafter, allowing for the effects of pit closures, the society continued to prosper. An average membership of 60,272 in 1913 represented 56 per cent of the county workforce. By contrast, 48,814 subscribers in 1930 constituted 65 per cent of a reduced constituency.[28] Such consistency reflected a widespread belief, validated by practical experience, that the use of company offices to collect contributions and distribute benefits offered the most economical method of relief. In the first decade of operations under the Compensation Act, administrative costs absorbed between 3 and 8 per cent of contributions. This compared with managerial reserves of 15 and 35 per cent maintained by a local friendly society order, the Bolton Unity of Oddfellows, and the Prudential Assurance Co., respectively. Such a differential was of particular importance given the actuarial adjustments required to reflect the risks involved in working underground. The Worsley and Walkden Moor Friendly Society, a sick fund for colliers employed by the Bridgewater Trust, near Manchester, was obliged to operate with a reserve 25 per cent in excess of average life estimates to ensure solvency. With the future of the trust in doubt in 1903, the society had faced dissolution. Only reconstitution of the trust under the Third Earl of Ellesmere, which ensured that relief arrangements would continue, enabled the society to survive.[29] Miners were thus reluctant to jettison a system which maximised benefits, and allowed funds to accumulate regardless of trade fluctuations. The issue of democratic control which so exercised Federation officials appeared of marginal concern to the rank and file. On this, as on other points, trade union arguments provide an unreliable guide to the outlook of the membership as a whole.

The work of relief societies offers the broader perspective required to capture the internal dynamics of Lancashire colliery society. All claimants to relief were subject to close supervision, an approach driven by concern that a system of payments supplementing basic benefits would reduce incentives to work. There was more to this than a narrow desire to secure financial economies. Society rules embodied a deeper moral imperative. The Atherton Collieries Sick and Burial Society penalised those suspected of 'any unlawful practice or evil course of life ... or of gross or immoral conduct'.[30] Respectability was particularly required of women widowed by pit accidents, who were enjoined to remain chaste and behave 'with becoming propriety'.[31] The supervision required to regulate personal conduct operated at several levels. In addition to the provision of medical certificates as proof of continued inability to work, occasional visits were made to claimants' homes by society stewards, many of whom were working colliers. Much the most effective resource at the societies' command, however, was the internal discipline of working class neighbourhoods. A particular instance illustrates the point. In 1924, officials of the Lancashire and Cheshire Society investigated claims that Ada H., widowed by the Pretoria Pit disaster, was associating with a married man. When confronted on the point, Ada proved unrepentant and 'proceeded to say that there are others round about doing the same as she had been doing, and she mentioned the name of Mrs Albert H. ... and then added quickly "but I mustn't say any more"'.[32] Unfortunately for Ada, not all were as reticent as she. Information from neighbours and the estranged wife's family enabled officials to collate a detailed catalogue of her irregularities, ranging from her drunken appearance at Bolton's New Year fair, to her absence from work during the Blackpool carnival of 1923. As a result of this information from neighbours, Ada was judged to have forfeited her right to benefit.[33]

Several points emerge from this. Firstly, relief administration rested on a coincidence of interests whereby neighbourhood values were mobilised to assist employers in their efforts to check peculation and demoralisation. A capacity for social cooperation is indicated, a feature of local society which a narrow concentration on trade union rhetoric and the practical functioning of the industrial relations system serves to obscure. Yet cooperation clearly had its limits. Rather than upholding elite values, the neighbourhood largely acted in defence of its own precepts. Society records materially assist in de-crypting the moral code by which life in densely populated, working class districts was regulated. 'Neighbourliness' involved more than a readiness to cooperate in ameliorating distress, it also demanded conformity to a common standard of behaviour, deviation from which, through sexual promiscuity or the misuse of funds to which all had contributed, could result in the isolation and ostracism of suspected individuals.

Central to the neighbourhood's moral sense was the family, the most important source of moral and material support in working class life. In analysing kinship links, an immediate contrast presents itself. Abundant employment opportunities across the bulk of the Lancashire coalfield generated household economies fundamentally at variance from those encountered in more 'traditional' colliery societies. In the Durham mining township of Stanley, surveyed by Bowley and Burnett-Hurst in 1913, 60 per cent of households subsisted on one, male wage. Barely 6 per cent of local women were employed outside the home. In Lancashire, the potential for supplementary contributions was much greater. Over 45 per cent of families affected by the Pretoria Pit disaster drew on three or more sources of income each. So although individual shift earnings in Lancashire were among the lowest in the country, the multiple nature of household incomes ensured most families a comfortable sufficiency over at least part of their life course. To cite one, admittedly extreme, example, 9 of the 12 members of the Gerrard family of Westhoughton were in work in 1910, bringing home a combined wage of £6 3s a week.[34] The capacity to render financial assistance was considerable. Support frequently extended well beyond the conjugal household and gained from a readiness to adapt residential arrangements to changing circumstances. For dependent parents, co-residence with married children offered the most effective guarantee against impoverishment in old age, even after the introduction of state pensions in 1908. Additional support, both in money and in kind, was provided by non-resident children. Each week during 1910, William Potter, a Westhoughton collier with six children of his own to maintain, sent 3s 6d along with food to his parents, both of whom lived with his sister in Leigh; his actions were not unusual.[35]

Such behaviour owed little to calculations of individual gain. Rather it conveyed a powerful moral sense. Commitments were often undertaken at great personal cost. Daughters, in particular, were frequently called upon to give up work to care for an elderly or infirm relative. The sacrifice involved was described in a report prepared by the secretary of the Lancashire and Cheshire Miners' Permanent Relief Society in 1927, which summarised the problems faced by women who were 'approaching middle age, and partly owing to ... attention required by their mothers, their present and future prospects have been greatly injured either as regards work, and in other ways such as marriage'.[36] A broader observation derives from this. High levels of female involvement in paid employment were recorded across much of the coalfield. Within the Pretoria sample, almost one-third of women of working age were wage earners. Yet women's perceptions of their own social role appeared broadly unaffected by this experience. For the majority, full-time work beyond the home ceased on marriage or the birth of their first child. Even across the central part of the coalfield, where cotton and coal were both sizeable employers, only between 10 and 15 per cent of wives were recorded as being in waged work by the census.[37] However economically active before marriage, women's aspirations thereafter centred on the home and a marital relationship in which maternal skills, including the management of household resources and child-rearing, would complement the husband's wage earning role. As custodians of neighbourhood values, women were often fierce critics of those whose economic ambitions were thought to derogate from their 'natural' sphere as mothers and managers of the family purse.[38] The family's place at the moral centre of working class life was confirmed.

This point also assists an understanding of the survival of national identities across the coalfield. Irish migrants gained their first experience of work underground as contractors' men. Employed in gangs of up to 20, they were hired by sub-contractors, many of whom were fellow nationals, to undertake repair work once the main day shift had ended. Separate recruitment networks ensured that, to an extent, national differences were reproduced underground. At least 50 Irish were among the 75 miners killed in the explosion at the Maypole Colliery at Abram, near Wigan, in August 1908, which occurred one hour into the afternoon turn.[39] However, the absence of craft controls on labour dispositions within the pit ensured that, with the passage of time, occupational assimilation became the norm. The 26 victims of the Pretoria Pit disaster associated with the Catholic Mission of the Sacred Heart included 21 face workers. Yet although no longer differentiated by work, a distinct Irish identity endured, sustained by residential segregation and extensive family ties and given material form by various national and denominational organisations operating within the neighbourhood.[40]

A sense of 'community', that is of associations and values held in common, is revealed, structured more around ties of kinship and neighbourhood, than around the solidarities of work. The progress of political change across the coalfield endorses the point. For much of the nineteenth century, elections, particularly in west Lancashire, had revolved around religious and national divisions. Violence between English and Irish colliers had marked contests in Wigan in the 1880s. From that date, although such differences endured, they rarely acquired the force which so disfigured the politics of west coast ports and the Scottish coalfield. Various factors contributed to this trend. Firstly, the pace of migration slackened over time, reducing the number of Irish-born within the region. Secondly, Ulster orangeism was of limited significance: most Irish miners came from western agricultural counties, more especially Mayo and Leitrim. Thirdly, across large parts of the coalfield, patrician political elites sought to contain national animosities, a policy which owed much to the fourth factor: west Lancashire's strong recusant tradition, maintained by local catholic gentry.[41] In such circumstances, Conservatives were circumspect about playing the orange card. Rather, encouraged by the presence of a large English catholic community, they projected an alliance between anglicans and catholics, based on shared religious concerns. In Wigan, political realignment was precipitated by the question of voluntary education, a potent issue given the lack of Board school provision locally. The 1902 Education Act exposed fundamental differences between former nonconformist and catholic allies, fatally weakening Liberal Party organisation within the borough. After 1906, across much of west Lancashire, the task of opposing the Conservatives passed to a labour movement with strong links with mining unionism.[42]

The LCMF's decision to affiliate to the LRC in 1903 was a pragmatic response to political divisions which permeated the coalfield. Wigan and Leigh, both constituencies with large mining electorates, were Conservative and Liberal strongholds respectively before 1900. Party divisions were also apparent on the Federation executive and among the rank and file. The death roll at the Pretoria in 1910, included members of local Conservative and Reform Clubs, as well as ILP activists.[43] In such circumstances, extended attempts at Lib-Lab cooperation were impracticable. Instead, through a strict policy of 'independence', prohibiting agreements with either of the established parties, Labour would come to define a distinct political interest, enabling Federation members to set established allegiances aside in favour of industrial unity.[44] However developments after 1906 ensured that attempts to restructure loyalties would be far from straightforward.

Labour's emergence as the dominant 'progressive' force signalled no immediate change in the terms of political debate. Rather continued interest in the education issue kept religion at the forefront of local politics throughout the Edwardian period. Nevertheless the return of Home Rule to the national electoral agenda revealed underlying tensions in the anglican-catholic alliance. At the first general election of 1910, the catholic vote split along national lines: while the English remained loyal in their support for voluntary education, United Irish League branches in Wigan and the neighbouring constituency of Ince declared for the Labour candidates, Henry Twist and Stephen Walsh, both of whom were sponsored by the LCMF. From that point, catholic unity both at local and national elections proved elusive. The momentum behind Labour's advance slackened, however, in the second election of 1910. Across west Lancashire the party's share of the poll fell. Nowhere was this decline more marked than in Wigan where victory in January was followed by defeat in December. Analysis of the causes of this defeat reveal much about the nature of popular politics in this period. For the chairman of the Wigan LRC, defeat occurred in spite of 'the Irish ... who were patriots more than anything else, and denominationalists second, and who, as they knew from the turning out of the boxes had so gallantly, almost unanimously, gone in favour of their comrade'.[45] However miners in the division had deserted Twist. Various explanations were adduced to account for the change, from the fall in earnings under the Eight Hours Act, a reform long advocated by the Federation, and the exercise of employer influence at the polls, to organisational deficiencies, exposed by injunctions prohibiting the use of union funds for political purposes. None adequately explains Labour's defeat. The effects of the Eight Hours Act were no greater in December than they had been in January, while constraints on proprietorial authority within and beyond the pit suggest that employers were unable significantly to affect voting behaviour. Equally the effect of any legal challenge to electoral activity was more than offset by the work of allied organisations such as the United Irish League and the Lancashire and Cheshire Liberal Federation.[46] For many, however, dependence on external agencies exemplified Labour's increasing identification with 'Progressive' forces. The ideal of 'independence' appeared to have been fundamentally compromised. In January 1910 both Twist and Walsh had refused to speak in support of Thomas Greenall's candidature in a three-cornered contest in Leigh. Their apparent concern to avoid offending Liberal sensibilities led branch delegates to claim that they had 'wandered from the principles of labour'.[47] Instead of promoting a distinct electoral interest, Labour had become identified with one strand of established partisan allegiances. In December 1910, therefore, the mining vote was disposed along traditional, religious, rather than occupational lines.

Corroboration of this point can be found in a survey of Wigan voters, undertaken by the local Constitutional Association in July 1914, which recorded the political and religious affiliations of each householder. Supplementing this information with occupational data derived from local directories, the mining vote was reconstructed in two wards: St Catharine, which had the largest proportion of heads of household employed in mining and which regularly returned a Conservative in Edwardian council elections; and Victoria, an inner ward, won consistently by Labour from 1912. In each case, attention was confined to the anti-Conservative vote, reflecting the views of householders sufficiently determined to give 'unfavourable' responses to questions, and so invite prolonged debate on the doorstep. In St

Catharine, 130 out of the 370 miners traced voiced opposition to the Conservatives; 84, or almost two-thirds, were catholics or nonconformists. In Victoria, the anti-Conservative vote was in the majority, accounting for 97 out of 152 colliers for whom an allegiance could be established. Almost three-quarters were catholics or nonconformists, predominantly the former. Support for Labour was thus denominationally consistent across two wards with contrasting political traditions.[48] Given that the returns betray their origins by consistently overstating the extent of Conservative support, such results cannot be regarded as definitive. Nevertheless aggregate polling data corroborate the impressions they convey. Throughout the period Conservatism was weakest in wards with sizeable catholic electorates (St George; St Patrick; Victoria). By contrast, the Party's candidates were still capable of winning the mining district of St Catharine well into the 1920s.[49] It is clear that the miners had yet to swing unequivocally behind the Labour Party.

Indeed in 1916, the LCMF remained sufficiently uncertain of the loyalty of Wigan's colliers to vote against contesting the seat at future elections. That decision was reversed in the following year, a change prompted not by political radicalisation in wartime, nor by the impending extension of the franchise, but by an alteration in constituency boundaries. From 1918 the township of Pemberton would be incorporated into the Wigan parliamentary borough. A colliery district in which almost 60 per cent of occupied males worked down the pit, Pemberton also had strong Lib-Lab traditions, sustained by a sizeable nonconformist population. A limited catholic presence blunted the force of religious controversies within the township. Federation officials were sufficiently confident of success on the new boundaries to recommend contesting the seat at the next election. Events justified their optimism. Labour won Wigan in 1918, retaining the seat through the 1920s, with between 56 and 58 per cent of the popular vote.[50] Yet even then traditional allegiances were not wholly eradicated. As the first wave of Labour's advance ebbed in the early 1930s, support held up best where deeper loyalties than those based on work alone were mobilised. Across west Lancashire, the party's most reliable constituency remained not the miners, but the catholic Irish, for whom the associations of class, family and neighbourhood broadly coincided.[51] Elsewhere, ethnic and cultural more than occupational factors remained the prime determinants of political developments in this period. The Labour Party's attempt to articulate a politicised consciousness drawing on the solidarities of workplace and trade union lodge enjoyed fitful success, at best.

Labour's difficulties reflected broader factors at work within the coalfield. In contrast to most other areas, the structuring of community ties around a single place of work was lacking. Instead occupational identities were refracted through a complex urban society in which domestic and industrial lives often occupied separate spheres. If anything, over time the difference between home and work became more marked as miners sought jobs for their children beyond the pit. In this context, 'conventional' approaches to mining history, in which analysis centres on the work experience and on the internal dynamics of labour organisations, fail to illuminate the broader realities of social and political life. The trade union perspective is particularly deficient in this regard, as labour protest across the coalfield more often assumed individual than collective form, while involvement in Federation affairs was confined to a small number of committed activists. An appreciation of the values underlying Lancastrian mining society requires that attention be directed not only at the workplace, but also at the world of family and neighbourhood. Particular facets of working class life thereby acquire a new prominence. Thus it appears that declining levels of attendance and the rise of alternative secular agencies failed significantly to diminish the influence of organised religion. The church remained both a leading source of cultural and educational provision, and the principal focus for political loyalties across much of the coalfield. Its continued importance owed much to the strength of the kinship tie. Throughout the period, the family remained the primary agent of moral and material support in working class life. If anything, its influence in this respect increased as the period progressed. In the interwar years the economic uncertainties induced by industrial decline delayed departures from the parental home and encouraged extended recourse to co-residence.[52] Yet the role of kin did not extend to the workplace, where the evidence indicates that direct familial employment was experienced by a steadily decreasing minority of Lancashire's miners. So while ethnic, religious and, the electoral record suggests, political allegiances drew strongly on the ties of family and neighbourhood, occupational identities appear to have been altogether more marginal to the broader pattern of social development.   Any attempt fully to comprehend the values and associations on which Lancastrian mining society was constructed should therefore take the home rather than the pit as its starting point.

Notes

Place of publication is London unless otherwise stated.

1.   *Census of England and Wales, 1911*, vol. 10, Occupations and Industries, Table 15; W.J. Naughton, *On the Pig's Back: an autobiographical excursion* (Oxford, 1987), p. 130, and *Saintly Billy: a catholic boyhood* (Oxford, 1988), p. 1.

2.   *Reports of HM Inspectors of Mines for 1929* (1930), 'North Western Division', p. 40; S.J. Chapman and W. Abbott, 'The tendency of children to enter their fathers' trade', *Journal of the Royal Statistical Society*, vol. 76, 1912-13, p. 600; John Rylands University Library Manchester, BCA/13/2/33, Bolton Operative Spinners' Provincial Association General Correspondence, Report of Conference on Juvenile Employment, 19 July 1928.

3.   D. Gilbert, *Class, Community and Collective Action: social change in two British coalfields, 1850-1926* (Oxford, 1992), pp. 9-53.

4.   *Census of England and Wales, 1911*, vol. 10, Occupations and Industries, Table 13; *Catholic Family Annual and Almanac for the Diocese of Liverpool* (Liverpool, 1886), pp. 48, 78; Board of Trade, *An Industrial Survey of the Lancashire Area* (1932), p. 164.

5.   Cited in R. Challinor, *The Lancashire and Cheshire Miners* (Newcastle upon Tyne, 1972), p. 235.

6.   R. Church, *The History of the British Coal Industry, volume 3, 1830-1913: Victorian pre-eminence* (Oxford, 1986), p. 3; *Mines Inspector's Report for the Manchester and Ireland District* (Parliamentary Papers, 1908, XIX), p. 6; *Report for the Liverpool and North Wales District* (PP 1908, XIX), p. 7; *Reports of HM Inspectors of Mines for 1932* (1933), 'North Western Division', p. 6; B.E. Supple, *The History of the British Coal Industry, volume 4, 1913-1946: the political economy of decline* (Oxford, 1987), pp. 210-11, 271-80.

7.   National Union of Mineworkers, North-Western Area Headquarters, Leigh, Lancashire and Cheshire Miners' Federation Records (hereafter LCMF), Minutes of Monthly Conference, 23 December 1911; *Departmental Committee into Conditions Prevailing in the Coal Mining*

Industry Due to the War, Minutes of Evidence (PP 1914-16, XXVIII), q. 2510.

8. *Report on Strikes and Lock-outs in 1909* (PP 1910, LVIII), pp. 95-6; I.F. Scott, 'The Lancashire and Cheshire Miners' Federation, 1910-14', unpublished DPhil thesis, University of York, 1977, pp. 320-1; LCMF Minutes of Special Conference, 15 December 1906.

9. LCMF Minutes of Special Conference, 23 November 1918; *Second Report of Departmental Committee into Conditions Prevailing in the Coal Mining Industry Due to the War* (PP 1914-16, XXVIII), Appendix C, p. 33.

10. LCMF Minutes of Joint Committee, 17 December 1923; *Commission of Enquiry into Industrial Unrest, No. 7 Division, Wales, including Monmouthshire* (PP 1917-18, XV), par. 22.

11. LCMF Minutes of Joint Committee, 10 January 1921, 13 March 1922; Minutes of Monthly Conference, 10 December 1921; *Labour Gazette*, vol. 30, 1922 , p. 377.

12. *Bolton Journal and Guardian*, 1 July 1921; LCMF Minutes of Adjourned Special Conference, 17 November 1926; Minutes of Monthly Conference, 26 March 1927.

13. R.A. Church, 'Edwardian labour unrest and coalfield militancy, 1880-1914', *Historical Journal*, vol. 30, 1987, p. 856; *Labour Gazette*, vols 27-40, 1919-32.

14. *Royal Commission on Labour, Minutes of Evidence before Group A* (PP 1892, XXXIV), q. 6105 (Caldwell); *Minutes of Evidence before Departmental Committee into Eight Hour Day* (PP 1907, XV), qq. 5157, 6460.

15. *Minutes of Evidence before Departmental Committee into Eight Hour Day* (PP 1907, XV), qq. 5182, 5287; LCMF Minutes of Executive Committee, 23 January 1926; Lancashire Record Office, Preston (hereafter LRO), NCWi 7/3, Wigan Coal and Iron Co., Ltd, Clock Face Colliery, Monthly Reports, February 1924.

16. LCMF Minutes of Executive Committee, 13 September 1924-27 March 1926; Minutes of Monthly Conference, 31 December 1927.

17. Bolton Library Archives (hereafter BLA), ABHC/5/1-344, 145, Hulton Colliery Disaster Relief Fund (hereafter HRF), Personal Files, Compensation Statements and Report, 20 March 1911; LRO NCHu 9/2, Hulton Colliery Co., Ltd, Disaster Inquest transcript, qq. 2491-2, 2848, 3000.

18. T.R. Threlfall (ed.), *Lancashire Miners' Federation Official Programme of the Second Annual Miners' Demonstration* (Southport, 1890); LCMF, Minutes of Monthly Conference, 7 October 1905.

19. LCMF, Minutes of Monthly Conference, 8 September 1906;

Commission of Enquiry into Industrial Unrest, No. 7 Division, Wales, including Monmouthshire (PP 1917-18, XV), par. 17.

20. Scott, (thesis), Table S14; LCMF, Minutes of Annual Conference and Membership Returns, 8 January 1921, 6 January 1923.

21. LCMF, Minutes of Monthly Conference, 10 November 1923.

22. Ibid., 8 November 1924, 31 January 1903; *Wigan Coal and Iron Co., Ltd* (Altrincham, 1908).

23. *Royal Commission on Labour* (PP 1892, XXXIV), q. 8273; LCMF Minutes of Monthly Conference, 30 January 1904, 19 July, 16 August 1924; *Bolton Journal and Guardian*, 8 April 1921.

24. *Colliery Yearbook and Coal Trades' Directory* (1924 edn); G. Simm, *Richard Evans of Haydock: a study of a local family* (Newton-le-Willows, 1988), p. 49; *Bolton Journal and Guardian*, 11 June 1920; LCMF, Minutes of Monthly Conference, 10 April 1915; LCMF Minutes of Excutive Committee, 15 October 1927.

25. LCMF, Minutes of Monthly Conference, 16 September 1922; Mines Dept., *Eighth Report of the Miners' Welfare Fund* (1930), pp. 30-1; *Reports of HM Inspectors of Mines for 1923* (1924), 'Lancashire and North Wales Division', p. 41.

26. Non-fatal accident figures calculated from relevant Mines Inspectors' Reports for the period, 1908-13; Wigan Archives, Leigh (hereafter WA) D/DS 22, Lancashire and Cheshire Miners' Permanent Relief Society (hereafter PRS) Minutes of Board of Management, 30 October 1914; LRO NCC1 20/2, Cliviger Miners' Relief Society, *Rules*, pars 6, 8.

27. *Royal Commission on Labour* (PP 1892, XXXIV), qq. 5833, 5919-26, 8316-17; *Minutes of Evidence before Departmental Committee on the Truck Acts* (PP 1908, LIX), q.7789; WA D/DS 22, PRS Board of Management, 5 May, 1898; *Farnworth Weekly Journal*, 30 April, 2, 9 July 1898.

28. *Departmental Committee on the Truck Acts* (PP 1908, LIX), q. 7765; *Farnworth Weekly Journal*, 9, 23 July 1898, 24 March 1900; WA D/DS 22, PRS Finance Committee, May 1913-February 1914; *Bolton Journal and Guardian*, 1 May 1931.

29. WA D/DS 22, PRS Finance Committee, 17 December 1908; *Farnworth Weekly Journal*, 12 March 1898; *Bolton Unity Magazine*, April 1912, p. 161; P. Johnson, 'Credit and Thrift: a study of working-class household budget management in Britain, 1870-1939', unpublished DPhil thesis, University of Oxford, 1982, p. 31; LRO NCBw 25/3, Worsley and Walkden Moor Friendly Society, Quinquennial Valuation, 31 December 1900, pp. 4-5; NCBw 24/3, Draft Minutes, 19 September 1903; NCBw 26/12, *Rules*, par. 7.

30. WA D/DZ A83/6, *Rules of the Atherton Collieries Sick and Burial Society* (Atherton, 1930), par. 15; LRO NCBw 25/5, Worsley and Walkden Moor Friendly Society, Report, par. 13.
31. BLA ABHC/2/2, HRF, information supplied by the Permanent Relief Society, *Rules*, pars 31, 37.
32. BLA ABHC/5/136, HRF Personal Files, David Shaw to Hon. Sec., 3, 19 June 1924; in cases where the files disclose information of an intimate nature, I have respected the privacy of the families concerned by not giving names in full; LRO NCHa 9/1, *Rules of Rossendale Collieries Accident and Burial Society* (1925), par. 17; WA D/DS 22, PRS Visitation Committee, 24 November 1904.
33. BLA ABHC/5/136, HRF, Personal Files, pencilled note, 20 June 1924; Peace and Ellis, solicitors, to Hon. Sec., 27 May 1925.
34. A.L. Bowley and A.R. Burnett-Hurst, *Livelihood and Poverty* (1915), pp. 145-6; BLA ABHC/5/1-344, HRF, Personal Files, Compensation Statements.
35. BLA ABHC/5/248, HRF, Personal Files, note, n.d.; Father A.L. Coelenbier to J.T. Cooper, 19 April 1911.
36. BLA ABHC/3/11, HRF, General Correspondence, 'Notes on the Visitation of Widows', 17 August 1927, p. 4.
37. BLA ABHC/5/1-344, HRF, Personal Files, Compensation Statements; PP 1913, LXXVIII, Table 13.
38. Although financially secure, many Pretoria widows chose to re-marry. BLA ABHC/2/12, HRF, Correspondence and Cuttings, Memorandum on the Remarriage of Widows, 28 June 1917; B. Harrison, 'Class and gender in modern British labour history', *Past and Present*, no. 124, 1989, p. 142.
39. *Wigan Observer*, 25 August, 1 September 1908; PP 1908, XIX, 16.
40. Westhoughton Library, Pretoria Pit Disaster Pamphlet Box, Rev. A.L. Coelenbier, *Priest's Story of the Pit Disaster*, p. 4; *Mines Inspector's Report for Manchester and Ireland District* (PP 1911, XXXVI), pp. 28-9; *Bolton Journal and Guardian*, 24 March 1932; Naughton, *Saintly Billy*, pp. 12-21, 57-62.
41. *Evidence and Notes on Wigan Election Petition* (PP 1881, LXXIV), qq. 299-300, 2139-40; *Wigan Observer*, 7 November 1908; J. Vincent (ed.) *The Crawford Papers: the journals of David Lindsay, 27th Earl of Crawford and 10th Earl of Balcarres, 1871-1940* (Manchester, 1984), pp. ll-12; F.O. Blundell, *Old Catholic Lancashire*, vol. 2 (1938), p. 48.
42. *Wigan Examiner*, 26 October 1898, 17 October 1903, 27 October 1905.
43. J. Hill, 'The Lancashire miners, Thomas Greenall and the Labour

Party, 1900-6', *Transactions of the Historic Society of Lancashire and Cheshire*, vol. 130, 1981, pp. 116-17; D. Howell, *British Workers and the Independent Labour Party* (Manchester, 1983), pp. 29-32; *Bolton Evening News*, 22, 23 December 1910.

44. LCMF Minutes of Monthly Conference, 15 August 1903.
45. *Wigan Examiner*, 10 December 1910, 3 November 1908, 30 October 1909, 4, 25 January 1910; F.W.S. Craig (ed.) *British Parliamentary Election Results, 1885-1918* (1974), pp. 177, 209, 319, 323.
46. LCMF, Minutes of Monthly Conference, 21 October 1916; Scott, (thesis), p. 254; *Report of the Eleventh Annual Conference of the Labour Party* (1911), pp. 3, 68; *Labour Gazette*, vol. 28, 1910; Manchester Central Reference Library, M390/1/1, Lancashire and Cheshire Liberal Federation, Minutes of Executive Committee, 28 April 1909.
47. LCMF, Minutes of Annual Conference, 22 January 1910; Minutes of Adjourned Annual Conference, 5 February 1910; Minutes of Monthly Conference, 7 May 1910.
48. WA D/DZ A68/13-15 (St Catharine Ward) and D/DZ A68/26-7 (Victoria Ward), Wigan Constitutional Association, Survey, July 1914; *Seed's Directory of Wigan and District* (1st and 2nd eds, Preston, 1909, 1925).
49. In six contested elections between 1919 and 1924, Conservative candidates secured 51.5 per cent of the poll in St Catharine (*Wigan Examiner*).
50. *Census of England and Wales, 1901.* County of Lancaster, Table 35A; Wigan Reference Library, Biographical Cuttings Book, vol. 1, p. 232; LCMF, Minutes of Executive Committee, 19 August 1916; Minutes of Monthly Conference, 15 December 1917, 12 January 1918.
51. *Wigan Observer*, 4 November 1930.
52 BLA ABHC/5/299, HRF, Personal Files, Shaw to Hon. Sec., 27 July 1927, 30 July 1929.

CHAPTER NINE

The politics of labourism in the Yorkshire coalfield, 1926-1945

Andrew Taylor

Compared to other coalfields Yorkshire seems uninteresting. Syndicalism was unimportant. Communism had little impact until after the war, Spencerism never took root, and there were no splits. Unity and solidarity were maintained and conflict was contained within the Yorkshire Mine Workers' Association (YMWA) which was reflected in the ideological dominance of a staunch labourism.

Leadership culture and politics

Coalfield politics were a complex mixture of consensus and conflict. Management-union consensus was promoted by mutual acceptance, adherence to agreements, the insulation of industrial conflict from politics, and (despite opposition from some employers) coalfield regulation. Conflict was ever-present, and despite mutual recognition, was used to resolve disputes which, in the case of 1926, politicised industrial relations. A further element was the tension in the YMWA between union politics (the mineworkers' collective goals) and pit politics (work-based conflicts).[1]

Union politics tended towards cooperation, collaboration and compromise with employers and management in the wider interests of the membership. These interests were expressed by the union as an organisation and their defence and promotion depended on preserving and expanding the union's strength. Pit politics were a complex and volatile mixture of accommodation and conflict in which the branch was the linkage between the membership and union officials. Branch officials were often, therefore, in a complex situation as mediators between the demands of union and pit politics.

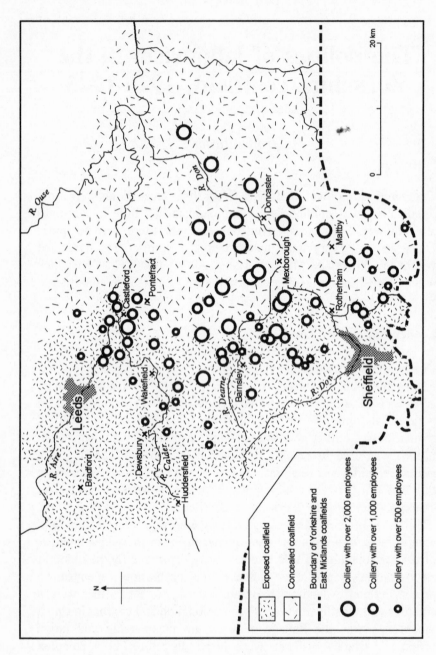

Map 6 The Yorkshire coalfield at nationalisation in 1947.

Colliery with over 2,000 employees
Colliery with over 1,000 employees
Colliery with over 500 employees

Exposed coalfield
Concealed coalfield
Boundary of Yorkshire and East Midlands coalfields

20 km
0

R. Ouse
R. Aire
R. Calder
R. Dearne
R. Don
R. Don

Leeds
Bradford
Dewsbury
Huddersfield
Wakefield
Castleford
Pontefract
Barnsley
Mexborough
Doncaster
Maltby
Rotherham
Sheffield

As officials of a wider organisation they were required to conform to its policies but they were elected by a membership which expected them to represent their specific interests to both pit management and the union in Barnsley.

Union and pit politics could, and did, clash. This produced unofficial strikes which were invariably condemned by union leaders as disruptive and unconstitutional; but the conflicts of pit politics could also be official, recognised by the YMWA as being in conformity with its wider goals. This challenges simplistic notions of grassroots militancy versus leadership conservatism, or rank and file spontaneity challenging, or being crushed by, the official bureaucracy. In the Yorkshire coalfield after 1926 union politics were dominant. It was only with the economic recovery of the later 1930s that the union/pit politics tension and unofficial conflict re-emerged. This tension became endemic during the war and was carried over into nationalisation. The management of the union/pit politics tension was the task of the branch and area leaderships; how they approached their task was a product of both current conditions and the dominant political culture in the Yorkshire coalfield.

The political culture of the Yorkshire coalfield was labourist.[2] Labourism was not a fundamental challenge to the political and industrial status quo; rather it sought recognition of working class aspirations. In Yorkshire labourism's roots lay deep in the coalfield's history and development, and had evolved via Lib-Labism into the parliamentary socialism of the post-1918 labour movement which underpinned the YMWA's activity in industry and community politics. The purpose of this activity was two-fold: to build order and stability in the pits and mining communities and thereby improve the material conditions of the mineworkers and their families. Achieving order and stability demanded the maximisation of the mineworkers' collective strength, which in turn required unity and solidarity behind the YMWA. This was particularly important after 1926. But labourism was neither conformist nor collaborationist; it could sustain serious political and industrial conflict.

The labourist tradition and its implementation was expressed in, and by, the YMWA leadership, in particular Joseph Jones, Joe Hall, and Herbert Smith. Jones was YMWA treasurer (1922-4) and general secretary (1924-38); he was a member of the MFGB executive (1924-31), vice-president (1932-3), and president (1933-8). Jones was a 'leader lost'. He was appointed to the Coal Mines Reorganisation Commission in 1931. When in 1938 this was reorganised as the Coal Commission, he was offered a permanent post. He wished to accept but when the YMWA insisted he could not be both a permanent official and a Commissioner, Jones joined the Commission and resigned from the union. He was a strategist. His central concern was how the YMWA could derive maximum benefit for the minimum sacrifice and he was particularly anxious that the union should derive the correct lessons from 1926. This undoubtedly made him cautious but no less effective, arguing the union should not engage in any precipitate action which might undermine the YMWA's solidarity and stability. Action, Jones argued, should be based on careful preparation, a reasonable case, and a willingness to compromise. Of the three Yorkshire leaders, Jones was the only ideological anti-Communist.

Hall was YMWA financial secretary (1925-38), president (1938-52) and a member of the MFGB executive (1931-44). As financial secretary, Hall was responsible for securing the union's recovery after 1926 and he worked closely with W.E. Jones (Joseph Jones' successor as general secretary) to modernise the YMWA's procedures in preparation for nationalisation. Hall was prominent in safety questions, being personally involved in several disaster rescue operations, notably at Barnburgh Main (April 1942). Like Jones his experience reinforced powerfully his conviction of the supremacy of the union and the importance of solidarity. Both Hall and Jones were deeply hostile to any unrest in the pits which was outside the Association's rules or which undermined its wider, long-term interests. Hall believed in leading from the front and that the membership would respond when given a clear lead.

Herbert Smith (YMWA president, 1906-38) was in the twilight of his career during our period of study, but was a major influence on Hall and Jones. Not only was he a living link with the YMWA's formative years, he represented a leadership style which was particularly identified with the Yorkshire miners. Smith's pugnacious, at times authoritarian, leadership style derived from his profound belief that the union was the servant of its members and that the members owed a reciprocal obligation of loyalty to the union. He had little time for abstractions, what mattered was the delivery of material gains to the mining communities. Passionately committed to the YMWA and the miners, Smith inspired great loyalty, but this passion also made him intolerant of dissent.

Jones, Hall and Smith, in common with their members, were deeply influenced by 1926 and its legacy provided the basis for their policies. All three were committed to the Labour Party and had extensive local government experience. Their labourism, and that of the YMWA, had five elements: first, the supremacy of the YMWA as the expression of the miners' interests. Second, the belief that the union's industrial and political purpose was to secure the best deal possible for the mineworkers and deliver substantial material benefits. Third, sectional interests had to be prevented from eroding union solidarity but these interests could find expression within the union in conformity with the YMWA's rules and policies. Fourth, that private ownership was flawed fundamentally and must be replaced by nationalisation. Finally, the union was committed totally to the Labour Party and the conviction that a Labour government was the answer to the mineworkers' predicament. This chapter examines two key aspects of labourism; the relationship between management and union and the YMWA's role in community politics. Finally, it considers the emergence of conflict between union and pit politics and the impact of the war on the politics of the Yorkshire coalfield.

The character of the Yorkshire coalfield

Yorkshire was a large and diverse coalfield which had undergone massive development between 1900 and 1914. After 1906 the coalfield expanded rapidly to the east of Doncaster and Rotherham to exploit the rich Barnsley seam at 2,600 feet. These very deep mines were owned by large corporations and were expensive to develop. Geographically isolated, and with poor working conditions (heat was a particular problem) they were unattractive to local labour. They often had cosmopolitan workforces of Scots, Geordies and, to some extent, Welsh, as well as locals. New pits in the Yorkshire coalfield were still opening, for example, Thorne (1925) and Upton (1928). These pits are often contrasted with the 'family owned' pits of West Yorkshire which were older and shallower, and drew their workforces from established communities. In 1910 Yorkshire produced 38.3 million tons of coal (14.5 per cent of

national output); in 1925 45.2 million tons (18.6 per cent); in 1937
45.1 million tons (19 per cent); and in 1947 38.2 million tons (20 per
cent). The Yorkshire coalfield mainly supplied the inland market
(industry, gas, electricity, domestic, and the railways); between 1927
and 1935 exports from the Yorkshire coalfield halved to about 7
million tons which gave it a degree of stability denied the export
regions. Many South Yorkshire collieries were part of steel
companies who used their mines to supply themselves with relatively
cheap coal.

The differences between the West and South Yorkshire coalfields
were narrowing. Production in West Yorkshire was becoming more
concentrated. In 1930, the West Yorkshire coalfield produced 12.5
million tons from 113 mines owned by 71 companies, but 90 per cent
of this output was produced by 41 mines owned by 18 companies,
and 48 per cent of output was produced by only 4 companies. In
South Yorkshire 41 pits owned by 72 companies produced 32.5
million tons; 90 per cent came from 28 companies owning 54 mines,
11 of which had outputs of more than one million tons and 7 were
approaching this figure. Convergence can also be seen in machine
mining: in 1926, 30 per cent of West Yorkshire's output was cut by
machine compared to 11 per cent in South Yorkshire (the national
figure was 22 per cent). By 1938, 51 per cent of output in both
coalfields was mechanised (compared with 59 cent nationally). In
both parts of the coalfield there were, or were to be created, massive
agglomerations of mining capital such as J. Currer Briggs, Son & Co
Ltd; Airedale Collieries Ltd; Staveley Coal & Iron Co Ltd;
Yorkshire Amalgamated Collieries; and the United Steel Companies
Ltd. Differences in attitude to the workforce cannot be clearly
discerned in the behaviour of the West and South Yorkshire
coalowners' organisations and as the decade wore on the two
coalfields became even more similar. This was due to concentration,
interlocking directorships, the closure of very small mines in the
West, and the unifying pressure exerted by the YMWA. The West
Yorkshire owners continued to argue they were at a cost disadvantage
to those in South Yorkshire which led the YMWA to see the West
Yorkshire owners as less amenable than their southern counterparts.

1926: the confirmation of an ethos

The Lib-Labs bequeathed to the YMWA an ethos which saw union solidarity and discipline as fundamental to the pursuit of collective goals. From the 1890s industrial relations in the Yorkshire coalfield were institutionalised, and whatever faults were found with the system, both sides accepted the principle of joint regulation. This system was not created nor maintained easily, nor did it guarantee industrial peace, but management-union conflict was concerned with content, not structures or principles. Relations were based on a mutual recognition that coal production required management-union cooperation.

The Yorkshire owners blamed the 1924 wage agreement for 'crippling the industry' and after May 1925 the industry, 'struggling against tremendous economic adversities', was confronting the greatest crisis in its history. Joseph Jones, described coal in 1926 as a 'pauper industry, fed by the State, run at a loss, and swept by a thousand blasts of turbulent unrest'. Nationalisation, not wage cuts and longer hours, was the only solution to the industry's difficulties. His report closed by predicting 'an early struggle ... and a period of bitter internecine warfare'.[3] After the end of the General Strike, the miners endured a lockout with great fortitude. However, between 1 October and 15 October 1926 the numbers working in Yorkshire doubled from 10,902 (5.8 per cent) to 19,684 (10.8 per cent). Between 15 October and 12 November this doubled again to 37,680 (20 per cent), and by the end of November 60,905 (32.2 per cent) were back at work. On 15 November the YMWA Council voted to accept the MFGB's decision to recommend district settlements. The dispute had been about preserving national agreements, the MFGB had conceded on this, so what point was there in carrying on? Once the drift back began it would be unstoppable so the YMWA's leaders speedily negotiated an end to the dispute: in Council only one delegate voted against the settlement and the branches approved this by 2,947 votes with none against.[4]

The sudden collapse reflected a recognition of defeat and the YMWA's leaders accepted that to continue the struggle would seriously damage the union. As early as 4 October, when 500 men presented themselves for work at Askern, there were fears of a Nottinghamshire-type breakaway in Yorkshire which alarmed the

YMWA leadership.   Preserving union solidarity was their prime motivation and was reflected in the lenient terms for re-admission to the union of those who had returned to work before the 29 November settlement.[5] Treating more than 30 per cent of the miners as pariahs would have created a bitter and divided workforce in which the seeds of Spencerism might flourish; in any case, many of those who had returned did so only after the MFGB had admitted defeat.   Official leniency was not always reflected at pit level and there were instances of YMWA members refusing to work with strike-breakers.   This attitude was deprecated by the YMWA leadership, who feared the ensuring conflict would complicate management-union relations.[6]

1926 was never presented as anything other than a catastrophic defeat. Joseph Jones called for a hard-headed analysis of the union's strategy and an honest appraisal of its strengths and weaknesses. The first lesson he drew was that the miners were defeated by 'the most reactionary government of modern times', a government placed in office by working class votes, so all efforts must be directed at a Labour victory. Secondly, 1926 'proved conclusively that sufficient care and thought have not been given to the strike as an industrial weapon'.   Strikes should be used in the last resort, after very careful preparation and should have no hint of political motivation. Third, security could only come from nationalisation which required a majority Labour government.   These objectives required discipline in the labour movement but the fundamental prerequisite for union effectiveness was 'to have the manpower within the industry well organised and well disciplined'.[7]

The YMWA began 1926 with 164,196 members and ended it with 88,246. (See Table 9.1 for trends in union density.) Not only did this sharply reduce membership contributions, it undermined the YMWA's influence and authority.   So after 1926 the YMWA's strategy centred on maximising union membership:

> This reservoir of unorganised manpower represents a serious menace so long as they remain outside the organisation and constitute an immediate peril to their own well-being and that of their fellows. It is the duty of every member and Local Official to bring to the notice of these non-members the remarkable achievements of our organisation, and to spare no effort until 100% membership has been achieved.[8]

'Why have not your local officials today in the colliery office the

Table 9.1 Density of YMWA membership in the Yorkshire
coalfield, 1920-1946

Year	Density (%)	Year	Density (%)
1920	93.2	1933	69.4
1921	89.5	1934	73.4
1922	83.8	1935	83.7
1923	84.8	1936	93.3
1924	86.6	1937	98.4
1925	85.2	1938	98.0
1926	48.4	1939	96.4
1927	63.0	1940	91.8
1928	63.0	1941	na
1929	61.0	1942	97.1
1930	59.4	1943	na
1931	58.5	1944	94.6
1932	66.7	1945	90.0
		1946	96.2

Source: Calculated from data provided by the Yorkshire Area (NUM)
Finance Department and *The Colliery Year Book and Coal Trades Directory*,
annual.

Note: Density of Membership is calculated by dividing total employed
workforce by the number of union members and expressing the result as a
percentage.

power they had before?', Joe Hall, YMWA financial secretary, asked the 1933 Demonstration (Yorkshire's Gala), 'why cannot your local officials and permanent officials get the same return as in years gone by? The reason is that the manager in his colliery office is able to point to the fact that for every three men in the Union there are two outside'.[9]   The YMWA's attitude to non-unionists was uncompromising: 'they become, and rightly too, as outcasts among the workers, and as scapegoats for the employers. They are a menace to the well-being of the organised working class movement. They are the deathwatch beetle trying to destroy the magnificent fabric of Trade Unionism'.[10]

The YMWA leadership made the delivery of selective benefits (benevolent, death, and compensation payments) central to its strategy.   These benefits were, by definition, available only to YMWA members. Whilst the amount spent on selective benefits by the union varies, the sums are considerable and show an upward trend (from about 25 per cent of total union spending in the 1920s to 45 per cent in the 1930s). Their maintenance (and therefore prudent financial management) were regarded by the YMWA as a major responsibility. Another spur to recruitment was the continuing high level of bargaining activity at pit level. It is impossible to estimate the scale of bargaining but the amount spent by the YMWA on local deputations to resolve problems at pit level can be used as a crude activity measure. Increases in the amounts spent on local deputations might indicate a worsening of pit level relations (the source of any worsening cannot be discerned), but there is no obvious pattern. Between 1919 and 1940 an average of 29 per cent of local expenditure was spent by the YMWA on deputations to management, indicating a stable pattern of formal industrial relations at pit level. During the war there was a marked increase (an average of 41 per cent) in expenditure on local deputations which reflects the increased tensions of wartime industrial relations and an increase in the YMWA's influence.

The politics of industrial relations, 1926-39

After 1926 the YMWA remained a significant and legitimate element in the coalfield's industrial relations.   Estimating the YMWA's success is not easy, but wages as a percentage of total production costs indicates a high degree of 'stickiness'. Despite general downward pressure on costs in Yorkshire this was not reflected in wage costs. The stability of average earnings per shift suggests an ability to resist management but the economic pressure on the coalowners can be seen in the gap between the average numbers of days worked and percentage unemployed in Yorkshire compared to the national average: mining employment in Yorkshire was on average 4.5 per cent higher than nationally.

Although there was no anti-union offensive after 1926 the owners exploited their advantage. The South Yorkshire owners repudiated a union recognition agreement of November 1915. 'Your argument', thundered Herbert Smith, 'being that you believe men should have freedom of action as to whether they should join the (YMWA) or not ... you think the present is the most opportune time to take advantage'.[11] Joe Hall accused the West Yorkshire owners of short-sightedness: 'we ought to be taken more note of than we are as a society, and a time is coming when you will have to do it, whether you want to do it or not'.[12] Blacklisting and victimisation occurred. Nine branch officials, for example, were sacked by the South Kirby, Featherstone and Hemsworth Collieries, Ltd. The Barrow Colliery Co., Ltd, prosecuted five checkweighmen for distributing contracting-in forms on pit premises, and individual militants were sacked, some not returning to the industry until the war.[13] There was no organised attempt to insert non-political unionism from Nottinghamshire and the Yorkshire Miners' Industrial Trade Union (YMITU) had only a brief life: Spencerism 'put its head inside Yorkshire' but 'we were not long in taking away his strength ... we are not afraid of Spencerism'.[14] An essential precondition of Spencerism was disunity and fragmentation over 1926, but the YMWA's traditional solidarity blocked such a development.

Much of the YMWA's response depended on convincing managers that cooperation would help in running the pit.[15] Some obstructed branch efforts: 'a very vindictive attitude has been taken up by the management ... a letter has been sent to the (Branch) Secretary asking him to remove the Union Box out of the pit yard', while the Manvers Main Colliery Co., Ltd, would 'not allow organising on the colliery premises'.[16] Others accommodated the union. At Barnsley Main 'the Manager will allow us any facilities except the branch is not to interfere with a man and his work'; at Upton 'the Management asked for the names of those who were not joining and they would deal with them'. The Wentworth Silkstone management agreed, subject to a union contribution, 'to build them a small Brick Building' and 'in the meantime I have given them permission to collect in the tub repairing shop'.[17] This manager told the branch that non-unionism 'was something which ought to be a county question and not left for the individual managers at the various collieries to deal with, I promised to put in a word for them to get men to join whenever I had an opportunity'.[18] However even sympathetic managers would not compel membership. At Hickleton Main the YMWA was allowed to organise No. 2 pit but not No. 3 where there was a YMITU branch. George Probert, the YMWA branch secretary asked the agent to help them persuade the YMITU men to join but the management 'did not promise either way, but asked them to do the work themselves'.[19]

The dominant management attitude was not to challenge the YMWA but not to promote it either. The managements of Locke and Co., (Newland) Ltd, and the Victoria Coal and Coke, Ltd, told the YMWA 'that they intended doing nothing to facilitate men being in the Union or out of the Union'.[20] An inquiry into the Haigh branch agreed,

> the Management have lent a fair amount of assistance, but Mr Hinchcliffe has not been quite as whole-hearted as he might have been in the matter hitherto. A notice was posted on the pit-hill informing all men that they must be Members of 'a Union' ... He agreed, finally, to alter this to read that the men should join 'the Union', which, in effect, refers to the [YMWA]. In addition he gave us an understanding that he will set no more men on who are not Members ... Mr Hinchcliffe seems to have a sneaking fancy for other Unions, but it has been made quite plain to him that we mean the [YMWA] and shall insist upon all persons working in and about a mine joining this Society as far as we are concerned.[21]

By 1937 union density had surpassed that of the early 1920s and Herbert Smith threatened the South Yorkshire owners with a county wide stoppage if they recognised other unions.[22] Owners and managers might not have liked the YMWA but made no organised attempt to disrupt its activities.

The non-union question rumbled on into the war. So discontented was the workforce in 1941 that the YMWA telegraphed the Minister for Mines: 'Spontaneous stoppages at Individual Collieries threatened. Friction impedes production'.[23] In response the owners agreed to recognise the YMWA. In return for giving 'their sympathetic assistance and us[ing] their influence to secure the individual membership of all workmen employed in and about the mines,' the YMWA undertook 'to avoid all stoppages of work at the collieries and to operate Pit Production Committees ... in a full and proper manner'. The owners recommended, rather than instructed, their members to withhold the attendance bonus from non-union members but refused to deduct union dues from pay, an action which was subsequently declared illegal. The concessions made by the YMWA provoked substantial opposition to the agreements in Council. Voting was 1742 to 431 for the West Yorkshire agreement, and 1656 to 477 for the South Yorkshire one.[24]

As the industry recovered so did the workforce's confidence. 1937 was a turbulent year in coalfield politics. In the summer there was a long-running dispute over the pay of juveniles in West Yorkshire. In May notices were to be handed in over the recognition of the Nottinghamshire Miners' Association, and the MFGB pressed for a general wage increase. The owners accused the YMWA of upsetting trade with its new truculence: 'You had a ballot over the flat rate, a ballot over Harworth, and a ballot over something else, and it is all very unsettling. We have got to keep Yorkshire in a good position and we will not get it by having the District stopped'.[25] In 1937 the YMWA also began a campaign to equalise wage rates between West and South Yorkshire because of the growth of machine mining and the development of the interlocking ownerships between the two coalfields, even arguing for a single owners' association. This was resisted by the owners who expressed concern at the deterioration of industrial relations. The South Yorkshire Coal Trades Association (SYCTA) chairman, pointing to trouble at the Doncaster Amalgamated Collieries and in the Sheffield pits, complained 'we have had nothing but stoppages'.[26]

The rapid growth in machine mining in South Yorkshire required the re-negotiation of price lists and increased the ability of the workforce to extract concessions (using strikes and output restrictions) from owners anxious to derive maximum use from new and expensive machinery. There was a belief the YMWA was fomenting unrest: 'There is no reason why splendid results should not be obtained directly a price list is fixed. The workmen are obviously working to the YMA's instructions at present'.[27] SYCTA thought the YMWA's attitude to mechanisation was 'part of a policy to do away with piecework altogether ... It is imperative in their own interest that the owners should keep closely together in dealing with this question'. Furthermore, a labour shortage was developing in some pits.[28]

Out of this new assertiveness came unofficial unrest. This was condemned by the YMWA leadership for undermining their authority with the owners at a time when events were moving in the union's favour and strikers were called on to stand by their local and area officials. [29] After a dispute over the price list at Rossington, Joe Hall reported that 'it was a difficult task to get the men to work at all, and only for six weeks did they agree to work ... so as to place them in constitutional order' (that is, in conformity with YMWA rules).[30] The Wentworth Silkstone branch conceded 'the men had no justification for refusing to work, in fact they did their utmost to get the men to work and were sorry when they were not successful'. The branch agreed to obtain a promise from its members 'that in future any grievance or other trouble will be dealt with by a Deputation in a proper manner' as in the past, assuring the manager: 'there is no communism amongst the men'.[31] Smith and Hall persuaded the management not to prosecute after an unofficial strike at Grimethorpe, if the men abided by their contract. The YMWA and the company agreed this was 'the most satisfactory way of providing continuity of work and HARMONY'. Smith and Hall agreed with management that the men were in the wrong and 'we cannot uphold the practice of stopping the pit without notice and [we] expect our members to honour the assurances given on behalf of the [YMWA]'. Council agreed and over-ruled branch objections.[32]

Jones devoted a large proportion of his 1937-38 annual report to attacking 'the unwarrantable increase' in unofficial stoppages. This reappearance of direct action 'as a means of permanently improving working conditions or industrial relations is both futile and obsolete', and threatened 'advantageous collective bargaining'. Although unions were democratic, democracy was impetuous and had to be guided, otherwise it would be defeated by its own rashness, and it was both in the membership's interest as well as their obligation to support their leaders. He concluded, '*collective bargaining* is impossible unless backed by *collective acceptance* and *honourable adherence ... unofficial strikes humiliate union officials* and *weaken their chances of successful negotiation*'. The unofficial striker was 'an industrial anarchist rather than a trade unionist ... a flouter of rules, undertakings, agreements and official advice ... and who is, consequently, a positive danger'.[33] By the late 1930s the YMWA was secure in the politics of industrial relations but this authority was under challenge from pit politics. The next section will examine its role in the local polity.

The YMWA and community politics

Until the 1920s, the YMWA's involvement in coalfield local government was localised or confined to individuals. Before the reform of the local government franchise the YMWA had no scheme to finance local political activity, but after reform local government involvement increased. The YMWA's rationale for community politics was straightforward: concentrated numbers and a Labour-voting tradition enabled the mineworkers to exploit the opportunities provided by liberal democracy to deliver material benefits. The delivery of, in particular, housing, health and education was sufficient reason for local political activity and was portrayed as proof of the vitality of the labourist tradition. Miners were urged 'to vote for their own people' as 'it is quite as important, and in many respects more so, that Labour should be to the fore in the administration of Law as in the making of Law'.[34]

Of the 15 working men elected to the West Riding County Council (WRCC) between 1889-1914, eight were miners. Greater representation was inhibited not just by the franchise but by the problem of obtaining time-off from work, loss of wages and travelling expenses. The miners' presence in the WRCC was also limited by the greater social diversity of the area compared to Durham (where Labour secured a majority on the county council in 1918). In the 1913 election only two miners were elected. In March 1918 the YMWA appointed a committee to report on the financing of local politial activity. It recommended that 2d out of the 6d per member retained by the branches for local activity should 'form the

nucleus of a fund for stimulating local political interest'.[35]   In
December 1919 the YMWA council approved Rule 71 which
provided a subsidy of 50 per cent of lost wages and expenses to a
maximum of £50 a year to be paid by the branch or group of
branches covered by a WRCC member's ward.   But unless a
candidate had received prior endorsement from the YMWA, he
would not be eligible for funding.[36] This system proved difficult to
operate.   Before the 1922 WRCC elections, the YMWA executive
warned all branches that no support would be forthcoming unless a
candidate was formally endorsed by the candidate's branch and by
council.   By 1924 the YMWA was spending £1,490 on county
councillors out of a total political fund expenditure of £16,329 (9.1
per cent). Of the 19 YMWA councillors, 12 were newly elected and
they comprised two-thirds of the Labour group on the WRCC. Five
of Labour's ten aldermen were YMWA members.[37]

A Labour majority would mean 'that a determined assault can be
made on the TORY-CUM-LIBERAL administration'. Labour would
deliver education and health and ensure 'that SYMPATHY and
HUMANITY may no longer be excluded from PUBLIC
ASSISTANCE ADMINISTRATION; and that the SERVICE OF
HUMAN NEEDS as well as HUMAN HAPPINESS may be the
supreme object of the Council's activity'.[38]   This philosophy of
service and material improvement inspired many miners to enter local
politics. In 1918 Tom Williams became a member of the Doncaster
Board of Guardians, mostly employers and farmers who 'regarded
themselves as Guardians of the ratepayers rather than Guardians of
the Poor'. In April 1919 Williams was elected to the Bolton-upon-
Dearne Urban District Council (UDC), which, before 1914, had been
an 'advanced' council building many houses. This continued under
Labour and local government was seen by Williams as a natural
extension of union activity.[39] This philosophy of practical, working
class self-help was clearly articulated by the YMWA in 1925:

> However good Acts of Parliament are, they bring little advantage to
> Working Class folk unless administered in a humane spirit and for the
> good of the people. If you are anxious, therefore, to get *Good Houses*
> at *Economic Rents*, adequate *Medical Services* for your brains, *Good*
> *Sanitation*, and a healthy, happy contented *Communal Life*, then support
> your own Candidates who have *Brains* as good as their Opponents and
> *Intentions* - infinitely better. Labour's ideal is to redeem Cities, Towns,

and Parishes from their sordidness and squalor, and to do all within its power to Humanise the Poor Law. Since the Lock Out of 1921 there has been a growing revulsion of feeling amongst our people because of the treatment they and their dependents have received from Boards of Guardians.[40]

At the 1933 Demonstration Herbert Smith, president of the YMWA and mayor of Barnsley, articulated a vision of practical and active local government meeting the people's needs. Smith admitted their room for manoeuvre was limited by the central government and appealed for his audience's understanding that cooperation with government policy was the price for a degree of control in local administration.[41] The purpose of this local government activity was to deliver benefits and demonstrate the advantages of Labour rule. This commitment was reinforced by the social effects of 1926 and recession. By 1929 'the industry [had] been reduced to such a state of dependency on public charity' that a more sympathetic administration of the social security system was needed urgently and this required greater Labour representation.[42]

In 1930 a proposal to extend the provisions of Rule 71 to city and borough councils, local assessment committees and boards of guardians was amended to include urban and rural district councils. Although Rule 71 was intended to apply to all local public bodies, the YMWA redefined its policy. To finance it the £50 expense limit was reduced to £40 as the WRCC now paid travelling expenses and expenses of £25 per year were now to be paid to local councillors. This decision was taken at a time of financial stringency and testifies to the importance attached by the YMWA to local government. It was approved by council by 72 to 35, coming into force on 1 April 1933.[43] As a result of this decision YMWA representation in local government increased. In an effort to control costs a sub-committee on local representation recommended payments be only given for actual time lost on council service and also advocated capping YMWA local government representation. A YMWA survey found that on some councils, as many as 13 out of 15 Labour councillors were miners. Not only was this expensive, it enervated local Labour politics. By limiting YMWA representation and financial support to no more than a majority of the total strength of a council 'opportunity will at least be afforded to other Unions and affiliated bodies to obtain local representation'. These recommendations were accepted and council was empowered to accept or reject any nomination.[44]

Before 1918, colliery managers, small businessmen, and professionals dominated local government, but by the early 1920s this was changing. Wombwell UDC, for example, had in the 1900s been dominated by colliery officials and shopkeepers; by the 1920s the miners were on the verge of capturing the council.[45] The rise of Labour and the YMWA's prominence altered the temper of local politics. The Poor Law Guardians in Rotherham and Wath-upon-Dearne, for example, pursued circumspectly loans granted to miners in the 1919 dispute despite protests from ratepayers about subsidising industrial unrest. In Hemsworth local politics after 1918 speedily divided between ratepayers and rent payers, and Gabriel Price (YMWA official and councillor) dared the rate payers to challenge him at the WRCC election.[46] By the end of the 1930s, the colliery interest had been removed from local politics. In 1935 the SYCTA Propaganda Committee wrote to all members urging them 'to do all in their power to support suitable candidates (colliery officials)' in the local elections. This initiative flowed from the growing burden of local spending on colliery companies and the scale of Labour's representation: 'In the whole of the South Yorkshire area there are only two anti-socialist members on the (WRCC)'.[47]

It is not easy to demonstrate unequivocally if the YMWA's role in local politics improved material conditions in the coalfield. WRCC Medical Officer of Health Reports throughout this period refer frequently to the poor state of coalfield housing. This was particularly noticeable in the Rotherham and Doncaster RDCs where the industry was still growing. The miner-Labour dominated Thurnscoe UDC had a high birth rate and a low infant mortality rate which was ascribed to the development of a model colliery village by the UDC.[48] There is evidence of a steady improvement in the health of the mining communities. The spectacular decline in infant mortality was 'brought about by a combination of such factors as the improvement in environmental conditions', notably in water supply and sewage disposal, better health care, and mother and child welfare services. It is unlikely that non-Labour councils would have brought about such a degree of change. Nevertheless, despite these improvements, eight of the ten UDCs with the worst infant mortality rates were in mining areas.[49]

The wartime electoral truce meant that YMWA endorsement was only given to candidates replacing sitting councillors during the war. Nonetheless by 1945 the local polity was Labour dominated, and within this domination miners were the largest group. The YMWA's political philosophy was located unambiguously in the labourist political tradition, a tradition which had delivered substantial material benefits at local level and which was about to do so in national politics.

The war and YMWA politics

On the outbreak of war the Yorkshire miners were called on by the government and their leaders to maximise coal production but the latter noted with regret that unofficial unrest continued.[50] Appeals were of declining utility unless pay and conditions were improved, and despite immediate gains the legacy of the interwar years meant unrest was never far from the surface. The YMWA recognised war would shift the balance of power in their favour and were determined to exploit this. Furthermore the YMWA felt that cooperation in the war effort would strengthen the case for a postwar restructuring of the industry, although this was initially conceived of as compulsory reorganisation under the 1938 Coal Act.

Coalfield politics were relatively quiescent in 1940-41, although in early 1940 the YMWA was embroiled in a major dispute over war wage additions and unofficial strikes continued. During the war the YMWA became jointly involved in trying to enforce better workforce discipline. Some branches refused to operate the absentee committee system but the formation of the Yorkshire Joint Coal Production Committee (9 July 1940) which established Pit Production Committees (PPCs) meant the union and the owners were jointly responsible for enforcing workforce discipline. The consequences of interwar neglect became apparent in 1941-42 in the general production crisis. Labour shortages (in 1941 Yorkshire needed 11,274 more mineworkers) and the pressures of wartime production (reflected in the accident rate) fuelled a simmering discontent, as output per faceworker fell from 73.54 cwts per shift in 1939 to 70.30 cwts in 1941. An Essential Work Order (EWO) was applied to the coal industry on 25 May 1941.[51] However, whilst the EWO increased union influence and extended collective bargaining it also confined those employed to that industry. As a result discontent simmered on.

PPCs met at least weekly and were involved in achieving the pit's production target. PPCs considered questions arising out of the EWO, disputes, claims, stoppages, absenteeism, and, in particular, 'How to secure the maximum co-operation in the pit among the workmen and the officials'. PPCs were enjoined to remain in close contact with the workforce, be 'zealous in propagating the idea of co-operation (and) building up discipline in the pits'.[52] There was, however, resistance from some branches to playing a full role in both the PPCs and in controlling absenteeism. The PPCs lost their disciplinary functions to the Ministry of Labour's regional offices in 1943 but by that time they were identified by many mineworkers as pro-management, driving a wedge between the union and workforce.

The 1942 coal crisis led to government control of the mines, although day to day control remained with management. Joint conciliation procedures were created and the much resented EWO amended by the government. The YMWA resented the fact the miners were unjustly blamed for production difficulties when a thorough overhaul of the industry was needed. The branch and district leadership of the YMWA nonetheless condemned strikers for ignoring procedures and warned of the serious penalties under wartime regulations.[53] The YMWA leadership was generally satisfied with the wartime system of control and the enhanced role it gave union leaders, but a resolution approving this machinery in council attracted a considerable minority of critical votes (1090 to 446). In December 1942 the Cortonwood branch called for the resignation of all YMWA members from the disputes machinery. This was rejected by council by 2036 to 232.[54] The YMWA kept a very close watch for signs of dissent. This led to an official enquiry into the Cortonwood branch committee, some of whose members refused to operate the disputes machinery, flouted its decisions, and urged other branches to do the same. The inquiry led to the disciplining of eleven committee members.[55]

By 1943 the situation in the coalfield was deteriorating rapidly as the beneficial effects of state control and the Greene Award, which increased the national minimum wage to 83s (£4.15) for underground workers and 73s (£3.15) for those on the surface, faded.

Severe unrest in 1944 was inevitable.[56] Joe Hall was deeply pessimistic: 'Since the capitulation of France ... there have been many crises in the coal industry but I am firmly convinced that the crisis hour is with us now'.[57] The cause of the crisis was the pay anomalies (notably deductions for home coal) caused by the Porter Award which, many mineworkers felt, were not being resolved by the national negotiating machinery. Despite appeals from union leaders to their members, discontent boiled over into unofficial strikes. The YMWA leadership recognised that this unrest posed a major threat not only to the war effort but to the union's new status and influence in the industry. Hall repudiated criticism of the agreements,

> We assure you that ... we shall stand by that agreement as a society. Even if the local branch diverts, we shall stand by it, and it will be definitely then an unconstitutional stoppage ... [We] are anxious when we put our men on that [constitutional] machinery, which we have advocated since 1926, to carry out our obligations. It may be that a few, a small minority, may not want to follow out that machinery, but we intend to stand by that which we have signed and that which we have advocated.[58]

To unofficial strikers Hall was forthright: 'This strike is a crime because they are not striking against the colliery companies. I told them, "You are not striking against the Owners; you are striking against two particular organisations, one is the State, and the other is the (YMWA)"'.[59] There was more at stake than the immediate interests of the mineworkers.

Union leaders were in a complex position: they had struggled to create a national industrial relations system, they had made substantial gains, but an enormous fund of discontent had welled up in the coalfields. As Joe Hall told the owners, 'you take it from me that neither you nor I, nor the powers that be, can stop a wholesale stoppage in this County'.[60] But only two council delegates supported a call that the YMWA withdraw from the conciliation machinery; instead council passed a resolution calling on all its members to return to work and follow established procedures.[61] The War Cabinet gave Bevin a free hand to deal with the unofficial strikes and modify the Defence Regulations to prosecute instigators of unofficial strikes; Trotskyist agitators were blamed for fomenting unrest. A joint statement by Bevin and the TUC general council condemned the strikes in Yorkshire and elsewhere as a 'lamentable development', claiming that they threatened 'the entire policy that the trade union movement has pursued since the war began'.[62] Bevin warned the miners that unless there was a quick settlement they risked War Cabinet intervention. The strikes ended on the 12-13 April with a guarantee that all wage rates would stand for four years. This was portrayed as a vindication of orderly industrial relations and cooperation with the state. Tom Oakey (YMWA financial secretary), calling for loyalty to Bevin and the YMWA leadership, argued Bevin had done more for the miners 'in four years ... than we could have done in 25 years'.[63] So valuable were the benefits won after 1940 believed to be, union leaders supported the system even when management was wrong: 'I know perfectly well our men are stopping for their rights, although I tell them to keep at work'.[64]

Coalfield, like national politics, moved to the left. One day before the declaration of war, a Clayton West resolution calling for the government's resignation and closer relations with the USSR attracted 13 votes in council; in 1943 delegates voted by 81 to 18 to support the Communist Party's application for Labour Party affiliation.[65] The YMWA's enthusiasm for the Beveridge report was tinged with suspicion: 'It goes further than anything done in the social security world, and when it reaches the floor of the House will have the united opposition of many million pounds-worth of vested interests ... I do not think the present-day Government could shelve it or seriously mutilate it without volte face in view of the publicity they have given it'.[66]

Not surprisingly the 1945 general election was seen by the YMWA as epoch making: 'This election will prove to be the most vital and far reaching one in our history, and dependant upon its result the future welfare of the working class community for generations to come will rest'.[67] A majority Labour government committed to the welfare state, full employment and the nationalisation of the mines was the culmination of everything for which the YMWA had been working since 1926. So significant were these gains, the YMWA was determined that nothing, including the discontents of its own members, would be permitted to jeopardise the successful realisation of the labourist project.[68] As there was no official industrial action in the coalfield until the overtime ban of 1971, the 1940s mark a dramatic simplification of the tension between union and pit politics, a simplification which was institutionalised by nationalisation.

Conclusion: 'The needs of the many outweigh the needs of the few'

The history of mining politics is understandably dominated by 1926. The scale of defeat and the subsequent hardships have, however, obscured both elements of continuity and the creativity with which mineworkers responded to their predicament. For the Yorkshire miners, 1926 did not produce a major strategic or policy rethink, rather it confirmed the validity and vitality of an ethos which had underpinned mining unionism in the coalfield from its earliest years. This ethos, or political culture, stressed, first, the necessity for the formalisation of management-union cooperation in an industrial relations system. Second, political activity (local and national) was an essential part of union activity to circumvent the owner's economic power; and third, the immediate justification of industrial and political activity was to deliver substantial material gains. The *sine qua non* of this was workforce solidarity and unity behind agreed collective goals, even if these seemed opposed to the immediate interests of significant numbers of mineworkers. The primacy of the collective was justified by the conviction that all mineworkers were victims of the market and that salvation lay in circumventing the market, the ultimate expression of which was nationalisation. Successful collective action to minimise market turbulence and introduce an element of stability and predictability into the mineworkers' life was so obviously in the interests of all as to be hardly worth debating.

Management was clearly dominant in this period, but this did not result in passivity on the part of the YMWA. After 1926 the YMWA mediated relations between management and workforce, its object was to establish a defined and understood set of responsibilities to the mutual benefit of management and union. In this branch and fulltime officials played a central role and this often provides the basis for accusations of 'bureaucratisation' or the growth of a Michelsian oligarchy acting against the 'real' interests of the workforce. This charge has an element of truth. By 1937 the

YMWA was moving perceptibly from the forging and maintenance of solidarity and unity to becoming involved in questions of labour discipline. This became a permanent feature of union politics during the war and with nationalisation, but accusations of oligarchy obscure more than they reveal.

Maintaining workforce discipline and obedience to due process is a core function of the union hierarchy as a prerequisite for collective action in the industrial and political systems. The tension between pit and union politics, though muted until 1937, was ever present in YMWA politics, becoming the motor of union politics after 1939. Management, and after 1947 the state, had an interest in the union providing coherence in an often highly volatile environment. After 1937 the YMWA was in a complex position, representing the members while exercising wider responsibilities, a situation which mirrors national developments as the unions were drawn into a closer relationship with the state.

The study of coal politics is implicitly (and often explicitly) informed by a conflict model of power with a zero-sum view of industrial and political relationships. This might seem appropriate for a period in much of which the YMWA was subordinate. However union subordination is normal, so analytically what matters is not inferiority *per se* but the strategies used to challenge this. The YMWA exploited managerial dependence on the workforce to maintain collective bargaining, and in politics deployed its numbers and organisation to colonise much of the local polity. War increased YMWA influence markedly but also introduced new factors, notably 'the national interest', which further complicated the YMWA's situation. The pattern laid down between 1926 and 1945 dominated union politics until 1969 when an explosion of unofficial conflict in Yorkshire fuelled a dramatic shift to the left in the NUM.

Notes

Place of publication is London unless otherwise stated.

1. See P. Gibbon, 'Analysing the British miners' strike of 1984-5', *Economy and Society*, vol. 17, part II, 1988, pp. 152-4 for a similar distinction.
2. A.J. Taylor, '"Trailed on the tail of a comet": the Yorkshire miners

and the ILP, 1885-1908', in D. James, T. Jowitt and K. Laybourn (eds), *The Centennial History of the Independent Labour Party* (Halifax, 1992), pp. 230-6.

3. South Yorkshire Coal Trades Association (SYCTA) 19th Annual Report, 1924-25 (11 May 1925), pp. 9-10; NUM Office, Barnsley, YMWA Records (hereafter YMWA), YMWA Annual Report 1925-26, pp. 3-5.

4. YMWA, Special Council Meeting, 27 November 1926.

5. YMWA, Special Council Meeting, 20 December 1926. Strike-breakers were to be readmitted on paying contributions for the period they had worked.

6. Sheffield Central Reference Library, NCB Yorkshire Region Archives, (hereafter NCB) NCB 1137, Hickleton Main Deputations, 21 December 1926. The depth of feelings can be seen in the Goldthorpe Working Men's Club's 1956 decision to continue to exclude those who worked in 1926.

7. YMWA, Annual Report 1926-27, pp. 2-5 and p. 9.

8. YMWA, Executive Committee Minutes, Circular to all Branch Officials, 11 June 1928.

9. YMWA, Report of the Annual Demonstration, 19 June 1933, p. 22.

10. YMWA, Annual Report 1927-28, p. 6.

11. Joint Meeting of SYCTA and YMWA, 4 January 1927, p. 2. A similar recognition agreement applied in West Yorkshire for the duration of the war.

12. Joint Meeting of WYCOA and the YMWA, 28 July 1932, p. 13.

13. YMWA, Council Meeting, 22 December 1927, and interview with Dick Kelley, 14 June 1982.

14. MFGB Special Conference Report, 2 June 1927, p. 48. YMITU membership: 1,300 (1927); 780 (1928); and 750 (1929). YMITU branches existed at Hickleton Main, Bentley, Askern and Bullcroft.

15. YMWA, W. Auty to J. Jones, 18 November 1933 for an example of this argument.

16. YMWA, Report on the Goldthorpe Branch by E. Hough to the YMWA Executive, 6 June 1934, and T.J. Critchley, 13 April 1935.

17. YMWA, G. Martin (Barnsley Main) to J. Jones, 17 July 1936, H. Hall to J. Jones, 31 July 1936; NCB 1267, Wentworth Silkstone Colliery Deputation Book, entries for 23 October 1928.

18. NCB 1267, Wentworth Silkstone Colliery Deputation Book, 11 February 1936.

19. NCB 1137/a, Hickleton Main Deputation Book, 3 March 1927 and 12 April 1937.

20. YMWA, Report on the Newland Branch by Herbert Smith and J.

Hibbert to the YMWA Executive Committee, 5 December 1936.

21. YMWA, Report on the Haigh Branch by E. Hough to the YMWA Executive Committee, 20 December 1937.

22. Joint Committee Meeting, 7 February 1937, p. 2 for this threat.

23. YMWA, Ordinary Council Meeting, 27 October 1941. Telegram to President of the Board of Trade and Minister for Mines.

24. YMWA, Circular, 'The Non-Union Question', 10 November 1941, and YMWA Ordinary Council Meeting, 22 November 1941.

25. Joint Board, Meeting of SYCTA and YMWA, 1 October 1937.

26. Joint Board, Meeting of WYCOA and YMWA, 22 July 1937, and Meeting of SYCTA and YMWA, 13 September 1937.

27. NCB 1137/5, Hickleton Main Deputations, Report of Manager to J.T. Greensmith, 30 July 1932.

28. SYCTA, 31st Annual Report 1936-37, p. 8.

29. YMWA, Executive Committee, 28 July 1937.

30. YMWA, Joe Hall to Joseph Jones, 5 August 1937.

31. NCB 1267, Wentworth Silkstone Colliery Deputation Book, 7 November and 26 October 1937.

32. YMWA, Ordinary Council Meeting, 4 February and 28 February 1938. Original emphasis.

33. YMWA, Annual Report for 1937-38, pp. 3-4. Original emphasis.

34. YMWA, Circular, 'Borough Elections', October 1923.

35. B.J. Barber and M.W. Beresford, *The West Riding County Council, 1889-1974: Historical Studies* (Wakefield, 1974), p. 191; YMWA, Ordinary Council Meeting Minutes, 18 March and Executive Committee, 9 April 1918.

36. YMWA, Ordinary Council Meeting Minutes, 5 December 1919 and 'Payment of County Councillors', 20 December 1919.

37. YMWA, Branch Circular, 'County Council Candidates', March 1922 and Annual Report 1923-24, Report on the Political Fund, pp. 22-23.

38. YMWA, 'Let Labour Rule the Riding', YMWA Manifesto for the WRCC Elections, 3 March 1934.

39. Lord Williams of Barnburgh, *Digging for Britain* (1968), pp.37-8,43.

40. YMWA, 'Labour Marching On', Circular to All YMWA Members, Local Elections, 4 April 1925. Original Emphasis.

41. YMWA, Report of the Annual Demonstration, 19 June 1933, p. 7. Labour's influence was further restricted by a Liberal-Conservative electoral pact to deny Labour control of the WRCC. Nonetheless, Labour's strength did force the ruling group to make concessions.

42. YMWA, Annual Report 1928-29, p. 2.

43. YMWA, Yearly Council Meeting, 22 December 1930 and 19 December 1932; Council Meeting, 20 February 1933.

44. YMWA, Report of the Sub-Committee re Rule 71 (March 1936), pp. 1-2 and YMWA, Special Council Meeting, 16 March 1936.
45. *Barnsley Chronicle*, 18 September 1920.
46. Ibid., 11 October and 25 October 1919.
47. NCB 208, SYCTA Correspondence with Newton Chambers, R. Clive to all SYCTA Members, 29 January 1935.
48. WRCC Clerk's Department, RD 17, *35th Report of the Chief Medical Officer of Health, 1923* (15 December 1924), p. 13.
49. WRCC Clerk's Department, RD 17, *47th Annual Report of the Chief Medical Officer of Health, 1935*, p. 24.
50. YMWA, Annual Report for 1939-1940, p. 2.
51. The best account of the coal industry at war is W.H.B. Court, *Coal* (1951).
52. South Yorkshire District Production Committee, *Guide for Pit Production Committees* (1941).
53. YMWA, Ordinary Council Meeting, 23 March and 1 June 1942.
54. Ibid., 22 December 1942.
55. Ibid., 22 February and 5 April 1943.
56. Ibid., 18 October 1943.
57. *Sheffield Star*, 3 January 1944.
58. YMWA, Ordinary Council Meeting, 1 April 1944, and West Yorkshire Joint Board, 25 January 1944, p. 8.
59. West Yorkshire District Conciliation Board, 7 February 1944, pp. 7-8.
60. Joint Meeting of the West and South Yorkshire Coalowners' Associations and the Executive of the YMWA, 10 February 1944, p. 17.
61. YMWA, Ordinary Council Meeting, 1 April 1944.
62. PRO CAB 65/42, 3 April 1944 and CAB 64/42, 5 April 1944; *Daily Herald*, 6 April 1944.
63. MFGB Special Conference Report, 12-13 April 1944, pp. 30-31.
64. Joint Meeting of the West and South Yorkshire Coalowners' Associations with the Executive of the YMWA, 12 September 1944, p. 12.
65. YMWA, Ordinary Council Meeting, 2 September 1940 and 22 February 1943.
66. YMWA, Circular, 'The Beveridge Report', 9 January 1943.
67. YMWA, Ordinary Council Meeting, 11 June 1945.
68. Ibid., 6 September 1945.

PART THREE
Outcomes

CHAPTER TEN

Learning from bitter experience: the making of the NUM

Hywel Francis

Twenty-five years ago I wrote a pamphlet. I made a beautiful draft with diagrams of one Mineworkers' Union. I drafted it believing I had a nice flat floor on which to build a lovely union. I have learned from bitter experience that it is not a flat floor; it has different District interests with different District conceptions, different degrees of development. This we are now proposing is an attempt to make a superstructure over what already exists, and we cannot do it independently of what exists. (Arthur Horner, MFGB Annual Conference, July 1943.[1])

Arthur Horner was speaking on behalf of the Reorganisation Sub-Committee which the MFGB executive appointed in 1937. Its two members, Horner and Sam Watson from Durham, laboured valiantly for two years. In January 1939 the executive abandoned their blueprint for one national union. Their plans had foundered on the opposition from the district unions affiliated to the MFGB. The different, often conflicting, interests of the district unions originated in the nature of the industry. The official historians of the National Coal Board described coalmining on the eve of nationalisation in 1947 as 'an extraordinarily varied industry in which most national generalisations had to be qualified because of the many differences in natural conditions, working practices, social traditions and business organisations'.[2]

The National Union of Mineworkers (NUM) was made by war and the coming of nationalisation: its constitution was a creative tension between coalfield traditions and the imperative of national unity. The visionary speeches of Michael McGahey, vice-president of the NUM, many decades later, with the often repeated slogan, 'there is only *one* union, the National Union, and only *one* coalfield, the British Coalfield', sums up that tension over generations.

The Second World War and its centralisation of coal production in Britain provided the final impetus towards nationalisation, and in anticipation of that momentous achievement, pushed the Miners' Federation of Great Britain (MFGB) towards a similarly more unified structure. That unification was to be a balance between district interests and long-standing centralising tendencies.

For all its significance then and later, the actual creation of a National Union of Mineworkers in 1944-45, viewed in isolation and from a distance now of half a century, appears to have been something of a non-event. At the time, there was little tangible transfer of power to the centre. So much was in turmoil in that crucial period: the imminent victory over fascism in Europe and Asia; the subsequent Labour landslide victory at the polls which raised universal expectations for social reform and public ownership; the crisis in the coal industry of underinvestment, recruitment and conditions of work and their resolution (or as it seemed) by nationalisation and the implementation of the new Miners' Charter. All of this somewhat overshadowed the creation of the NUM. Indeed it was certainly the case at pit level that the changeover from the Miners' Federation to the National Union was achieved so quietly in many areas that it barely merited a mention. At the Bedwas miners' lodge in South Wales, inextricably and always linked with the long term and ultimately successful battle to defeat a local breakaway in the 1930s, the chairman concluded the year's end in December 1944 by wishing members' ... sincere greetings for a Happy New Christmas and Bright New Year'. He made no mention of the impending birth of the NUM on 1 January 1945.[3]

The new union's rules and structure were indeed the product of learning from bitter experience. Mining activists had been pursuing the ideal of a unified miners' union for two generations. For much of that time trade unionism had been in mortal danger in the coalfields. In the course of responding to the serious threat presented by the post-1926 breakaway unions, thoughtful MFGB leaders recognised the need to make provision for particular differences between the district unions which could not be submerged into a united union. Over forty years later, Michael McGahey spoke in the same vein about the very same problems of unity: his phrase 'anger is not enough' (over scabs and breakaways, in the 1980s as in the 1930s) was an echo of Horner's haunting words.[4]

Horner's notion of 'learning', the need to combine experience with some intellectual energy, a 'scientific strategy', needs closer scrutiny. The exhaustive consultations with district unions, MFGB executive meetings and special delegate conferences in 1943-4 were precisely about that: how to devise an incorporating, 'embracing' strategy which brought more firmly onboard the Nottinghamshire coalfield, within a stronger national structure. This achievement, and it was a significant one, arose out of that synthesis of decades of experience and collective intellectual understanding. The nature of the consensus, the compromise or the settlement enshrined in the NUM constitution, proved durable. The strength of the national union - based upon a delicate balance between local, area and national interests - stood the test of time. It lasted four decades and it required a massive assault by the state to crack it.

The abstract ideal of 'one Mineworkers' Union', Horner's 'nice flat floor', would have swept away any lingering district autonomy. The union which Horner and Watson constructed in their sub-committee was something quite different.

> The old district unions became administrative areas of a single National Union of Mineworkers, and the salaries of Area officials were now paid from bank accounts controlled by the national body. Of the 21 Areas, 15 were geographical and 6 were occupational, catering for winders, craftsmen and electrical power workers. The new union had control over all questions of industrial policy, including strike action, which needed a two-thirds majority on a national vote.[5]

But was this 'settlement' a mere tactic or a long-term strategy? It would not be fanciful to describe Horner and his then ally Sam Watson as emblematic of the many rank and file 'organic intellectuals' who had over many generations suffered, survived, struggled and constantly thought through questions of local, district, national and indeed international unity. The complex strategic settlement they achieved in 1944-45 involved, of necessity, both the left and the right. The more progressive elements (broadly described as the left) saw it as a step towards an eventual 'one Mineworkers' Union' to be achieved over time through organisational restructuring, national initiatives and national agreements.

The more conservative elements focused mainly, but by no means exclusively, around George Spencer, president of the former breakaway in Nottingham and since September 1937 president of the fused Nottinghamshire Miners' Federated Union. These elements, existing undoubtedly in every coalfield, whether on the left or the right, were still proud, even jealous, of their own relative independence and would have seen the arrival of the NUM as an end in itself.

What neither progressives nor conservatives appeared to recognise was that inherent in these different perceptions was the central truth of Horner's reflections in 1943: the distribution of power contained in the compromise settlement between local, regional and national foci was actually a strength, rather than a weakness. The left in the NUM has always subsequently and erroneously believed in abstract organisational and political unity. The durability of the 1944-5 constitution lay in its combination of the ideological commitment to unity with the local coalfield pride characteristic throughout the MFGB. It was this mixture which made the NUM such a potentially powerful organisation.[6]

But all this was a long way from the MFGB in 1943 when it began the final push towards a slightly more centralised organisation: Ebby Edwards as general secretary and Sidney Ford, administrative officer, were the only national officials in the old Russell Square offices of the MFGB in the London of the blitz. The young Labour Research Department writer, Margot Heinemann, recalled an organisation at this time which still suffered from the great battles and defeats of the interwar period. The real strides for unity were not made at MFGB conferences, but off stage in the national policies, awards and agreements being conceded by a government desperate for the coal to fuel its war economy.[7]

The long haul

To the men who seized the opportunity presented by the wartime emergency, the NUM was the culmination of a long historical process lasting over a century. They themselves had participated in many of the organisational struggles for unity and democratic control at all levels, as well as the related political struggles, eventually for public ownership and a range of socio-economic demands which were codified into Miners' Charters. The strong ideological commitment to unity was forged and maintained through the educational activities conducted by district unions. The opportunities for workers' education, in its broadest sense, both formal and informal, within all the coalfields, underlay activists' continuing pursuit of unity. Within the non-contentious educational setting, they were able to explore the inter-related issues of unity, democratic control and political activity. As a result of their searching questions and reflections, they developed practical and sophisticated views and strategies.

Each coalfield had distinctive educational institutions which reflected the district unions' predominance in the life of what were typically single industry communities. Union-sponsored classes were part of a monoculture serving what Kerr and Siegal famously described as 'isolated masses'. When asked why the Kent coalfield was distinctive in its militancy, its veteran secretary, Jack Dunn, identified educational opportunities as the key factor, particularly the provision of a miners' library, as in other coalfields, particularly South Wales.[8]

Similarly there is no doubt that the Durham Sunday Schools, pioneered by Sam Watson, were important in helping to develop a regional coherence and a strong coalfield consciousness in the long years after the defeat of 1926, prior to the creation of the NUM. That coalfield identity, exemplified by the Durham Miners' Association (DMA), built in part on formal and informal educational opportunities allied to wider political strategies, was to be so influential in the shaping of the future National Union.[9]

And again, as if to emphasise this 'learning' culture so deeply ingrained in the coalfields of the interwar period, there is the classic case of Will Paynter. General secretary of the NUM in the period 1959-68, he was very much shaped, indeed scarred, by the disunity after 1926 and placed great emphasis on the educational dimension. He had been a part-time lecturer for various educational and political organisations including the National Council of Labour Colleges (NCLC), the Workers' Educational Association (WEA) and the Communist Party, of which he was a long-standing member. When asked what his personal achievements were in his period as national secretary, he modestly explained them entirely in educational terms which intriguingly related directly to the creation of a national culture of unity: the establishing of a national newspaper, *The Miner*, and the founding of the first ever national educational programme, bringing together miners from all coalfields. At the very last Gala he ever addressed, in South Wales in 1981, raising consciousness through education was again his theme.[10]

Historians of the miners have frequently remarked upon the phenomenon of leaders, especially on the left, whether national or rank and file, who strove to display in the postwar period a strong commitment to, and understanding of, the need for an educational role for the union which linked inextricably to the desire for greater national unity. The union school, locally and increasingly nationally, was a central part of their strategy. More than that, as Vic Allen has written, there was a wide appreciation of the need to discuss intelligently a good book or a political idea as well as the current industrial strategy. The debates over unity over many generations within the miners' organisations can only be properly understood if set against this intellectual background.[11]

The debate over unity actually begins in 1912 with the publishing in South Wales by the Unofficial Reform Committee of *The Miners' Next Step* which was far more than a proposal for the reorganisation of the South Wales Miners' Federation, as the sub-title indicated. In one sense, the conclusion of the debate came with the key rule 3(a) of the NUM constitution:

> To secure the complete organisation in the Union of all workers employed in or connected with the coal mining industry of Great Britain, and membership of the organisation shall be a condition of employment in the industry.[12]

That objective, such a central tenet of that era of industrial unionism and syndicalism up to 1926, ingrained in 'organic intellectuals' like Ablett, Harvey, Horner, Watson and Paynter a recognition that the organisation should be all-inclusive. It was the synthesis of the theoretical ideas of *The Miners' Next Step* and the ongoing problems of non-unionism and subsequently the breakaways by the right and the left which enriched the otherwise arid debate on the need for a more centralised national organisation.[13]

The Miners' Next Step provided three pointers for the future in terms of the reorganisation of the MFGB, all of which had a bearing on the founding of the NUM. Firstly, the pamphlet identified the key internal issues which preoccupied the MFGB and the NUM for the rest of the century: the need for a streamlined industrial union, with leaders democratically accountable. Secondly, it recognised the central problem of nationalisation and the power of the state and proposed a form of industrial democracy through socialisation. And finally, its own text became an important political and educational tract for subsequent generations. The overlapping memberships and indeed overlapping revolutionary ideologies of such educational and quasi-educational bodies as the Unofficial Reform Committee, the Plebs' League, the Labour College and even, to an extent, the emerging Communist Party, included leaders like Ablett and Cook. They and many others ensured that the debate over the reorganisation of the federation was broadened beyond mere constitutional wrangling to include wider political issues, and always in an educational context.

Published in an age before the Labour Party was a mass organisation, *The Miners' Next Step* reinforced the syndicalist outlook of miners. A phenomenon developed which became known as 'lodge politics'. This was the belief that the miners' organisation, not the Labour Party nor any other body, could and should deal with all matters political. This was also mirrored by the lodges' independent approach to the political education of their members.[14] The defeat of the MFGB in 1926 served only to underline the fundamental weakness of the loose federal structure: the affiliated county associations were left to their own devices now that national negotiations and national agreements had come to an end. Worse than that however, the very existence of some associations was called into question. From its inception in 1889, the MFGB had always been weakened by the scourge of non-unionism. Now however another phenomenon, the so-called non-political union, emerged as an alternative, non-striking, company-backed union. It prospered and became the major union in Nottinghamshire under the leadership of George Spencer MP. A similar but separate breakaway established itself in the North Wales coalfield, surviving until 1942, and most surprisingly of all, the South Wales Miners' Industrial Union, the infamous 'scab union', established itself in the most militant coalfield of all and remained a threat until its final elimination in 1938.[15]

All these internal and external divisions were compounded by problems with the Communist Party. Its old strategy of what was in effect 'boring from within', with the success of the Miners' Minority Movement in the mid 1920s, was replaced by the more sectarian 'class against class' policy of establishing 'red unions'. The only major splits were in Scotland, with the creation of the United Mineworkers' of Scotland, and the expulsion of Maerdy, 'Little Moscow', in South Wales. Nevertheless these internal problems served to focus, over time, on the inadequacies and weaknesses of the old, archaic, miners' agent-dominated federation.[16]

In the post-1926 period, the main critique of the MFGB's policies and structures came from the Communist Party. It was a critique without an audience, disconnected from most coalfields and not fully understanding the depths of despair which arose out of defeat, disunity and the subsequent slump. Its revolutionary rhetoric did not take account of the vast economic and cultural differences between the coalfields. These differences were crucial: some relying on internal markets, some on overseas markets. Durham and Northumberland were centuries old and reflected the generations of influence of the great land-owning and coal-owning families and the church with a fairly well defined and powerful local state. South Wales and Kent were new, cosmopolitan, self-confident and carried the revolutionary optimism of the early twentieth century. Then there were the Dukeries in eastern Nottinghamshire, born in the age of defeat, in a period and a local context when it was difficult to develop a labour movement.[17]

Set against this diversity, Horner's 'flat floor' (in his pamphlet written with Nat Watkins entitled *One Mineworkers' Union - Why?*, published in 1927) was idealistic and naive in its highly centralised and rank and file focus. These views were also outlined in a chapter in his book written with Allen Hutt, *Communism and Coal* (1928). These writings under-estimated the different cultures, histories and the vested interests of coalfield leaders and ultimately low morale following 1926. They did however identify the general lack of democracy throughout the federation in what they called the 'fortress of bureaucracy' and the 'voiceless rank and file'. But the tone was sectarian and anti-leadership, not unlike the Unofficial Reform Committee in an earlier period.[18]

Horner's career in the 1930s mirrored a growing recognition of the need for local reorganisation and coalfield unity as pre-requisites for national unity. In South Wales, the federation of districts gave way in 1933 to a periodically elected rank and file central executive (to which agents came as non-voting observers) in line with the spirit of

The Miners' Next Step

Further coalfield unity was achieved by a new wages agreement in South Wales in 1937 which reduced to four the number of grades of payment: this was the forerunner of the 1955 National Third Day Wage Structure and the 1966 National Power Loading Agreement which achieved 'trans-coalfield' unity through the erosion of differentials and piece work. Perhaps most significantly of all, major compromises in Nottinghamshire (in 1937) and South Wales (in 1938) saw the end of company unionism, but at some cost. In South Wales it was at the price of a 'no strike' agreement, the non-return of some militants and the acceptance of the elimination of long-established customs and practices. In Nottinghamshire, it was the return of the 'Spencer' union under the leadership of George Spencer himself: more a merger or even a local takeover rather than apparent elimination.[19]

The journey which Horner and the Communist Party travelled is instructive. By 1936 he had been elected president of the SWMF, was the main architect of the wages and 'company union' strategies in subsequent years. In 1936, too, he had written his pamphlet *Towards a Popular Front* which located these local developments within a national and international framework, the essence of which was the pre-eminence placed on unity at all levels in the face of fascism at home and abroad: this led to 'less conflict and more cooperation with the more progressive coalowners'.[20] It was this strategy that paved the way for a new realism in the conference discussions of 1943-44 which led to creation of the National Union.

The opportunities of war

The strategic new realism which Horner pursued in South Wales was also being embraced at national level by the three MFGB officers, Joseph Jones, Ebby Edwards and Will Lawther. Their conduct of the national wages dispute in 1935-6 was astute and pragmatic. As a result, substantial concessions were gained. At the MFGB conference in July 1936 which followed the dispute's successful conclusion, Jones raised the issue of unification: 'I believe it to be the firm desire of our members that this task should be taken in hand, and I hope, therefore that the work will go forward without delay'.[21]

However the MFGB did not apply its collective mind to it until the following year. The MFGB conference convened in July 1937, in the aftermath of the Harworth strike and the elimination of the 'Spencer' union. Earlier in the month, 'a circular suggesting the formation of a national union had been drawn up by the Secretary (Edwards) and sent to all districts'.[22]   Jones' presidential address declared:

> In the coming months ... let us make organisation both from the structural and from the individual point of view, one of our chief objects, and let us try to ensure that the virility and enthusiasm which now characterise our best-organised areas are extended throughout the Federation ... If you expect to carry on successfully the Mineworkers' Federation on the present basis, I say it cannot be done ... You have the Annual Conference.   Districts come along and determine the policy of the Federation, not from the wider outlook of the Federation, but from the district outlook. When the Executive meets, our actions are based upon our own district views ... If you expect a national organisation to function nationally in these circumstances I say frankly it will not work.[23]

The circular had hardly been received with eager enthusiasm in the district unions. At the conference, Jones reported that the Yorkshire council had discussed it and decided against any change to the current district structure. The South Wales delegation had to report that their executive had not yet considered the circular. Jack Williams, a veteran leftwing activist from the Forest of Dean, observed: 'It wants courage to come up and say anything in favour of this when you see progressive districts like South Wales have nothing to say about it'.[24]

At this juncture, there was a concerted demarche conducted by proponents of unity. The South Wales delegation reported to conference on the next day that they had considered the matter and were now keen for a unification initiative to be mounted. The mood of all delegates had clearly been swayed by the discussions - both formal and informal. Conference passed a motion from Kent instructing the executive to prepare a scheme for one national association to be placed before a special conference for consideration and endorsement.[25]

The executive subsequently appointed a reorganisation sub-committee of two, Arthur Horner and Sam Watson. They produced an ambitious plan which provided for the incorporation of the existing district unions into eight areas. Lobbying for the plan was undertaken by the sub-committee, MFGB officers, and those districts supporting unification. The Communist Party also lent its support. But at the MFGB conference in July 1938, it was clear that the mood in favour of change had dissipated. The conference postponed any serious consideration of the report until the districts had time for further reflection. Even this tactical expedient was opposed by Leicester, North Wales, Somerset, Scotland, and Yorkshire.[26]

Faced with overwhelming evidence of entrenched district opposition, the MFGB resolved in December that the special conference on unity, scheduled for January 1939 be not held.[27] At its first meeting of the New Year, the executive adopted a minimalist position. The sub-committee were instructed to 'consider what can be done to secure greater central organisation for the MFGB and to present a scheme to that end'.[28] The prospect of unity had faded and seemed unlikely to be revived in the immediate future.[29]

The real momentum for unity was resumed only with the arrival of the war economy, the MFGB's consequent renewed economic power and the need for a national coal strategy by the government. The coalowners, through their Mining Association and their alliance with the Conservative government, had destroyed the national strength of the MFGB in 1926 by the imposition of district agreements. Now the opportunity arose to retrieve the situation.

The miners' new found importance in the public perception had been revived on the eve of war in books and films. Lewis Jones' novels *Cwmardy* (1937) and *We Live* (1939), as well as B.L. Coombes' widely acclaimed Left Book Club edition *These Poor Hands* (1939), both idealised and soberly chronicled the struggles of miners and their communities. The appearance of Paul Robeson in *Proud Valley* (1939) and the world-wide popularity of Hollywood's *How Green Was My Valley* (1941) confirmed that the miners, if not yet their union, were no longer beyond redemption.

The desperate shortage of mining manpower from 1940 and the related failure to increase coal production significantly led to government control of the industry in 1942. Advisory boards were established at national, regional and local levels. The boards, with union representation at all levels, considered the key questions of wages and conditions. The fundamentally changed circumstances of

collective bargaining raised very sharply the matter of a new
organisation to meet the challenge of what was already in effect one
employer.   Suddenly the miners were helping to prepare for the
postwar reconstruction, not trying to retrieve the pre-1926 world:
pneumoconiosis was recognised as an industrial disease, closed shop
agreements were beginning to be signed in individual coalfields, and
major national wage advances represented by the Porter and Greene
Awards (for all the criticisms of the time caused by rising
expectations) were being won.[30]

The Labour Research Department's work on the wartime coal crisis
(the evidence it gathered for the MFGB to present to the Greene
Tribunal), was published in Margot Heinemann's *Britain's Coal*
(1944), a Left Book Club edition whose real political objective was
to prepare the way for nationalisation. It complemented the Reid
Report of March 1945 by highlighting the inefficiency and the
underinvestment of private enterprise and the terrible human neglect
and exploitation in mining communities consequent upon it. *Britain's
Coal* also symbolised the way in which the MFGB was now once
again behaving like a national union, engaging on a national stage
with government and coalowners, and harnessing all the intellectual
and educational resources of the coalfields. Its moving accounts of
working conditions and industrial relations at pit level were based on
handwritten personal accounts by miners of their own daily lives; all
this was very much rooted in the independent working class
educational traditions of the coalfields.[31]

A 'new realism'

These changing fortunes, set against a backdrop of government
control of the industry, provided a more conducive environment for
an emerging national union. Indeed, on reading the proceedings of
the wartime conferences of the MFGB, there is the distinct
impression that matters are really being decided elsewhere. MFGB
officers were now negotiating nationally. They needed a more
effective and democratic national forum which could relate to the
second half of the twentieth century rather than the archaic and
paternalistic structures of the late Victorian age, what Lawther in
1942 had called 'the Bow-and-Arrow Trade Union ... [against] a

dive-bomber coal organisation'.[32]

Horner's cautionary words at the 1939 MFGB conference when he had urged full agreement with the districts rather than imposing organisational change from above, set the tone for the wartime discussions. The pace quickened in 1942 following the winning of the national weekly minimum wage, the imminence of national conciliation machinery and the improved prospects for public ownership. The 1942 MFGB conference accepted the executive's recommendation for unification. The reorganisation sub-committee again set out to meet representatives from district unions and produced fresh proposals in time for the 1943 conference. The historian J.E. Williams described them as 'similar' to the 1938 plan. They were actually substantially diluted.[33] Unity and agreement were more important than homogeneity and compulsion. The compromises of Nottinghamshire in 1937 and Horner's moderation in 1939 were acknowledgements of this. But circumstances were changing. Again Horner's haunting description of unity growing out of a bitter learning experience were echoed by MFGB vice-president James Bowman's reference in the 1942 conference to 'the bitter history of splendid district isolation', when districts undercut each other's coal prices.

The ghost of Spencerism was, nevertheless, ever present: at the same conference, George Spencer emphasised that district peculiarities were best dealt with by district leaders. Handing responsibilities over to the Federation would, he claimed, be one of the 'greatest and gravest mistakes that has ever been made ...'.[34]

Spencer's offensive came from the rearguard. It was answered by both Horner and Watson. A picture of a postwar world was painted by them which rightly assumed nationalisation, one state employer and one miners' organisation to deal with it. At the 1943 MFGB conference, Watson reminded delegates:

> Has not the war experience taught us, on wages, on holidays, on compensation or rehabilitation ... that you have only been able to get satisfaction from a national angle and on a national basis? ... The industry is tending not towards control by private enterprise, but towards public or State ownership ... I submit to delegates that if when that discussion (on the future of the coalmining industry) takes place in Parliament we are divided into districts, with district organisations and district Unions, we will not be able to bring to bear upon the people of

this country, through our Members of Parliament, the force we could
bring if we were organised into one Miners' Union.[35]

The principle was overwhelmingly carried at the 1942 conference.
The detail which would deliver maximum unity was to be worked at
over the coming two years, in the midst of war and the growing rank
and file confidence indicated by unofficial disputes including boys'
strikes and imprisonment, as at Betteshanger (Kent) and Tarreni
(South Wales). Nevertheless, whilst these debates and discussions
proceeded nationally, at pit and coalfield level reorganisation was by
no means the major issue. Only two resolutions on the issue for
example came before the SWMF annual conference between 1943
and 1945. The progress of the war, wages, living conditions and
public ownership were the burning issues of the time. Is it more
likely to assume that all miners believed in the inevitability of a
national union and that it would be achieved by whatever
compromises that were necessary?[36]

Crucially, the recommendation of the national executive committee
of the MFGB, following its reorganisation sub-committee's
deliberations in 1942-43, was to maintain the structures which existed
in the districts - to build on what already exists were Horner's words
- rather than dismantle them and start afresh. Industrial activities
(primarily wage negotiations and working conditions) however would
mainly be dealt with nationally and paid for through a levy whilst the
variety of benefits and varying contribution arrangements would
remain essentially untouched. Two other thorny problems needed
addressing. Firstly, relationships between over forty districts and
craft organisations and also their possible merger was to remain a
problem until the national union had come into being. Secondly, the
positions of the full-time officials and staff of all the districts were to
be protected. These recommendations had been achieved through a
careful process of consultation with district officials. All the twisting
and turning involved was described by Horner in 1943 as an
emasculation; it was also a recognition by 'realists' that the ideal for
the members (one thorough-going union) had to be reconciled with
the vested interests of the districts. The scheme was recommended
to the districts for discussion and amendment at the 1943 MFGB
conference by acclamation.[37]

The founding conference was held appropriately, and obviously by design, at Nottingham on 16 August 1944, paralleling the holding of the MFGB founding conference at Newport in 1889 to address South Wales' lack of enthusiasm for a national organisation in the 1880s. There were differences over the pace towards one national union (Yorkshire wanted it immediately); over fees to the centre; over the abolition of capitalism (now enshrined in the objects for the first time); and over the closed shop (again for the first time). Yet the widespread air of optimism and unity ensured that the compromise between the districts and the centre was at the heart of the new constitution. In particular, the two-thirds requirement in a ballot vote for a national strike was a clear indication that the new union was to continue the cautious approach of the old organisation. An amendment from Cumberland that the two-thirds be changed to a simple majority did not even find a seconder.[38] Under the new rules, MPs were now to be sponsored nationally. The salaries of area officials were also to be met by the national union. But significant financial autonomy was to be retained by new areas and their branches, particularly with regard to property and local benefit schemes.[39]

For one participant, the proceedings seemed to have been 'cut and dried' before the event. James Bowman (in the chair in place of Will Lawther) and Arthur Horner appeared to have sorted out the key decisions beforehand. A combination of the platform, South Wales (Horner) and Durham (Watson) successfully achieved the necessary compromises. The ten to one majority was a vindication of the strategy of accommodation: even more significant was the achievement of a clear majority in each of the districts, including Nottinghamshire. By their votes the miners immediately turned the thirty-seven existing districts and craft organisations into twenty-one areas or groups.[40]

Continuing the compromise

With the Allied victory and the Labour victory in 1945, the miners having created their new organisation, now focussed on much bigger issues. The NUM's main objectives of the postwar world were the nationalisation of the coal industry and the implementation of the new Miners' Charter which had largely been drafted by Horner on the eve

of his becoming the general secretary of the NUM. According to
Will Paynter, a relatively young miners' agent of the time, the sense
of achievement was immense, almost millenarian: '[For the
generation of Edwards and Horner] ... Release from the old
coalowners ... was not only progress, it was paradise!'

Paynter succeeded Horner as NUM secretary in 1959. He imitated
Horner's tactical footwork but not his romantic view of
nationalisation nor his view of the creation of the NUM. Paynter
however did acknowledge that they were important first steps and his
praise for that was fulsome. Horner would be remembered for:

> Standards of oratory; of negotiating skills; of introducing significant
> agreements that became historic, like the Day Wage Structure which led
> onto other things; creating patterns that would stand the test of time; his
> contribution in the formation of the NUM and his contribution to the
> establishment of the Coal Board. Creatures of time and circumstances
> we are in the end, aren't we? He was a man of his time but he made
> a terrific contribution *to* his time *and* to the working class principles
> that guided him.[41]

The structure of the NUM, despite the intentions of many of its
founders, did not evolve organically. For the most part it ossified in
the postwar period and did not change fundamentally, although some
neighbouring areas did successfully merge (Forest of Dean and
Somerset became part of South Wales). Strategically, Horner and
Paynter, faced by a rightwing majority on the national executive
placed their faith in achieving greater national unity through national
wage agreements, and especially the Third Day Wage Structure
(1955) and the National Power Loading Agreement (1966) which
eliminated piece work and thus disparities between coalfields.
Undoubtedly the latter agreement provided the platform for the
successful national strikes of 1972 and 1974.

The historic demand for a streamlined and centralised
democratically accountable national industrial union remained elusive.
In 1961, Paynter attempted to take up some of the issues left on the
Nottingham table in 1944, but all his proposals (including better
representation for craftsmen and more professional central staffing)
were rejected out of hand. The real reasons emerged later:

> Not until some time later was I told in confidence that the real reason
> for the rejection of the document was that the suggested reforms would

have upset the balance between left and right in the union and would have strengthened the position of the left.[42]

In 1944-45, strategies were devised to maintain the delicate distribution of power between local, regional and national interests. The pedagogy of the miner combined with his capacity to learn from experience, combined also with the fortunes of war, resulted in the organic emergence of the NUM. The compromise settlement took account of the historic bedrock of pit branches and coalfield unions within the culture of the national organisation. Unfortunately the achievements of 1944-45 have been obscured by the left-right struggle within the NUM from the Cold War through to the early 1980s. The left increasingly saw the resolution of the union's problems in terms of greater democratic accountability via majority rule and centralisation. The right, by contrast, used its built-in national executive majority, merely to defend the *status quo*.

Notes

Place of publication is London unless otherwise stated.

1. Arthur Horner at the MFGB annual conference, July 1943, published proceedings, p. 336.
2. W. Ashworth (and M. Pegg), *The History of the British Coal Industry, Vol. 5, 1946-1982, The Nationalised Industry* (Oxford, 1986), p. 3.
3. South Wales Coalfield Archive, Bedwas Lodge Minutes, Vol. 5, 21 December 1944.
4. This was the theme of Michael McGahey's speech in the first full national debate on unity following the 1984-85 strike at the Tenby NUM Conference, July 1986.
5. J.E. Williams, *The Derbyshire Miners* (1962), p. 875.
6. This can be seen in the words of Dai Francis, General Secretary of the NUM (South Wales Area) between 1963 and 1976. He had been part of the process of achieving the NUM in 1944-45 but often proposed the toast: 'Long live the South Wales Miners, and long may they continue to influence the affairs of the National Union'.
7. Interview with Margot Heinemann, 7 February 1983.
8. For discussion of this term, see D. Gilbert, *Class, Community and Collective Action: social change in two British coalfields, 1850-1926* (Oxford, 1992), pp. 9-13.

9. For an estimation of Sam Watson's career in the DMA, see H. Beynon and T. Austrin, *Masters and Servants: class and patronage in the making of a labour organisation* (1994), pp. 357-62.

10. These comments were made frequently by Will Paynter at schools and conferences which he attended in his retirement, particularly in his capacity as President of Llafur, the Welsh Labour History Society.

11. V.L. Allen, *The Militancy of the British Miners* (Shipley, 1981), *passim*.

12. National Union of Mineworkers, *Rules* (1947), p. 3.

13. For a discussion of the importance of *The Miners' Next Step* and subsequent tracts on industrial democracy, see K. Coates, *Democracy in the Mines* (1974), pp. 7-30, and H. Francis and D. Smith, *The Fed: a history of the South Wales miners in the twentieth century* (1980), pp. 13-16.

14. R. Lewis, *Teachers and Leaders* (Cardiff, 1991), *passim*, provides the most detailed discussion of these educational and political developments. *The Miners' Next Step* was reprinted with 'a note of explanation' in October 1964 by the South Wales Area's Cymric Federation Press. In the foreword the then general secretary wrote that there was a clear educational purpose behind the reprint: 'This pamphlet could very well be the subject of discussion at our Weekend Schools and at classes that could be organised in the mining villages'.

15. R.J. Waller, *The Dukeries Transformed* (Oxford, 1983); R.M. Jones, 'A note on 1926 in North Wales', *Llafur*, vol. 2, no. 2, pp. 59-64; Francis and Smith, *The Fed*, pp. 113-144.

16. See S. McIntyre, *Little Moscows* (1980) for a series of local studies which reveal the strength and limitations of communist influence.

17. Beynon and Austrin, *Masters and Servants*; M. Pitt, *The World on Our Backs* (1979), pp. 20-36; Waller, *The Dukeries*.

18. A. Horner and G.A. Hutt, *Communism and Coal* (1928), pp. 185-217.

19. R. Page Arnot, *The Miners in Crisis and War* (1961), pp. 194-243; Gilbert, above, Chapter 7 of this volume.

20. N. Fishman, 'Coal: owned and managed on behalf of the people', in J. Fyrth (ed.), *Labour's High Noon: the government and the economy, 1945-51* (1993), p. 72.

21. MFGB conference report, 1936, p. 23.

22. Williams, *Debyshire Miners*, p. 609.

23. MFGB conference report, 1937, p. 311.

24. MFGB conference report, p. 131.

25. MFGB conference report, p. 150.

26. MFGB conference report, 1938, p. 343. For the Communist Party, see *Daily Worker*, 18, 19, 20 July 1938.

27. MFGB Executive Minutes, 15 December 1938. See also *Daily Worker*, 25 October, 17 November 1938.
28. MFGB Executive Minutes, 12 January 1939.
29. Durham, Northumberland, and South Wales stood to gain substantially from a national wages agreement which the MFGB hoped to manoeuvre the coalowners into accepting. These coalfields were less profitable than Yorkshire, Midlands and East Midlands. Their wages would be substantially increased by a national agreement, whilst miners in the profitable coalfields would gain much less. A unified union would be in a much better position to pressurise the coalowners to concede a national wages agreement.
30. T. Hall, *King Coal* (1981), pp. 52-63; Francis and Smith, *The Fed*, pp. 392-419.
31. M. Heinemann, *Britain's Coal: a study of the mining crisis* (1944); Margot Heinemann interview.
32. Quoted in Arnot, *Miners in Crisis*, p. 354. It is very likely that Lawther's colourful phrase had been given to him by Margot Heinemann who wrote many of his speeches and articles at this time, but never Horner's. (M. Heinemann, interview.)
33. Williams, *Derbyshire Miners*, p. 874.
34. Arnot, *Miners in Crisis*, p. 356.
35. Quoted in W.R. Garside, *The Durham Miners, 1919-1960* (1971), p. 383.
36. A thorough search of the vast South Wales Coalfield archive reveals very little discussion on the reorganisation issues, in stark contrast to the era of *The Miners' Next Step* or even the early 1930s in the run-up to the creation of the rank and file executive council.
37. MFGB Conference proceedings, 1943, pp. 312-338; Arnot, *Miners in Crisis*, especially pp. 404-430.
38. MFGB Special Conference Report, 16 August 1944.
39. MFGB Conference proceedings, 1944, pp. 455-611, *passim*.
40. Interview with Will Paynter, 8 February 1983; Arnot, *Miners in Crisis*, *passim*.
41. Paynter interview.
42. Will Paynter, *My Generation* (1972), p. 149. Paynter's concern for industrial union structures, rooted in syndicalist theory and practical experience is reflected in his *British Trade Unions and the Problem of Change* (1970).

CHAPTER ELEVEN

The beginning of the beginning: the National Union of Mineworkers and nationalisation

Nina Fishman

After the Labour Party's stunning victory in the July 1945 general election, it was assumed that the Labour government would nationalise the coal industry. The three main players in the process, the government, the 'progressive' managers of private coal companies who largely staffed the National Coal Board (NCB), and the National Union of Mineworkers (NUM) who represented the vast majority of miners, invested substantial political capital in the venture. They also had correspondingly high expectations. It was pressure from the NUM which determined that the government opted to centralise the industry rather than a devolved scheme of the sort suggested by the Coal Commission in 1938. It was the 'progressive' managers support for radical change which ensured that nationalisation was well received by public opinion. The Cabinet gave coal nationalisation higher priority than most other parts of its domestic programme. The spectre of coal shortages which would hamper reconstruction loomed very large in their minds.

On Vesting Day, 1st January 1947, the NCB acquired about a thousand pits and 700,000 miners. Its chairman, Lord Hyndley, aged 63, had been managing director of Britain's largest mining company, Powell Duffryn, in South Wales. Commercial adviser to the Department of Mines from 1918-38, he then administered the government's wartime controls on the coal industry in 1942-3. Two other managers of private coal companies became Board members, Charles Carlow Reid and T.E.B. Young. Reid was a mining engineer, and had been manager and director of the Fife Coal Company: 'Since 1942 he had been Production Director of the Ministry of Fuel and Power and had chaired the committee which brilliantly analysed the technical problems of the coal industry and pointed the way to specific drastic reforms'. Young was a mining engineer and had been managing director of the Bolsover Colliery Co. in Derbyshire.[1]

The Board member for industrial relations was Ebby Edwards, previously secretary of the Miners' Federation of Great Britain (MFGB) since 1932, and secretary of the newly unified NUM in 1945. Edwards accepted the NCB post with great reluctance, after powerful pressure from Emmanuel Shinwell, the Minister for Fuel and Power. The subsequent election contest for NUM Secretary resulted in a decisive, if predictable victory for the communist South Wales miners' leader, Arthur Horner.

The coal industry's transition from 800 privately owned companies to one centralised corporation 'owned and managed on behalf of the people' is usually depicted in dramatic terms.[2] Contemporary participants and observers certainly viewed coal as a test case for Labour's commitment to build democratic socialism. However, ideological commitment was not the primary motivation for the government's expropriation of the coalowners at the earliest opportunity. The wartime coalition government had been dogged by the likelihood of severe coal shortages. The coal problem seemed set to continue, even intensify.[3] Even if the Conservatives had won the election, it is highly unlikely they would have restored the industry to its pre-war pattern of private ownership.

Since 1915, successive British governments had been compelled by political necessity to apply their minds to the recurring vicissitudes of the coal industry. Cabinets usually delayed putting coal on their agendas. Eventually, they all reluctantly engaged with the notoriously complex and politically explosive issues. Coal matters affected large numbers of MPs and their constituents since working coalfields were to be found in most parts of the island. From 1921 there was persistent structural unemployment in the exporting coalfields of South Wales, Scotland, and the North East of England. The attendant problems, extreme poverty, severe social dislocation and community demoralisation were unending. Concern at this social distress and the prospect of social unrest persuaded the 1929 Labour government to make a serious attempt to enforce reorganisation on the industry.

The 1930 Coal Mines Act established a compulsory marketing

scheme for domestic coal. The industry was divided into districts, each of which received a production quota from a central committee. Minimum prices were set by district committees to further restrict competition. The scheme met with considerable opposition in the industry, and there were many unexpected difficulties in enforcing it. Further government intervention was required in 1934: administrative procedures were tightened; separate production quotas for inland sales were established; and moves initiated towards national price coordination.

After the national wage claim of the MFGB had been settled in 1936, the coalowners themselves took the last steps towards cartelisation. With their support, a further amendment to the Coal Mines Act was passed. District selling organisations were set up and machinery provided for their national coordination: 'Slowly, but none the less surely, and spurred by state initiative and the relaxation of official inhibitions, the industry's marketing moved from competition to control'.[4]

The effect of a nationally regulated system of district cartels was to restrict competition both within each district between collieries and also between districts. Yorkshire and Nottinghamshire collieries produced coal more cheaply than pits in South Wales or Lancashire. However coal companies in Yorkshire and Nottinghamshire were constrained to limit their production, allowing the more expensive coal from the other coalfields to 'compete'. The advantage for Yorkshire and Nottinghamshire owners was that the price at which their coal was sold was 'artificially' high, and therefore their own profit per tonne was higher.

It was the consumer, not the taxpayer, who paid for the statutory cartel. There has been little research on this aspect of the interwar industry, but it seems that there was little public opposition to the element of subsidy built in to the price of consumers' household coal. In the 1935-6 national wage dispute, the MFGB national officials capitalised on the public's willingness to pay a higher price for their coal to ensure that miners received a living wage. Major purchasers of coal, led by ICI and the cooperative societies, signified their willingness to pay a higher price for coal provided that the increase was used finance miners' wages.[5]

Reorganisation was the second important feature of the 1930 Coal Mines Act. The act provided for the appointment of a Coal Mines

Reorganisation Commission to promote best practice and amalgamations of the smaller coal companies. The commission proceeded with enthusiasm and misplaced optimism. Its members evidently believed that because the case for reorganisation was economically unanswerable, reason and good will would prevail. However, their reports and recommendations proved dead letters, despite the best efforts of the chairman, Sir Ernest Gowers, an energetic and somewhat eccentric civil servant and his fellow commissioners including the MFGB president Joseph Jones.

Reorganisation continued to pre-occupy successive governments. The impasse created by the coalowners' refusal to cooperate with the commission involved the Chamberlain government in yet another attempt to reorganise the industry. Legislation passed in 1938 provided for the nationalisation of the mineral rights for coal and created a new Coal Commission with greater statutory powers than its unfortunate predecessor.[6]

Willingness to act against the market was not unusual for Conservative cabinets of the time. Baldwin's government had bypassed market mechanisms to ensure that electrification proceeded quickly and affordably throughout the whole of Britain. Their determination to act despite the market was a modernising one. The same rationale prevailed for coal. The large coal companies were clear that an efficient industry capable of paying its own way would never result from the workings of unbridled *laisser faire*. Too many small coalowners existed who could make an acceptable profit without investing in coal cutting machinery or mechanised transport.

The remit of the revamped Coal Commission was never tested. War intervened before Gowers and his fellow members could flex their institutional muscles. Nevertheless the wartime emergency did not mean that the government could postpone the more mundane coal problem. By 1942 the coalition government found itself as intimately involved in the coal industry as its wartime predecessor. In 1915 state intervention was triggered by 'industrial unrest' at the manifest failure of miners' wages to keep pace with the rampant inflation. South Walian miners refused to produce coal out of altruistic patriotism whilst the owners reaped allegedly colossal profits.

David Lloyd George, Minister of Munitions, moved swiftly to impose the radical solution of state control in all the coalfields. Nationalisation and centralisation of the coal industry's forward planning, distributive and administrative mechanisms were carried out under duress. Overseeing production remained the owner's prerogative, but administration, including wages, the allocation and distribution of production, and coal prices, became the government's province.

Churchill and Bevin, like Asquith and Lloyd George before them, had previous bitter experience of the coal problem. However they too were eventually drawn into the labyrinthine complexities which the industry continued to present. The decisive factor was again miners' willingness to strike in defiance of wartime emergency legislation. This time the law was Order 1305.

Miners were being exhorted from all sides to work intensively and enthusiastically in unsatisfactory conditions for pre-war wage levels which reflected the industry's straitened circumstances. Not surprisingly, there was 'disaffection over pay ... [which] became a serious threat to production, and therefore the war effort, fairly early on'.[7] In the first five months of 1942, there was a rash of unofficial strikes, including miners in usually moderate coalfields. Led by equally disaffected union lay officials, the strikers acted outside the law to take opportunist advantage of their greatly enhanced bargaining power. Their self-interested action could be (and was) criticised. Nevertheless, despite strong pressure from the MFGB and district union officials, the strikes continued.[8]

There was no question of the Ministry of Labour initiating prosecutions after the debacle in January when summonses served on hundreds of Kent miners for a strike lasting 19 days at Betteshanger colliery had to be withdrawn and their imprisoned union leaders released through the intervention of the Home Secretary. Instead, the government appointed a commission under the chairmanship of the Master of the Rolls, Lord Greene. Its recommendations, produced at high speed, awarded a substantial wage increase to all miners and provided for a return to the pre-1926 conditions of national collective bargaining.[9] The MFGB's arguments for the national determination of wages were based upon principles of fairness and equity. They proved unanswerable in the atmosphere of people's war and equality of sacrifice.

But the Greene award did not buy much time. Coal soon re-emerged as a problem for the coalition government. Increased wages did not produce the anticipated increase in coal production. Patriotic propaganda and the Communist Party's best efforts to inspire miners to defend the Soviet Socialist Fatherland met with little response. As Supple notes, '... coal *was* exceptional in being crucial to so many aspects of the war and civilian economy; and the prospect of disaster seemed real enough to those directly involved'.[10]

The government commissioned the Technical Advisory Committee to report on production in 1944 in order to be seen to be doing something about the anticipated coal crisis. Reid, the committee's chairman, was flanked by a bevy of other technical experts and owners from the 'progressive', highly profitable sector of coalmining. The report embodied their view, as scientific managers and large capitalists, that the industry must be substantially reorganised to ensure the rational and profitable exploitation of coal reserves. Its findings were hardly new, but its recommendations were certainly sweeping. The report's message to owners of the smaller and/or older pits was that their time had come.

The Reid Report had a revelatory effect upon public opinion, similar to the impact of the earlier Beveridge Report. Not surprisingly, the MFGB national officials seized upon its findings as vindicating their case for nationalisation. The myth is still current that Reid recommended nationalisation. In fact the report confined itself to a meticulous account of the enormous capital investment necessary to modernise the British coalmining industry, to enable it to compete on an international market and provide coal for domestic use at competitive prices.

What is fascinating is the persistence to the end of the fiercely *petit bourgeois* outlook which had dominated the Coalowners' Association throughout the interwar period. The absence of a detailed history of the association and its internal politics is a surprising lacuna in business history. The 'progressive' owners apparently made no serious attempt to convince their anachronistic brethren that they too could benefit from embracing the Reid Report.[11] When the Labour government nationalised coal, its justification was neither socialism nor class vendetta, but rather the need to transform the coal industry along lines recommended by its most efficient capitalists.

Given the uncontested consensus in favour of the Reid Report, the Labour government acted without delay to solve the coal problem. Their prime motivation for pressing forward was expediency. The Labour Party's election manifesto, *Let Us Face the Future*, pledged to socialise the fuel and power industries. No White Paper on coal was issued and none evidently was expected. There were no protests of constitutional impropriety when the Coal Industry Nationalisation Bill was introduced in December 1945. It passed through all its stages within six months and received royal assent in July 1946.[12]

The Coalowners' Association offered no serious opposition to the bill throughout the parliamentary debates. Owners who intended to bail out of the industry were mollified by Shinwell's pledge of generous financial compensation. Those who planned a future in coalmining could see that their technical and managerial skills would be required by the National Coal Board, whose designated members met daily during the summer of 1946 to plan the new public corporation's structure.

At this stage, the 'progressive' capitalists may well have concluded that they had received the best deal of any of the players. In return for the surrender of formal title to possession, they gained not only ample monetary compensation, but also the near certainty that they would be redeployed by a new state enterprise in which their leadership would be unquestioned. After all, they were the only ones who knew how to run it. In the euphoria accompanying the Allied victory and the attendant atmosphere of collective commitment to domestic reconstruction, these new NCB managers had hardly incurred an irreparable loss.

The NUM's indifference to the nationalisation bill's lack of detail on the structure and remit of the National Coal Board is notorious. There is no evidence, however, that their lack of attention to formal details was either imprudent or due, as is commonly supposed, to lack of foresight. The NUM Executive of 26, including five Communists, had no reason to doubt that Shinwell and his colleagues in government would ensure that the NCB provided acceptable terms and conditions of employment.[13] In 1912 *The Miners' Next Step* had addressed the issues of control and administration in the coal industry. Twenty four years later in 1946, the NUM were pre-occupied by a very different problem.

It had been assumed by coalowner and coalminer alike in 1912 that the future prosperity of the industry was assured. Miners' wages were moving steeply upwards and miners were winning industrial conflicts.[14] By 1946, after over a generation of poverty, uncertainty and unsettled industrial relations, NUM leaders were preoccupied by

very different questions.   They showed great perspicacity and
determination in pursuing them through to a favourable conclusion
well in advance of Vesting Day.

Coincidentally with the bill's first reading in the Commons, Horner
produced a new Miners' Charter.   At the time he was the NUM's
National Coal Production Officer, a post created in response to a
request from Shinwell, who was evidently concerned to show that the
union was responsibly addressing a thorny problem, which was
taking up so much of his own ministerial time.   Horner linked the
question of production with miners' economic and social conditions.
His analytic and propaganda point was that coal shortages could only
be alleviated if miners' living standards and status were radically
improved and the new levels then maintained.

> This time it was different.   I was not setting down the minimum
> demands of the miners.   I was setting down the minimum conditions
> which would enable the industry to go on functioning.   We were not
> presenting an ultimatum; we were simply setting on record the
> conditions which must obtain in the mines, if the men were to be there
> to dig the coal.[15]

The Charter's rationale provided the cornerstone of the NUM's
approach to the nationalised industry until the late 1960s.   It accepted
the requirement for the Coal Board to produce sufficient coal to meet
the nation's needs in an efficient manner.   But it was also an
affirmation that the union would continue to seek the best possible
wages and conditions for its members from a nationalised employer.
Its first demand made oblique reference to the need for miners to
accept   pit   closures,   by   supporting   the   Reid   Committee's
recommendations for modernising the industry.[16]

Its other 11 points included a guaranteed weekly wage; the
restoration of the 7 hour day and the introduction of a 5 day week
without loss of pay; a comprehensive occupational pension scheme;
and extended holidays with pay.   Management were also expected to
provide for 'the adequate and careful training of youth in the various
phases of mining operations and [to establish] ... a clearly defined
scheme of promotion, [and] ... provision of further training and
tuition, in cases where workers desire to enter for a colliery
technician's career.[17]

After the Charter was accepted by the NUM executive, it was sent to Shinwell with a note 'to the effect that the NUM, having in mind the manpower crises and recognising the complete dependence of the country's economy upon coal production, "calls upon the Government through the Minister of Fuel and Power to give guarantees that effect will be given to the foregoing measures in accordance with a timetable and a progressive plan"'.   Shinwell replied on 11 March with an official letter saying 'one of the principal objects of Government policy' in nationalising the coalmining industry was to achieve 'the kind of far-reaching reforms and improvements contained in the Charter'.[18] The union had thus secured the principal objectives which it sought from nationalisation well before the actual transition to public ownership took place.

In signing up for the Charter, the cabinet responded as astute politicians. In the government's view, the NUM and its members were the last part of the equation which they required for securing the nation's coal supplies. The NUM executive promised that the Charter would bring increased productivity, efficiency, less absenteeism, less industrial conflict and more young men coming into mining. Miners had been blamed by much of public opinion and many experts for the wartime coal shortages. By agreeing to the Charter, the government could plausibly claim to be solving the coal problem. Expediency aside, Attlee's government felt a moral commitment as socialists. The vision offered by the Charter of the industry's future accorded with their own. It balanced the Reid Report's call for modernisation and pursuit of efficiency with humane improvements in wages and conditions along with egalitarian opportunities for advancement within the nationalised industry.

Even though the cabinet's pledge to the NUM seriously violated the NCB's managerial autonomy, their consciences evidently remained untroubled. The cabinet's tendency to interfere in the coal industry continued in the summer of 1947. Having suffered severe political damage during the previous winter of record cold and coal shortage, the government was determined to take pre-emptive steps in good time. A cabinet committee met with NUM officials in a bid to prevent another winter of discontent.

Bevin spoke for the committee, putting forward a proposal for a modification to the five day week agreement recently concluded between the NUM and the NCB. They wanted the NUM to agree that all miners should work an extra, sixth shift every week. (The fact that the NCB had only conceded the early operation of the five day week agreement under duress from the cabinet made the situation even more poignant.[19]) Horner described the negotiations which ensued when Bevin deployed his old skills on the other side of the table:

> Bevin, who appeared to think he was going to have an easy victory, got angrier and angrier as we went on making conditions. Finally he said, 'You have got a damned cheek. You've got your five-day week on a basis that is not unreasonable, and now you are offering to sell us the sixth day at overtime rates.' I replied, 'It is you who are asking for the overtime. We don't want it, and that is why we are insisting that if we give you overtime it must be on a voluntary basis ... While these discussions were going on, members of the Coal Board, including the Chairman, Lord Hyndley ... were waiting in an adjoining room, having been summoned there by the Cabinet. After we had reached our agreement, an official went to tell them they would not be required any more. They were sent away without any further information.[20]

It must have seemed in the early summer of 1947 that the NUM were seeing more of their expectations fulfilled than either the government or the 'progressive' managers. Though nationalisation had been mining unions' principal political goal in the interwar period, few activists believed they would live to see it. The prospect of its finally coming to fruition produced heady euphoria in NUM delegate conferences and executive meetings throughout 1946. The atmosphere of self-congratulation continued through much of 1947. Underneath the surface, however, there was evidence of disorientation.

Since the 1890s, British socialists had eagerly anticipated the first steps being taken towards abolishing wasteful and inefficient capitalist production. Public ownership provided an opportunity to develop the new morality of collective responsibility which was an essential complement to socialist production. The question of how socialist enterprises would function had been reflected upon and debated in the abstract. But miners' officials were facing a problem, which the early pioneers had not foreseen: how to pursue their members' interests when conflicts of interests occurred with their nationalised employers the NCB, whose shareholders were 'the people'.

The lead in arriving at a solution was given by Horner. He drew on a precedent which was familiar to British union leaders, the situation of unions in the socialist USSR. The Webbs' journey to the Soviet Union and their enthusiastic description of the success of the First Five Year Plan were well known. Many influential union officers, including Jack Little, president of the Amalgamated Engineering Union, had themselves visited the USSR as guests of the Soviet unions and paid particular attention to their place in the 1936 'Stalin' constitution.[21]

At the inception of the Soviet state, Lenin acknowledged the need for autonomous unions. They had, of course, a socialist responsibility to ensure that their members carried out their duties as workers in a workers' state, but they also had to defend their members' collective interests in potential conflicts when the employer might well be a state-owned enterprise. It was recognised that the nature of the production process, of industrial work, continued under socialism; unions must therefore continue to safeguard workers against exploitation.

The theory of how Soviet unions operated allowed for the inevitability of conflict when the proletariat in individual factories and industries had interests at variance with the state. Their structure allowed for a formal independence from the state with which successive leaderships had not tampered.[22] With hindsight, (and to many contemporary observers), it is clear that the actual practice was routinely at variance with these theoretical constructs to the grave detriment of workers on the ground. At the time, the USSR was the only example of socialism in practice. Most British union leaders who visited the USSR in the 1930s and early 1940s were thoroughly impressed by the examples they were shown of the role which unions played.

Horner followed the Soviet example and argued that, on the one hand, the NUM had to defend members' interests against exploitation and abuse by the NCB. On the other hand, the union also had to ensure members fulfilled their responsibility to make the publicly owned industry successful and efficient. He outlined this dual role at the NUM's conference in July 1947, the first gathering of the union since Vesting Day.

> ... these things we want, this new wages structure, this new minimum [wage] - all these reforms, which represent in their totality the change in the status of the British mineworkers, have got to be got by one means or another out of the coal which is produced in British pits ... If

this Coal Board fails, we cannot succeed in realising our objectives, and as an Executive we have got to tell you so. We cannot hope, as the men expect us to do, to go week by week, securing one concession after the other, if at the back of us there are elements who are robbing the Coal Board of the very means that would enable them to give us what we are asking for - especially when those elements belong to our own ranks.[23]

Most miners' working lives were not substantially different in Year One of the new Board. From the end of the phoney war, the official priority for colliery management had been to maximise coal production, not profits. In 1942, management prerogative was further modified by the regime of dual control imposed by the coalition government.[24] Under this disposition, union officials sat alongside management on pit production committees and arrived at joint approaches to absenteeism, welfare and pit safety. Though the committees functioned with indifferent success, many union activists tried to address production problems for the sake of defeating fascism, (and, in some cases, helping the Soviet Socialist Fatherland).

The historiography of coal nationalisation highlights the failure of the rank and file miner to identify with the Coal Board. The evidence, both contemporary and recollections recorded recently long after the event, is marshalled to show that the NCB failed to live up to socialist expectations that a publicly owned industry would show itself superior in efficiency and industrial relations to its private predecessors. However, whilst many union activists undoubtedly had disappointed expectations, it is not obvious that 'ordinary' miners were overly concerned with the unchanging nature of their daily work experience.

Since 1942 rank and file miners not been subjected to the rigours of a cost-cutting management. They also had protection against the vicissitudes of arbitrary or capricious managers. Their wages had increased significantly and they had been guaranteed security of employment. They had certainly been continuously exhorted to produce coal to the maximum extent of their physical capacity. The pursuit of increased output by both management and union men was unremitting. If anything, the union campaign for more production was intensified after Vesting Day.

Greasley's recent examination of labour productivity failed to substantiate perceptions of miners' poor work performance which were current at the time.[25] This is an important conclusion and goes a long way towards dispelling the stereotype of the 'slacking' miner which loomed so large in popular perceptions of the time. Nevertheless when contemporary 'experts' applied their minds to coal, the problem of low productivity appeared not only to be a key issue, but also intractable. The sociologist Ferdynand Zweig visited most English coalfields and also South Wales between July and October 1947. He concluded that for many young miners, there was no material advantage to be gained from working a full week of five shifts: the last day's wage was only taken by the taxman. Shortages meant that there was little choice of non-essential goods and pleasures on which to spend their increased money.[26]

The disparity between Greasley's analysis and contemporary experts' may be explained by the observation, made by both Ashworth and Greasley, that in most pits there was little physical scope for increasing productivity above its existing levels. It is true that many miners in many coalfields did not work full weeks. However even if they had worked full weeks, output per man shift, the measure of labour productivity in the industry, would not have increased proportionately.[27] This comparatively nuanced conclusion is not difficult for a scholar to make with the benefit of an abundance of statistical evidence and also without the pressure of contemporary politics. At the time, it was, however, far from obvious. The Labour government continued to place increased coal production high on its own list of priorities. Union leaders continued to feel responsible for ensuring that this goal was met. In the circumstances, it is only surprising that there was not more reaction from the rank and file to this unremitting pursuit of Stakhanovism.

Contemporaries and subsequent historiography have pointed to the fact that management personnel in the pits remained largely unchanged after nationalisation as another source of disillusion with the NCB.[28] Zweig noted the common observation of working under the same management, but he also recorded that: 'The miners have no doubt that nationalization was both necessary and beneficial, and has brought them a great many improvements ...'. A more recent investigator conducted twenty-seven interviews with South Wales miners who had started work before 1947. She found that: '... the overwhelming majority ... thought that nationalization was "a good thing" ... "a wonderful thing" ... "the best thing that has come into the mines" ... because ... "we had a better deal, we've had more fair play"'.[29]

During the debates on the Coal Industry Nationalisation bill, no one, except Harold Macmillan as a half-serious devil's advocate, suggested that rank and file miners should run their pits as direct democracies and abolish management. In July 1948, G.D.H. Cole, a veteran advocate of guild socialism, wrote a Fabian pamphlet justifying the NCB's management structure. He argued that it was unrealistic to expect nationalisation to transform capitalist enterprises into workers' control at a stroke. He looked forward optimistically to the contribution which colliery consultative committees could make towards industrial democracy:

> Whatever wider forms of workers' cooperation may develop at a later stage, the foundations must be laid by creating in each pit the right atmosphere of cooperation and the right machinery for promoting that atmosphere ... Consultation is nothing, unless it reaches the individual directly; but it is also very nearly nothing unless, in addition, it gives the individual the sense of being really represented by persons who are close enough to him in his actual work to be able to express his views, and of a real willingness on the part of the lower as well as the higher management to give these representatives a sympathetic hearing.[30]

Cole's description of how consultation should operate was highly ambitious. His hopes for the process were shared by more orthodox 'state socialists', who were committed to giving the human element in management a high priority. The NUM viewed the NCB's intention of employing ex-NUM officials as Labour Officers at all levels of its structure as an additional guarantee that the union's viewpoint would be influential. The TUC had strongly advocated that all nationalised industries should adopt this practice to ensure that boardrooms and management were thoroughly imbued both with a democratic atmosphere spirit and trade union viewpoint. In its foundation years, the NCB was probably the most conspicuous practitioner of this philosophy. Cole noted:

> As a plain matter of fact, the NUM, nationally, regionally and locally, is reckoning on playing a part in the control of the coal industry, without any corresponding responsibility, through the ex-miners who hold office as members of the Board or in divisional or local positions under it ... The key position occupied by the ex-Trade Union leaders on the NCB itself was a principal factor in inducing the NUM not to press for direct representation ...[31]

In addition to Ebby Edwards' position as the member of the NCB for labour relations, the Board actively sought capable union officials to become Labour Officers at the regional and divisional level.[32] Many of the activists who accepted jobs were were not only committed socialists, some were also members of the CPGB.[33] From the outset, they approached their duties with a strong sense of idealism. The first task for many of them was handling the unofficial strikes which broke out in the summer of 1947 in some coalfields over the operation of the five day week agreement. It was to prove a real baptism of fire. Their cause was clear: miners were unwilling to work harder in order to earn the same amount of money.

Under the five day week agreement, to qualify for the guaranteed weekly wage, miners now had to complete a full week of five shifts. Only union business or industrial injury qualified for exemption. This was an attendance bonus in all but name. The NUM had also agreed that miners should work their full shift, or stint. At one level, this 'concession' appears trivial. It was merely a formal acknowledgement that miners had to work the hours of work specified in their contacts of employment. However, in practice, the union had signed away the long-standing *de facto* custom of job and finish operating in many coalfields, notably Yorkshire.[34]

The NUM officers signed the agreement in good faith but also with open eyes. They were committed to the union principle of a five not a six-day week even though they knew full well that many miners would have to work harder during those five shifts than they had done previously. The officers also believed the proper operation of the agreement would safeguard the future of the coal industry. The difficulties in recruiting young men to mining which had emerged in the late 1930s in the profitable coalfields had been exacerbated during the war by the expansion of engineering, including war factories in the South Yorkshire and South Wales coalfields, providing easier and more lucrative job opportunities.[35] NUM leaders believed that a guaranteed five-day week was required to make coalmining an attractive, 'modern', well-paid career for youth.

In the first months of the agreement's operation, their expectations were justified. Recruitment to the industry improved and total output of coal increased. But unofficial strikes, many concerned with men refusing to work the full stint, also increased. Ashworth observes: 'In general, though there were many local exceptions, the response to the appeals by both the NCB and the NUM for men to take on greater tasks [to work the full stint] was disappointing'.[36]

The NUM's annual conference in July 1947 was held in the background of the agreement's adverse consequences. By this time, coal production was well below the target set by the NCB. It is remarkable that delegates did not challenge the leadership, indeed they affirmed with virtual unanimity that the officers had done the right thing in negotiating the agreement. They evidently shared the officers' clear conception of the union's new dual role and their strong commitment to fulfilling it. Speaking in private session on behalf of the executive, Horner was candid.

> The losses which might have been reduced or evaded following the five-day week are not being evaded, because of the downward tendency of output ... But the position is made worse by something which is curable, and for which we are responsible, and that is the unsatisfactory relations within the industry expressed in unconstitutional stoppages ... following on the greatest single concession in our history [the 5 day week agreement] we have had little or no diminution of the losses. It is intolerable, and the Executive Committee wishes it to be clearly understood that if a minority violate the policy of this Union, and thereby reduce the capacity of the Board to concede the reforms which we are asking for, then that minority must be regarded as an alien force, and treated as an enemy of the true interests of the majority of the miners of this country.[37]

As soon as he sat down, Sammy Watson from Durham moved that the union print a transcript of Horner's speech and distribute it to the membership. This was agreed without debate.[38] The Yorkshire area president, Ernest Jones, then delivered a ringing affirmation of Horner's 'excellent statement':

> I was never prouder of the moral courage and the moral leadership of some of our local officials in my own district ... those of our men who have never been prepared to bow the knee to Baal or to sacrifice responsibility to expediency - men who have been prepared to stand up to their responsibilities, prepared to take the unpopular point of view if it was right in the interests of this Movement and the common good of the men employed in the coalmining industry ...[39]

Despite this official optimism, the longest, most notorious unofficial strike began at Grimethorpe colliery in South Yorkshire on 11

August. It was precipitated by an attempt to enforce the full stint on faceworkers. At the end of August, when the divisional manager, General Mickie Holmes, signified his intention to summons the strikers for breach of contract, intermittent sympathetic strikes began in neighbouring pits. At one point, nearly one-third of the men working in the South Yorkshire coalfield came out.

The Grimethorpe strike was proof for the sceptical political establishment that British miners and the public were disillusioned by nationalisation, which they had always believed to be a misguided and dogmatic adventure. Its contemporary notoriety has survived into the historiography of the NCB.[40] The strike, coming so soon after Vesting Day, is cited as evidence of the NCB's failure to fulfil the sanguine predictions made by the government and NUM in anticipation of Vesting Day. A different interpretation of the strike and the strong public interest is warranted after an examination of its protracted course.

Prior to Holmes's decision to prosecute the Grimethorpe strikers, their action attracted no national interest and very little local attention. It was merely the latest episode in an unexceptional rash of unofficial disputes over the operation of the five day week agreement.[41] The sympathy strikes were well reported because they began in the week before the TUC met, that year in Southport. Congress convened in an atmosphere thick with rumours that Ernest Bevin was about to make a bid to unseat Attlee. The strikes added to the drama of the occasion by appearing to call in question the miners' allegiance to nationalisation.

During Congress week, Holmes made a statement that the men would be sacked unless they returned to work. Horner and Alwyn Machen, a leading Yorkshire area official, dashed across the Pennines to reason with the Grimethorpe strikers not to rise to this provocation. They also began behind the scenes manoeuvres to induce the NCB to bring Holmes to heel.[42] Over the next fortnight, Horner and Yorkshire area officials nearly succeeded on several occasions in arranging a return to work. Each time, some maladroit management action or inept statement of intent which could be misinterpreted as provocative by the local lodge intervened.

The summer of 1947 was glorious. An unbroken run of hot sunny weather had followed the big freeze-up of the previous winter, when record cold temperatures and acute coal shortages produced worse working conditions for millions than they had endured during the war. In addition, there was the full calendar of horse racing meetings, being run for only the second time since their wartime disruption. The combination of high-handed management, glorious sun and racing was evidently sufficient to produce a protracted industrial battle in South Yorkshire.[43]

The Grimethorpe strike attracted a great deal of publicity compared to the other unofficial strikes earlier in the summer. This was partly due to its protracted length and the numbers of men involved in sympathy strikes. But I think the media were also responding to strong public interest. The strikers were the embodiment of a reaction shared by so many people at the time: they were making hay while the sun shone. Government and opposition benches might condemn them, but the strikers reflected an element in the popular mood. For most people, unremitting toil and the luxury of moral rectitude seemed meagre and unfair rewards for the sacrifices of the war years. The strike afforded the opportunity to indulge in vicarious hedonism at the expense of the puritanical cabinet pronouncements.

Despite the political establishment's pronouncements that the strike presaged the downfall of the socialist experiment, there was no discernible backlash against the Labour government or the NCB in any of the coalfields from either lodge officials or their rank and file. In the wider society, there was disgruntlement and dissatisfaction with the present state of affairs. But the summer of 1947 was not a watershed signifying a profound rejection of Labour. The popular interest aroused by Grimethorpe merely showed that the British people could not live by morality alone.

Nevertheless predictions of the NCB's imminent collapse continued into 1948. The gloom merchants could certainly find some evidence for their portents of doom. Many NUM activists were finding their dual role a difficult one to play. They had endured the problematic war years on the assumption that victory would bring an end to their crises of conscience in having to urge their members to work harder and fulfil their contractual duties. But from the current mood in many, though hardly all coalfields, it seemed that there would be an unending succession of tricky double binds which lodge officials would have to negotiate.

The mixed reaction to nationalisation on the ground was reinforced by the Communist Party leadership's change of attitude. Having been enthusiastic and unqualified supporters of nationalisation, the CPGB began to provide strong backing for the pessimistic and dissilusioned view. The *volte face* was a belated response to the Cold War. Communist membership in the coalfields was negligible. But the influence of communist officials and activists inside the NUM was disproportionate to their numbers.[44] If these Communists had faithfully followed the public party line, the NUM might have become irreparably divided over nationalisation.

Despite the external pressure generated by the intense propaganda battle being waged between the Communist and Labour leaderships, the NUM continued to operate as a united, coherent force. Its national and area officers and lodge officials continued to support the NCB. Their suport was not unqualified. Their response to national-isation was inevitably tempered by the learning curve which ex-perience provided. But there was no indication that the union intended to back out of its dual role.

The Labour cabinet recognised the value of the union's support for the NCB. When Ernest Bevin addressed the NUM's annual con-ference in the summer of 1948, he made no reference to the rapidly intensifying Cold War. It was an outstanding omission. As Foreign Secretary, he had recently organised a British diplomatic offensive against what he perceived to be the threat of Soviet expansion westwards. At the NUM conference, he refrained from attacking the British communists who held union office. His speech was finely judged and apparently calculated to reinforce the consensus across political lines on economic issues.

> ... you have a new employer, and I do not think you ought to regard yourselves as being employed by the Coal Board ... You are really employed by the British public. It is the public who are the employers, and the Coal Board are the Managers on behalf of the British public ... I beg of you miners of Great Britain, don't blame the Managers. I say to the Managers in the industry, don't just evade your responsibility, and say, 'Oh, that is the men.' You are both in it ... The miners, with that great, generous soul you have always shown, will not let us down. (Applause)[45]

The NUM could not, however, be wholly immune from the political divisions in the Labour movement caused by the Cold War.

The acid test for the union occurred in the winter of 1948. Horner went to Paris as an NUM fraternal delegate to the congress of the CGT, the communist-dominated union. The congress coincided with a CGT mining strike in the northern region of Pas de Calais. After Horner had, predictably enough, expressed solidarity with the strikers at the congress, he returned home to face 'an army of reporters, photographers and press cameras' at the airport.[46] He then weathered a full-scale confrontation inside the NUM, probably orchestrated by Will Lawther. It was probably Sammy Watson who brokered the compromise. It was an elegant union fudge, which allowed Horner to save face. He remained a communist and also continued in his post as NUM secretary, apparently enjoying the full confidence of Labour loyalists.

The Cold War certainly precipitated complicated changes inside the NUM. But activists of all political complexions continued to work together. Their mutual and overriding priority was domestic; they wanted to prove coal nationalisation a success. In 1948-50, the NUM conference reports and the resolutions submitted by areas for debate revealed confusion and frustration about the failure of nationalisation to give rise to any socialist transformations. There were similar reactions inside the Labour Party to the experience of nationalisation across the board.[47] However the disquiet soon subsided inside both institutions, and did not re-surface until after Labour had won the 1964 general election.

Though successive Conservative governments in the 1950s never contemplated denationalising coal, NUM officials and activists were evidently concerned to defend what they had won. They were content to build upon the foundations of the NCB and the union's complicated relationship laid down in 1945-8. They did not seriously pursue the case for any structural changes in the NCB's management structure. Opting for consolidation meant that the joint consultation committees at pit level became the principal instrument through which the NUM made its influence felt. There has been no serious investigation of the operation of these committees in the NCB but impressionistic evidence confirms the view that the coal industry did indeed approach the vision of industrial democracy which Cole sketched out in 1948.

It was not until the late 1950s that the NCB had the resources to embark upon the ambitious modernisation programme which the 'progressive' managers of the Reid Report had declared was essential to assure the industry's future. By some supreme irony, this was also the point oil completed the conquest of the energy market. International and domestic demand for coal steadily declined. The NCB did not abandon its investments in new super pits. It did, however, embark on an accelerated programme of pit closures in the older export coalfields.

For the first time since 1945, the NUM faced adverse material circumstances and declining prospects for its members. The union was slow to respond to the negative turn of events. When it did so, there was no question of jettisoning the relations which had been established in good faith with colliery management. The union's strategy was defensive. Will Paynter, Horner's communist successor as secretary, organised well-ordered retreats which enabled the NUM to keep its substantial power inside the industry. When the oil price rise decreed by OPEC occurred in 1974, both NCB and NUM were ready to take advantage in the sudden upturn in the market for coal.

In 1947, when the NUM had staked its claim to play a major part in the nationalised coal industry, most activists assumed that they were helping to build an institution which must not only be able to stand the test of time. They were clear that the NCB must serve the needs of the British people, but were determined that it must also meet the interests of their members. It is difficult with the benefit of hindsight to find their efforts misplaced or their construction faulty.

Notes

Place of publication is London unless otherwise stated.

1.   W. Ashworth, *The History of the British Coal Industry, Vol. 5, 1946-1982, The Nationalized Industry* (Oxford, 1986), pp. 3-6, 122-3.
2.   On Vesting Day, notices were displayed throughout the coalfields announcing that: 'This colliery is now owned and managed by the National Coal Board on behalf of the people'. (B. Supple, *The History of the British Coal Industry, Vol. 4, 1913-46, The Political Economy of Decline* (Oxford, 1987), p. 696.)
3.   D. Greasley, 'The coal industry: images and realities on the road to nationalisation', in R. Millward and J. Singleton (eds), *The Political Economy of Nationalisation in Britain 1920-1950* (Cambridge, 1995),

pp. 37-9, and A.J. Robertson, *The Bleak Midwinter 1947* (Manchester, 1987), pp. 34-7.

4. Supple, *Coal Industry*, p. 340; see also pp. 35-40 for an analysis of the pre-1913 structure of the industry; pp. 45-57 and pp. 86-9 for the wartime measures taken to control the industry in 1914-18. For the 1930 Coal Mines Act and subsequent developments, see pp. 209-13, 297-300 and 333-41.

5. R. Page Arnot, *The Miners in Crisis and War* (1961), pp. 171-3 and Supple, *Coal Industry*, pp. 348-9.

6. Supple, *Coal Industry*, pp. 341-7. Jones was a qualified mining engineer who had a strong trade union commitment to modernising the industry. See J. Jones, *The Coal Scuttle* (1936). The question of whether reorganisation was an economically efficient method of 'solving' the coal problem has been examined most recently by Greasley, pp. 44-5, pp. 51-3.

7. Supple, *Coal Industry*, p. 534. The official wartime history is W.H.B. Court, *Coal*, (1951).

8. Supple, *Coal Industry*, p. 526: 'In the second week of May the man-days lost had risen to 75,235, a week later they were 88,008 - eight times the pre-war average'.

9. 'The Greene Board confirmed that between 1938 and early 1942 weekly earnings in coal had increased by significantly less than those in other major industries [including vehicle manufacture, engineering, shipbuilding, and metals and metal fabrication], and that miners came 49th in a list of wages in 97 industries or industry groups'. (Ibid., p. 534.)

10. Ibid., p. 538.

11. Supple deals with the coalowners' response to wartime pressures and the Reid Report, in ibid., pp. 609-624. However, he is either diplomatically silent or too discreet to delve closely into the Coalowners Association's internal conflicts. It is not clear whether any of the major players in the Coalowners' Association left private papers. Supple's bibliography does not cite papers from either Hyndley, Reid or Evan Williams, the interwar leader of the Coalowners' Association. The apparent absence of these sources is remarkable given the importance of these men in determining the coal industry's fate. It is also surprising that neither Hyndley nor Reid published an autobiography.

12. The manifesto observed: 'For a quarter of a century the coal industry ... has been floundering chaotically under the ownership of many hundreds of independent companies. Amalgamation under public ownership will bring great economies in operation and make it possible

to modernise production methods and to raise safety standards in every colliery in the country'. (*Let Us Face the Future*, May 1945, p. 6.) Labour's nationalisation plans were made in the spring of 1945 in concert with the NUM and the TUC General Council. See R. Page Arnot, *The Miners: one union, one industry. A history of the National Union of Mineworkers 1939-46* (1979), pp. 113-4. For the passage of the bill through Parliament see ibid., pp. 127-60 and N. Fishman, 'Coal: owned and managed on behalf of the people', in J. Fyrth (ed.), *Labour's High Noon: the government and the economy 1945-51* (1993), pp. 61-6.

13. The five Communists were Willie Allan, representing the Northumberland area, Alf Davies from South Wales, Abe Moffat from Scotland, Jim Hammond from Lancashire, and Arthur Horner, as general secretary.

14. Greasley, 'Coal industry', pp. 46-50 and p. 57.

15. A. Horner, *Incorrigible Rebel* (1960), p. 176. Ashworth assumes that Ebby Edwards wrote the Miners' Charter on the basis of Arnot's description of its gestation. Arnot's account is formally correct. He states that the workers' side of the Coal Industry Joint National Negotiating Committee on 8th January 1946 'accepted a memorandum prepared by Ebby Edwards and this on 10 January 1946 was adopted by the National Executive Committee [of the NUM]'. Edwards' apparent authorship of a document for which Horner claimed responsibility is explained by the fact that Edwards was secretary of the union at the time. As the chief administrative officer of the union, Edwards name appeared on documents, memoranda, circulars and letters, though they originated elsewhere inside the union. It is unclear why Arnot omitted to attribute Horner's responsibility for the Charter. (Ashworth, *Coal Industry*, p. 147 and Arnot, *One Union, One Industry*, p. 125.)

16. Horner, ibid., pp. 176-7. The demand was for 'the provision of adequate compensation for the men who became redundant'.

17. Horner, ibid.

18. Arnot, *One Union, One Industry*, pp. 126-7. In 1960, Horner observed that Shinwell's letter 'addressed to the President of the NUM, Will Lawther, is kept at our new headquarters in Euston Road, and we regard it as a solemn pledge to the miners of Britain'. (Horner, *Incorrigible Rebel*, p. 179.)

19. 'After Hyndley had seen Shinwell on 16 December 1946, he told his colleagues that the five-day week was coming even if it cost four or five shillings a ton and that Shinwell had passed on the information that the NUM wanted to be able to tell a delegate conference later that

week that there was a good prospect of the five-day week being introduced on 1 May 1947'. (Ashworth, *Coal Industry*, p. 148.)

20. Horner, *Incorrigible Rebel*, pp. 181-2. See also Ashworth, *Coal Industry*, pp. 149-50. Ashworth comments that Horner's account is seriously misleading: 'a faulty memory seems to have led him to telescope the events of several weeks'. However he concurs with Horner's substance. He concludes that 'the conduct of the negotiations for extended hours ... seemed at times to threaten a serious limitation to the authority of the NCB'. (p. 154.)

21. See N. Fishman, *The British Communist Party and the Trade Unions 1933-45* (Aldershot, 1994), p. 233. A Soviet miner had attended the MFGB conference in July 1938 as a fraternal delegate. (*Daily Worker*, 20 July 1938.)

22. See E.H. Carr, *The Bolshevik Revolution 1917-23*, volume 2, (1966), pp. 105-20 and pp. 317-30.

23. NUM Annual Conference Report, 1947, pp. 70-5.

24. Supple, *Coal Industry*, pp. 528-32.

25. Greasley, 'Coal industry', pp. 40-5.

26. F. Zweig, *Men in the Pits* (1948), pp. 49-70. He visited Yorkshire, Durham, Northumberland, Cumberland, Lancashire, North and South Staffordshire, Warwickshire, Derbyshire, Nottinghamshire, Leicester, Kent, the Forest of Dean and South Wales. He had talks with 'several hundreds of miners ... school teachers, librarians, policemen, managers of hostels, welfare institutes or working-men's clubs, and also with miners' wives'.

27. Greasley, 'Coal industry', pp. 43-6, and Ashworth, *Coal Industry*, p. 154, 159-62, 165-8.

28. J. Saville, *The Labour Movement in Britain* (1988), pp. 109-12; H. Francis and D. Smith, *The Fed: a history of the South Wales miners in the twentieth century* (1980), pp. 436-7; D. Rubinstein, 'Socialism and the Labour Party: the Labour left and domestic policy, 1945-50', in D.E. Martin and D. Rubinstein (eds), *Ideology and the Labour Movement* (1979), pp. 228-30.

29. Zweig, *Men in the Pits*, p. 158. He has a chapter on 'Nationalisation and the reaction of the miners', pp. 157-61. I. Zweiniger-Bargielowska, 'South Wales miners' attitudes towards nationalization: an essay in oral history', *Llafur*, vol. 6, no. 3, 1994, p. 77. Rubinstein notes, 'Industrial democracy was a subject of constant discussion during these years [1945-50], and steps towards its introduction were demanded in various parts of the labour movement. Yet such demands ran up against the hard fact that there seemed to be little desire on the part of workers themselves to run their industries'.

('Socialism and the Labour Party', p. 246.)

30. G.D.H. Cole, 'The National Coal Board, its Tasks, its Organisation, and its Prospects', *Fabian Research Series* No. 129, September 1948, p. 30. See also Fishman, 'Coal', pp. 71-3.

31. Cole, 'National Coal Board', p. 36. Jack Dunn remembered travelling up to London to see Arthur Horner when the nationalisation bill was going through parliament to argue the case for direct NUM representation in management. Horner had long discussions with him about the need to approach the transition to workers' control gradually. (Video interview with Hywel Francis, 1994, South Wales Miners' Library.)

32. Ashworth, *Coal Industry*, pp. 125-6, and Arnot, *One Union, One Industry*, pp. 188-90.

33. It is remarkable that there has been no research into this area of NCB administration. There are no reliable estimates of the number of ex-NUM officials employed by the NCB; nor has there been any attempt to follow the careers of these men in their new role as Labour Relations Officers. The veteran communist activist, Jock Kane, became a Labour Relations Officer against the advice of many of his peers. He resigned as soon as he had to deal with a strike from 'the other side'. (Interview with Jock Kane by Charles Parker, in Charles Parker Collection, Birmingham Reference Library.)

34. For the ubiquity of job and finish, see Zweig, *Men in the Pits*, pp. 49-56. He observes that in Cumberland, the word used for stint is 'darrick', in Lancashire, 'bread or breadth' and in many counties 'cut', which derived from the hewer's task of cutting a particular length of coal from the face.

35. Robertson, *Bleak Midwinter*, p. 48.

36. Ashworth, *Coal Industry*, p. 149. For the unofficial strikes, see p. 167.

37. NUM Annual Conference Report, 1947, pp. 70-3.

38. Ibid., p. 78.

39. Ibid., p. 91.

40. There are descriptions of the strike in Ashworth, *Coal Industry*, p. 167-8 and B.J. McCormick, *Industrial Relations in the Coal Industry* (1979), pp. 180-1. At the time, the *Economist* commented: 'The real issue which is being fought out at Grimethorpe ... can be summed up as a struggle between rationalisation and syndicalism. The argument over the extra working at the coal face appears to be merely the pretext for a show-down on whether control is to be exercised by an all-powerful Board or whether the workers are to be given a measure of influence in the management of their own pits. Many miners

expected nationalisation to result in workers' control; instead it has resulted in a large bureaucratic machine...'. (Vol. CLIII, No. 5428, 6 September 1947, p. 393.) A fortnight later, its comment was somewhat more measured. 'The basic case for the nationalisation of the coal industry still stands: without it the clash with labour would have been violent instead of veiled; the financial problem of the industry would have ben insoluble; and little or no progress could have been made with the technical reorganisation of the industry. But the general justification for nationalisation does not automatically justify its particular manifestation as is at present being evolved from Berkeley Square [NCB headquarters]'. (Vol. CLIII, No. 5430, 20 September 1947, p. 468.)

41. Ashworth also notes that on 30 June 1947 the NCB lifted a ban on changes in wage rates at individual collieries which had been in force since 1944 and 'this suddenly brought a backlog of contentious cases into the open ...'. (*Coal Industry*, p. 167)

42. Horner, *Incorrigible Rebel*, pp. 196-7.

43. See Fishman, 'Coal', pp. 67-70. The ebbing and flowing of the numbers on strike coincided with local race meetings. The first wave of sympathy strikes began on 27 August, when the Ebor, one of the biggest handicap races of the flat season, was being run at York. The number of pits on strike continued to rise during the final two days of the York race meeting. The climax of the flat racing season is the Doncaster meeting with the St Leger, the oldest and longest classic race in Britain. In 1947, the St Leger was run on Saturday 12 September. The Grimethorpe strikers finally returned to work on the 16 September. (In addition to York and Doncaster, there were race meetings at Beverley on 3-4 September and Manchester on 5-6 September.)

44. See my Chapter 4 in this volume.

45. NUM Annual Conference Report, 1948, pp. 113-19.

46. Horner, *Incorrigible Rebel*, p. 186.

47. See Labour Party Conference Report 1948, pp. 168-72, particularly the reply to the debate by Jim Griffiths MP, pp. 170-2; Conference Report 1949, pp. 127-31; Conference Report 1950, pp. 87-92; Scottish Area NUM Minute of Conference 1948, Resolutions 1 and 2, pp. 549-50. Rubinstein, 'Socialism and the Labour Party', pp. 228-30.

Index